Perspectives on

HCI

Diverse Approaches

Computers and People Series

Edited by

B. R. GAINES and A. MONK

Monographs

Communicating with Microcomputers. An introduction to the technology of man–computer communication, *Ian H. Witten* 1980
The Computer in Experimental Psychology, *R. Bird* 1981
Principles of Computer Speech, *I. H. Witten* 1982
Cognitive Psychology of Planning, *J.-M. Hoc* 1988
Formal Methods for Interactive Systems, *A. Dix* 1991
Human Reliability Analysis: Context and Control, *E. Hollnagel* 1993

Edited Works

Computing Skills and the User Interface, *M. J. Coombs and J. L. Alty (eds)* 1981
Fuzzy Reasoning and Its Applications, *E. H. Mamdani and B. R. Gaines (eds)* 1981
Intelligent Tutoring Systems, *D. Sleeman and J. S. Brown (eds)* 1982 (1986 paperback)
Designing for Human–Computer Communication, *M. E. Sime and M. J. Coombs (eds)* 1983
The Psychology of Computer Use, *T. R. G. Green, S. J. Payne and G. C. van der Veer (eds)* 1983
Fundamentals of Human–Computer Interaction, *A. Monk (ed.)* 1984, 1985
Working with Computers: Theory versus Outcome, *G. C. van der Veer, T. R. G. Green, J.-M. Hoc and D. Murray (eds)* 1988
Cognitive Engineering in Complex Dynamic Worlds, *E. Hollnagel, G. Mancini and D. D. Woods (eds)* 1988
Computers and Conversation, *P. Luff, N. Gilbert and D. Frohlich (eds)* 1990
Adaptive User Interfaces, *D. Browne, P. Totterdell and M. Norman (eds)* 1990
Human–Computer Interaction and Complex Systems, *G. R. S. Weir and J. L. Alty (eds)* 1991
Computer-supported Cooperative Work and Groupware, *Saul Greenberg (ed.)* 1991
The Separable User Interface, *E. A. Edmonds (ed.)* 1992
Requirements Engineering: Social and Technical Issues, *M. Jirotka and J. A. Goguen (eds)* 1994
Perspectives on HCI: Diverse Approaches, *A. F. Monk and G. N. Gilbert (eds)* 1995

Practical Texts

Effective Color Displays: Theory and Practice, *D. Travis* 1991
Understanding Interfaces: A Handbook of Human–Computer Dialogue, *M. W. Lansdale and T. R. Ormerod* 1994 (1995 Paperback)

EACE Publications
(Consulting Editors: *Y. WAERN and J.-M. HOC*)

Cognitive Ergonomics, *P. Falzon (ed.)* 1990
Psychology of Programming, *J.-M. Hoc, T. R. G. Green, R. Samurcay and D. Gilmore (eds)* 1990

Perspectives on
HCI
Diverse Approaches

Edited by

Andrew F. Monk
Department of Psychology, University of York

G. Nigel Gilbert
Department of Sociology, University of Surrey

ACADEMIC PRESS
Harcourt Brace & Company, Publishers
London   San Diego   New York   Boston   Sydney   Tokyo   Toronto

ACADEMIC PRESS LIMITED
24-28 Oval Road
LONDON NW1 7DX

U.S. Edition Published by
ACADEMIC PRESS INC.
San Diego, CA 92101

A catalogue record for this book is available from the British Library

ISBN 0-12-504575-1

Printed in Great Britain by the University Press, Cambridge

Contents

List of contributors

Frank Blackler,
The Management School,
Lancaster University,
Lancaster, LA1 4YX, UK

Jeanette Blomberg,
Xerox Palo Alto Research Centre,
3333 Coyote Hill Road,
Palo Alto,
California, 94304, USA
blomberg@parc.xerox.com

Peter Campion,
Department of Genenral Practice,
University of Liverpool,
Liverpool, L69 3BX, UK

John Carroll,
562 McBryde Hall,
Computer Science Dept.,
Virginia Tech.,
Blacksburg, Virginia, U.S.A.
carroll@vtopus.cs.vt.edu

Alan Dix,
School of Computing and Mathematics,
University of Huddersfield,
Queensgate,
Huddersfield,
West Yorkshire, HD1 3DH, UK
alan@zeus.hud.ac.uk

Nigel Gilbert,
Department of Sociology,
University of Surrey,
Guildford,
Surrey, GU2 5XH, UK
GNG@soc.surrey.ac.uk

David Greatbatch,
Department of Social Sciences,
University of Nottingham,
Nottingham, NG2 2RD, UK

Christian Heath,
Department of Sociology,
University of Surrey,
Guildford,
Surrey, GU2 5XH, UK
Christian.Heath@soc.surrey.ac.uk

Andrew Howes,
School of Psychology,
University of Cardiff,
P.O. Box 901,
Cardiff, CF1 3YG, Wales, UK
HOWESA@cardiff.ac.uk

Matthew Jones,
Management Studies Group,
Department of Engineering,
Mill Lane,
Cambridge, CB2 1RX, UK
mrj10@phx.cam.ac.uk

Paul Luff,
Department of Sociology,
University of Surrey,
Guildford,
Surrey, GU2 5XH, UK
luff.europarc@rx.xerox.com

John McCarthy,
Department of Applied Psychology,
University College,
Cork, Ireland.
McCarthyj@iruccvax.ucc.ie

Andrew Monk,
Department of Psychology,
University of York,
York, YO1 5DD, UK
am1@tower.york.ac.uk

Andrew Shepherd,
Cognitive Ergonomics Research Group,
Loughborough University,
Loughborough, LE11 3TU, UK
A.Shepherd@lut.ac.uk

Roger Took,
Department of Computer Science,
University of York,
York, YO1 5DD, UK
roger@minster.york.ac.uk

Preface

A discipline or research tradition is a powerful force that shapes and constrains the puzzles and the solutions to which it is applied. All research is embedded in one sort of discipline or another. As a field of study, human-computer interaction has attracted researchers from many disciplines: computer science, psychology and sociology, to name but three. Each offers a different perspective on the subject.

The field of human-computer interaction (HCI) is noteworthy because, as well as attracting the attention of researchers in different disciplines, these researchers have started to work together to form new inter-disciplinary approaches. This has not been without its difficulties. A discipline which is not your own is like a foreign culture. It is very difficult to understand, or sometimes even to identify, the assumptions made. However, making the effort is worthwhile. Coming to understand someone else's research tradition gives new insights into one's own. The inter-disciplinary research effort in HCI benefits all the disciplines concerned.

This book is a collection of tutorial chapters. Each sets out the assumptions and criteria of a different research tradition as it has been applied to HCI, written to be read by someone from outside that discipline. Each of the authors of these chapters has been touched by the inter-disciplinary enterprise and so understands the difficulty of communicating with someone from another discipline. Our editorial policy has been to cover a range of disciplines and subdisciplines and this has meant imposing a strict word limit on individual chapters. You should bear in mind that the normal way of being induced to a new discipline is through an extended apprenticeship, normally a university degree course. These short chapters can only be viewed as introductions, to tempt you to further study. For this reason each contains a section to guide further reading in the area.

Chapter 1 provides an overview of the book in the form of a comparative summary of the perspectives covered. Two chapters from computer scientists follow this introduction. Chapter 2 is an introduction to formal methods, a mathematical perspective on the topic. Chapter 3 is a discussion of how software is built using some of the concepts from Chapter 2.

The next two chapters come from the psychological tradition. Chapter 4 describes how empirical methods from experimental psychology can be put to work on applied problems like HCI. Chapter 5 introduces cognitive modelling. Chapters 6 and 7 develop the notion of a "task". Their aim is to analyse the work or goals of the user of a computer system. In Chapter 6 John Carroll describes the special approach he has developed. This has a direct link to psychological theory and can be contrasted with Chapter 7 on task analysis which comes from ergonomics and work study.

The next two chapters present a sociological perspective, Chapter 8 introduces an ethnographic view of the topic while Chapter 9 illustrates the micro analysis of interaction carried out by ethnomethodologists. Chapter 10 introduces activity theory. This Russian perspective is of particular interest in an interdisciplinary context as it presents a way of integrating a psychological view of the individual with a more sociological view of the group or organisation. Finally, Chapter 11 introduces organisational analysis. This is itself a multi-disciplinary approach drawing techniques from a variety of areas.

This book was written for a large audience. It will be valuable for HCI courses in each of the contributing disciplines: Computer Science, Psychology, Ergonomics, Human Factors, Anthropology, Sociology and Organisational Methods. We hope it will also be of interest to people contemplating interdisciplinary work in applied areas other than HCI. HCI was what brought the authors together but the chapters are essentially about the disciplines and the different perspectives they can bring to bear on any applied problem.

The editors would like to acknowledge the patience and help of Andrew Lloyd in preparing this text for publication.

Chapter 1

Inter–disciplinary research

Andrew Monk and Nigel Gilbert

All research is based on a discipline that shapes and constrains the arguments made and the methods used. In this way a community of scientists comes to agree on common criteria for judging good and bad research. A community of chemists, say, will agree broadly on the way theories should be formulated and the methods appropriate to test those theories. Kuhn (1962) has suggested that this consensus is needed in order for a discipline, or paradigm in his terms, to accumulate knowledge in an effective way.

The power of a scientific discipline should not be underestimated. The normal apprenticeship to be served is usually at least a degree course and may extend over many years. During this time the initiates absorb a framework of values, much of which may be implicit, that governs the way they think about research. While this framework of ideas and values facilitates communication with other scientists who share it, it makes it very difficult to communicate with others who do not. Many scientists are frankly xenophobic when it comes to the findings of other disciplines which are often simply dismissed as indefensible rubbish.

This lack of shared values and concepts is a difficulty when scientists from different disciplines come together to solve a common applied problem. This book is written by scientists and social scientists from several disciplines who have in common the goal of understanding HCI. This common goal is, ultimately, to provide designers with insights that will allow them to produce better computer systems. Just stating this common goal immediately brings out disagreements. What constitutes human–computer interaction? What do we mean by "better" and what evidence is needed to show that one thing is better than another?

Of course, this multiplicity of perspectives is the major advantage of multi–disciplinary research teams. Researchers from a Computer Science background have different concerns from psychologists and so will produce different contributions to the final result. A sociologist will have yet different contributions to make. So long as the recommendations can be reconciled, the advantages of casting the net widely in this way may be considerable. Our experience is that multi–disciplinary research soon leads to inter–disciplinary research. That is, under the right conditions, contact with scientists with very different backgrounds leads researchers to re–examine the assumptions of their own discipline and sometimes to changes in the way they think. The result is a merging of elements from one discipline into another, an inter–disciplinary approach to the problem.

So what is necessary to make multi–disciplinary research possible and to develop inter–disciplinary approaches? First, there has to be a willingness to cooperate and an understanding of the potential for misunderstanding. In many ways, explaining your research to someone from a different discipline is like talking to someone of a different nationality. The scientist explaining her findings has the obligations of a host, to make allowances for potential misunderstandings and be generally hospitable. The scientist listening to her has the obligations of a visitor to respect differences he cannot yet understand. Secondly, all parties have to work hard at creating inter–disciplinary understanding. If it takes the initiate several years to absorb the values and assumptions of a discipline one cannot, as an outsider, expect to understand anything but a limited aspect of that viewpoint without considerable effort. Thirdly, as intimated above, the catalyst that generates inter–disciplinary work is generally a practical problem. The more specific the problem, the easier it is for scientists from different disciplines to come together. Thus while the problem is specified as "human–computer interaction" there is plenty of room for disagreement and misunderstanding. If the problem is "designing an automatic bank teller for use in all the branches of bank X" then each contribution has a clear referent in the problem domain and communication is easier.

This book is meant as a guide for scientists embarking on a multi–disciplinary collaboration on some aspect of HCI. Each chapter introduces a different disciplinary perspective. We hope that these chapters will motivate the reader to find out more about the approaches described. We also hope that they will act as a guide to facilitate that process. What follows, in this chapter, is a high level introduction to the rest of the book in terms of the three parent disciplines: Computer Science, Psychology and Social Science.

1.1 Computer Science

The relatively new discipline of Computer Science is itself an inter–disciplinary enterprise borrowing from the older disciplines of Mathematics and Engineering. The ultimate goal is to build software. Hence software engineers face many of the same problems as arise in any engineering project. Broadly, these are: (i) to identify requirements, (ii) to specify a design and (iii) to build an implementation. The function of (ii), the specification, is crucial in understanding the way a software engineer sees this process.

A specification links the requirements, which say what the system is to achieve, to the implementation, the artifact delivered to the customer. The problem is that even something as apparently flexible as software is difficult to change. Once something that works is built, there are all sorts of political and practical obstacles to changing it. To get around this problem engineers construct a specification, colloquially a blueprint, between writing a requirements document and implementation. The specification is built to be changed, that is, to be analysed, evaluated, and improved as much as possible before implementation begins. This perspective from engineering led to the introduction of the "waterfall" model of software development. Here the process flows from requirements down through specification to implementation. In practice, this very top–down sequence has been found to be impractical for designing interactive systems. People now talk about "spiral" models of software development (Boehm, 1988). Here design is seen as essentially iterative. One might start off by writing an initial requirements document and then an initial specification, but writing the specification causes parts of the requirements to be revised and so on.

Computer systems can be extremely complex. Reasoning about a specification that included all the detail of the final implementation is generally impossible and so models are built. A model makes explicit certain aspects of the design and skims over others. This is where the mathematical perspective comes in, as many of the models built in the process of constructing a specification will be mathematical models. Mathematical models can be reasoned about formally, that is, one can exploit known mathematical techniques, such as graph theory or set theory, to prove things about the models. In Computer Science these mathematical techniques are known as "formal methods" and research into formal methods accounts for a large percentage of the output of university departments. Chapter 2, by Alan Dix, introduces this topic. In Chapter 3, Roger Took uses some of the formalisms developed to reason about the basic building blocks of an interactive system, so called "software architectures". Although well established in other areas of Computer Science, formal methods are only just beginning to be applied to HCI and so both these chapters are quite close to the research frontier.

1.2 Psychology

Like computer scientists, psychologists are concerned with abstraction and models, but there is a strong additional emphasis on measurement. Traditional Experimental Psychology proceeds by generating hypotheses that are then tested by collecting quantitative data. For example, a theory of human memory might predict that one kind of verbal material will be harder to learn than another. This hypothesis then has to be proceduralized as an experiment. This involves devising a comparison of people learning the two kinds of material and a quantitative measure of performance. The experimental method should rule out any alternative explanation of the observed differences. If another psychologist can think of plausible alternative explanations, further experiments are carried out to rule them out.

The quantitative measures used by psychologists generally suffer from high error variance. The same measurements made on different individuals in the same situation often give results that vary considerably. Even measurements made on the same individual in the same experimental context will vary. For this reason hypotheses are formulated in terms of averaged results and statistical tests are applied to assess the probability that the observed difference could have arisen by chance.

Through ingenious experimental controls and the application of sophisticated statistical techniques, experimental psychologists have been able to make generalisable statements about phenomena in a variety of areas of human and animal behaviour. In Chapter 4 John McCarthy explains how the experimental method can be used to answer applied questions such as those posed in the design of computer systems.

The emphasis on data in Experimental Psychology is a product of its history, as a reaction to the theories of "armchair" psychologists at the turn of the century. Because these theories had no mathematical basis they could not even be defended on the normal grounds of formal consistency or completeness. However, abstractions and notations from Computer Science are now being used to construct formal models of how behaviour arises. Andrew Howes introduces this new area of cognitive modelling in Chapter 5. In order that they be readily falsifiable, the theories used by experimental psychologists to generate hypotheses have tended to be rather simple, often not more than the yes/no hypothesis that is finally tested in an experiment. Cognitive modelling offers the possibility of much more sophisticated accounts of how behaviour is generated but makes testing the many individual assumptions that are included in the model very difficult. Chapter 5 includes a framework for including empirical data in the process of constructing a cognitive model that goes some way towards meeting this criticism.

1.3 Work

Most computer systems are built to support work and so successful design depends on understanding the tasks carried out by people as part of their daily work. Chapters 6 and 7 are both concerned with thinking about users' tasks. In Chapter 6, John Carroll describes the approach he has developed with colleagues at IBM's Thomas J. Watson Research Center, in New York. This is constructed around the notion of a task–artifact cycle. When they are not developing new abstractions, computer scientists build demonstration systems. By using these artifacts they get an understanding of what new problems are to be solved. The process of invention is a slow piecemeal business. Each innovation is invented to support some perceived task, but the innovation itself changes the way people work and the tasks they want to do. One is thus locked into a cycle of identifying tasks, supporting them with an artifact, identifying further tasks, supporting them and so on. Carroll's approach seeks to give this process a theoretical basis, using current theory from Experimental Psychology.

Andrew Shepherd introduces us to the topic of Task Analysis in Chapter 7. This has its roots in Work Study and Ergonomics. The major concern here has been to develop notations for describing the structure of work. Whereas Carroll's approach depends on the use of scenarios, loosely speaking stories of typical work, Task Analysis decomposes work into component tasks, components of these components and so on. Task Analysis has been developed for very specific purposes such as the design of training and safety procedures. As such it takes a very flexible and pragmatic approach compared with some of the more academic disciplines described in the book.

1.4 Ethnography

While work is often composed of the kind of tasks studied by Task Analysts, to focus only on tasks would be to miss out on a crucial aspect: that work is nowadays done in an organization, in a context in which other people are providing inputs, taking the outputs and managing the process. Although human–computer interaction as a research field started by considering individual humans more or less in isolation, it is now widely believed that knowledge about the social context of the work is vital in designing computer systems.

The problem is how to study that social context and how to bring what one learns to bear on the design process.

Jeanette Blomberg describes a tradition of collecting data on social practices and customs that was first developed by anthropologists who went off to study strange cultures. Ethnography, as this mode of research is called, involves close observation and interviews with people going about their normal, everyday business, with the aim of understanding not only what they do, but also why they do it; that is, to get an appreciation of the "culture" in which they work. Ethnography stresses the need to make detailed observations and not to make assumptions about what is going on in a social situation. Ethnographers have often found that what might be expected is not in fact what happens and, of course, designing on the basis of expectations when the reality is different is a recipe for failure.

David Greatbatch, Christian Heath, Paul Luff and Peter Campion continue the theme of detailed observation, but take it a stage further. They introduce a style of analysis that is called "conversation analysis" (CA) because it was originally applied to the examination of audio recordings of ordinary, everyday conversation. CA aims to describe the conventions that speakers use to make their talk understandable and the conventions that hearers use to understand what is said. Greatbatch et al. show that the same kinds of analysis can be applied to the study of video recordings of people using computer systems. The explanations that such analyses provide help designers appreciate the work that users have to do in order to make systems understandable to themselves and to the people with whom they are working.

1.5 Organizational perspectives

The theme of examining people's interaction with computers in its social context is continued in the final two chapters of this book, but here the main focus is on the role of computers in organizations. Frank Blackler in Chapter 10 reviews an approach called Activity Theory which, although it originated in the work of a Russian psychologist in the 1920s, draws in ideas more usually thought of as belonging to sociology. Activity Theory has become influential recently in studies of Computer Supported Cooperative Work (CSCW). CSCW systems are intended to help groups of people in organizations work together more effectively. Perhaps the best known CSCW application is electronic mail, but others under development include shared drawing tools and editors that several people can use simultaneously. Blackler makes the point that introducing such tools may not simply enhance existing work practices and increase collaboration as intended, but may instead disrupt the organization and lead to quite new patterns of working and relationships between people. Activity Theory aims to embrace an understanding of such changes.

There are many different perspectives on organizations, Activity Theory being one, and Matthew Jones, in Chapter 11, provides an overview of them. He identifies positivist, interpretative and conflictual undercurrents in the approaches that have been applied to the analysis of HCI in an organization context. The common feature of all these approaches is that, rather than focusing on the fine detail of interactions, they consider the whole work setting, inevitably with a rather broad brush. In organizational analysis, concepts such as role, status and power come into play. The recommendations for design include considerations of who is to use the system, for what purposes and who benefits. As Jones notes, such analyses are best employed as a preliminary to the detailed interface design, as part of a process of defining what the user's task is and what impact it has on the rest of the organization.

1.6 Inter–disciplinary research

All of the chapters that follow are organised in the same general format: an initial historical introduction to a perspective on HCI, an example of the approach applied to a problem or issue in the design of human–computer interaction, an account of the main features of the approach, and a comparison of the approach with others. By following this common format, we have tried to ensure that it is easy for readers to find their way around the book and to see what each perspective can bring to bear.

As will become clear, inter–disciplinary research will not result from an unreflective mixing of a few of these approaches, picked at random and stirred well. The concerns and, in particular, the grounding assumptions of the different disciplines are too often incompatible if not actually in conflict. To return to the linguistic metaphor with which we began this chapter, inter–disciplinary research is not the equivalent of "Franglais", a mixture of French and English that has neither the power nor the elegance of either. Thus, we see no value in trying to develop, for example, a hybrid discipline combining computer science and sociology; the assumptions of the two disciplines are so different that the enterprise is bound to fail (cf. Hughes et al., 1993).

Inter–disciplinary research involves an openness to different ideas and concerns, and a willingness to communicate with scientists who have not been brought up to speak the language. Often it is best done by those who have the capacity to operate at different times in different disciplines. From the placing together of the different disciplines, new ideas may develop that would not otherwise have surfaced. However, these ideas will still need to be located within some existing disciplinary framework. That is why, despite our desire for disciplinary pluralism within HCI, there is no chapter in this book describing "inter–disciplinary research" itself. Inter–disciplinary research can only be effective when it involves the creative juxtaposition of different approaches around a specific problem, so that each can shed its own light on the issues. It must be left for you, the reader, to see which particular approaches will be the most illuminating for the specific problems in which you are interested, and for you to apply these approaches in a creative way to the solution of those problems.

Chapter 2

Formal methods

Alan J. Dix

2.1 Introduction

For many years I have worked on the interplay between formal methods and human–computer interaction. This area of research originated with (present and past) workers from York, but over the last few years there have been several international workshops on the subject and there are now several books on aspects of this area. For further reading in the area the interested reader can consult the chapters on Dialogue and Formal Methods in Dix et al. (1993), my previous monograph Dix (1991) and the collection by Harrison and Thimbleby (1990).

2.1.1 Why use formal methods?

Formal notations and mathematics are used in several areas of human–computer interaction, including cognitive modelling and task analysis. However, this chapter will focus on those more connected with the engineering and analysis of interactive systems. These notations all try to abstract away from the way the system is programmed, but still be precise about some aspect of its behaviour. Of course, an informal description does the same, but with a formal description you can (in theory) say precisely whether or not a real system satisfies the description. Because of this, one can perform precise analyses on the description itself, knowing that any conclusions one comes to will be true of the real system.

One value of this precision is that it exposes design decisions which otherwise might not be noticed until the system is being implemented. It is clear in many systems that obscure interface behaviour could not have been designed that way, but has occurred as the result of some programming decision. The specification of an interactive system should not determine the algorithms and data structures used to build the system – that is the proper domain of the programmer. But, it should describe precisely the behaviour of the system – the programmer may not be qualified to make such decisions and the level of commitment at the time that the issue is uncovered may mean that the design choice has been determined by foregoing implementation choices.

2.1.2 Uses of Formal methods

We will consider three major strands of formal methods, each of which fulfils a different purpose:

Specification of individual interactive systems

This usually concentrates on a specific system and the complete specification of all aspects of its behaviour. Its purpose is to clarify design decisions, to expose inconsistency and to act as a "contract" with the implementor. User interface software can be extremely complex and so being able to deal with it at a more abstract level is even more important than for general software.

Generic models of interactive systems

The second strand models classes of system, for example one might have a general model of window managers as opposed to a specific model of the Macintosh window manager. Their purpose is to give new insight into general problems as the properties of the problem domain are analysed. For example, we will see later how general questions about the meaning of the undo command can be addressed without recourse to a specific system. In addition, they can be used as part of a formal development process to constrain the design of specific systems. That is, results of the analysis of generic models can be applied to formal specifications of specific systems.

Dialogue specification and analysis

Finally, dialogue notations are again used to describe specific systems, but at a different level of detail than a full formal specification. They concern the steps of the user interaction but typically do not fully specify the meaning attached to the user's actions. For example, the dialogue specification of a graphics editor may say that the user must always enter two positions (by mouse clicks) after selecting the "draw line" icon. However, it will not say that a line appears in the screen, except perhaps by way of informal annotation. Dialogue notations are used for various reasons, but this chapter will emphasize the way the formal element in the dialogue can be analysed in order to expose potential user interface problems.

2.1.3 What is formal anyway?

Of these three strands, dialogue specification is perhaps least mathematical, but most easily used by the non–formalist. Indeed, although Formal methods can be extremely powerful they do require a high–level of expertise. Most computing courses now include some element of formal methods and so the level of formal expertise will increase in coming years. However, it is unlikely that there will ever be a large community of people expert in both human factors and formal methods.

This suggests that formal methods need to packaged so that non–experts can get some of the benefits without negotiating the steep learning curve. One way this can be achieved is through "engineering level" notations which have formal underpinnings, but where simplified analysis and heuristics can be applied. This is as in other disciplines where the practising engineer does not use the theoretical methods and analyses directly, but instead more pragmatic and approximate versions of them. In the user interface domain, dialogue notations are one example of an engineering level notation and are amenable to both simple hand analysis and automated tool support. The fact that many dialogue notations have a graphical form also makes them more palatable! Another example of an engineering level notation is *status/event analysis* which uses simple timeline diagrams together with design heuristics based on a combination of formal analysis and naïve psychology (Dix, 1991, Ch. 10; Dix, 1992; Dix et al., 1993, Ch. 9).

Sometimes the benefits of formal analysis can be presented informally. For example, a purist might argue that an undo button should always undo the effects of the last command – even if the last command was itself undo. However, we shall see later that this is in fact impossible, thus removing the cause of long arguments and allowing more constructive debate over the purpose of undo. Not only can we state the result "it is impossible"; in this case the formal proof can be rendered in a reasonably informal, but convincing manner – which is as well as no–one ever believes the result!

Of course, we can all recognize a bit of formal notation – simply watch out for the $\lambda \forall \exists$! However, you will find that the dialogue notations are mostly diagrammatic. Can a graphical notation be formal? In fact, a diagram can be formal, informal or somewhere in between, depending on the meaning which is attached to the elements of the diagram. This is obvious when we think of an engineering diagram. When it says that the diameter of a rod is 13.7 mm it means precisely that! The dialogue notations discussed in this chapter will be semi–formal in that they have textual annotations on the diagrams which require informal interpretation. However, the structure of the diagrams will be perfectly formal and capable of formal analysis. The counterside of this also needs to be considered. Just because a paper is filled with Greek and upside down letters doesn't mean it is formal!

Any formal notation abstracts in some way. In being very precise about some things it completely ignores others. The important thing is to be aware of what is being abstracted and whether the abstraction is appropriate for the purpose for which it is required.

In the next chapter a computer game is specified in Z, a particular formal notation. It is thus an example of the first strand of formal methods.[1] In the rest of this chapter we will look at the other two strands in more detail. We will begin with a short introduction to the language and concepts used in formal methods.

2.2 The language of mathematics

The notations used for formal specification in computer science are based on a few key concepts from mathematics. Mathematicians care a lot about the meaning of these concepts, but are typically not worried about the notation used. Indeed, for the same concept, say the application of a function f to a value x one may see any of the following notations (and probably more besides):

$f(x)$
$f x$
$x f$

As you see, even the order may change! Furthermore, mathematicians will invent notations for specific purposes, even just for one paper. A piece of mathematics is written for a human reader (well, a mathematician anyway) and all that matters is that it is understood by the reader.

Computer science formalists are far more starchy. Different notations exist for the same concepts, but one is normally expected to stick to a particular notation and the proponents of essentially similar notations can become quite tribal at times. The reason for this stickling for notation is that computer science formalisms are written against the background of computer programs where the reader is not another human (or even a mathematician) but a computer. This punctiliousness can be a pain when the notation seems a poor match for the problem but has the advantage that automatic tools can help to check some aspects of a specification.

Unfortunately, several aspects of interface design fit badly with the standard notations and so several specific formalisms have been

---

[1]In fact, the purpose will be to expose general architectural concepts and thus also has aspects of the second strand.

developed aimed specifically at interface design. The advantage of such domain–specific notations is that they can have features specifically customized for interface design. However, each new notation requires work in establishing its formal foundations and if required the development of new support tools.

As a mathematician at heart, I will try in this chapter not to be too heavy on new notation. Where there is a choice of symbol or notation I will use those adopted in the Z notation (Spivy, 1992) which will also be used in the next chapter. However, I will not follow Z slavishly, especially where the Z notation becomes obscure and over–complicated for the examples used here.

Mathematics is like a pyramid stood upon its head: there are a few basic concepts forming the foundation and on these concepts are built successive layers of abstraction. From counting coconuts one moves to the use of numbers, to algebra (talking about numbers in general) to various forms of number–like things and so on. Only the tip of this pyramid is required to understand most formal specifications.

I will assume the reader is familiar with numbers (ordinary numbers!) and with basic logic. I will use the following logical symbols:

$p \wedge q$	–	logical and,	also sometimes written			$p.q$ or $p \, \mathrm{I} \, q$
$p \vee q$	–	logical or,	"	"	"	$p + q$ or $p \cup q$
$\neg p$		logical not,	"	"	"	$\overline{p}$
$p \Rightarrow q$	–	p implies q	"	"	"	$p \subset q$

Logic is the glue that joins together mathematics, but the heart upon which mathematics is based are sets and functions. Upon these virtually everything else is built.[2] Many readers will be aware of some set theory possibly from school days, so the following descriptions may be familiar.

2.2.1 Sets and other collections

A set is a collection of things which is *unordered* and *without repeats*. The simplest sets are finite ones, for example:

Primary	=	{ *red, green, blue* }
Secondary	=	{ *blue, green, cyan, red, magenta, yellow* }
Sea	=	{ *green, cyan, blue* }

This says that *Primary* is a set with three *elements*, namely: *red*, *green* and *blue*. we say that *red*, *green* and *blue* are *members* of *Primary*. This is written *red* ∈ *Primary*, *green* ∈ *Primary*, etc. The second set, *Secondary*

---

[2]In fact, sets are sufficient on their own, but why save on shoe leather by walking on your hands?

is a set with six elements, those in *Primary* and in addition *cyan*, *magenta* and *yellow*. The third set, *Sea* consists of the palette one might want for a seascape. Note that as sets are unordered we could have written the elements in any way and had the same set:

Primary   = { *red, green, blue* }   = { *green, red, blue* }
              = { *blue, green, red* }   =   ...

In addition, as the set does not count repeats we can only have one of each colour. If we wrote:

BlueSet = { *blue, red, blue, green, blue* }

this would be regarded as exactly the same as *Primary*, the repeated *blue*s are ignored. Alternatively, the definition of *BlueSet* might be regarded as ill–formed.

As *Secondary* contains all the elements that *Primary* does, we say that *Secondary* is a *superset* of *Primary*, or equivalently that *Primary* is a *subset* of *Secondary*. This is written:

Secondary ⊃ *Primary*   or equivalently   *Primary* ⊂ *Secondary*

In addition, note that *Sea* ⊂ *Secondary*.

We can build new sets from existing ones. This is done using set *union* (written ∪) which puts two sets together and *intersection* (written ∩) which extracts those elements common to two sets. For example:

Primary ∪ *Sea*   =   { *red, blue, green, cyan* }
Primary ∩ *Sea*   =   { *blue, green* }
Sea ∩ *Secondary*   =   { *blue, green, cyan* }

Note that because *Sea* is a subset of *Secondary* the intersection of *Sea* and *Secondary* is the same as *Sea*.

Not all sets are finite, for example the set of all *natural* numbers (non–negative integers) or the set of all integers:

ℕ   =   { 0, 1, 2, 3, 4, 5, ... }
ℤ   =   { ..., −3, −2, −1, 0, 1, 2, ... }

Usually infinite sets represent something abstract, after all it is difficult to really gather together an infinite collection of things. In fact, as infinite sets go, the set of natural numbers is relatively small and concrete.

In addition to sets it is sometimes useful to deal with *bags* which are unordered, but do allow repeats and *sequences* which are both ordered and have repeats.[3] So, one can write:

$$BlueBag \quad = \quad [\![\, blue, red, blue, green, blue \,]\!]$$
$$= \quad [\![\, red, blue, blue, blue, green \,]\!]$$
$$= \quad [\![\, green, blue, blue, red, blue \,]\!]$$

You can think of a bag as precisely that, a sack containing things in no particular order, but more of one thing than another. So *BlueBag* contains three *blues*, one *red* and one *green*.

One can have a similar blue sequence:

$$BlueSeq \quad = \quad \langle\, blue, red, blue, green, blue \,\rangle$$

However, this time the order is important. A sequence is like a list on a piece of paper. The first item on the list is "blue", the second is "red", the third is "blue" again. So, if we swop the first two colours we get a different sequence:

$$BlueSeq \quad \neq \quad \langle\, red, blue, blue, green, blue \,\rangle$$

Similar to a sequence is a tuple. It too is an ordered collection. However, the elements of sequences (and bags) are all the same type of thing, for example, *BlueSeq* consists solely of colours. A tuple may contain different sorts of things. For example, if we wanted to describe the colour and size of a dress, we might do so using a tuple:

$$dress = (\, red, 10 \,)$$

When specifying systems, tuples will be used to describe the state of a system in terms of its component parts. Often the components of a tuple are given names; for example, we may want to talk about *dress.colour* and *dress.size*. The notation for describing named tuples varies more than most although the use of a dot to access components is quite widespread.

I said that mathematics was like an inverted pyramid. We start with sets of things and other sorts of collections. However, from these one then goes on to talk about sets of sets, sets of sets of sets, ..., not to mention sets of sequences, sequences of sets etc.

---

[3] You could also have a collection which is ordered but has no repeats, a sort of prioritized set. Z calls this an injective sequence (**iseq**), but I have never found a use for one!

Lets start with the set $X = \{ x, y \}$. From this we can obtain $\prod X$, the *power set* of X – the set of all subsets of X, and **seq**X – the set of all finite sequences of elements of X.

$$\mathbb{P}\, X \quad = \{ \{\}, \{ x \}, \{ y \}, \{ x, y \} \}$$
$$\mathbf{seq}\, X \quad = \{ \langle\rangle, \langle x \rangle, \langle y \rangle, \langle x, x \rangle, \langle x, y \rangle, \langle y, x \rangle, \langle y, y \rangle, \langle x, x, x \rangle, \dots \}$$

Note that the power set of a finite set is also finite, but that the set of all sequences is infinite. However, even with finite sets power sets grow very rapidly in size and hence are used to describe problems but are rarely actually computed within a program. Note also that the empty set $\{\}$ (also written $\varnothing$) is the set which contains nothing. It is a subset of every set including itself.

We can also construct the set of all tuples using *Cartesian product*. So, if $A = \{ a, b \}$, the Cartesian product of A and X is the set of all tuples whose first component is from A and whose second component is from X: $A \times X = \{ (a, x), (a, y), (b, x), (b, y) \}$. Note especially that this does *not* contain (x, a) – which is a member of $X \times A$. The set of all dress styles could then be written as *Styles = Primary* $\times \mathbb{N}$(recall that $\mathbb{N}$ was the set of all natural numbers). Of course, one could argue with this as we may want to have dresses in non–primary colours. Also some of the sizes in this set do not represent reasonable dresses (have you ever seen a size 593 dress?). This is precisely the value of a formal specification. Often this sort of decision is taken while a system is being programmed rather than by the designer.

When a name is introduced in a specification it is usually given an explicit type to say what sort of thing it refers to. For example, we might introduce the name *sty* which is going to be a specific dress style. This can be declared as:

$$sty : \; Primary \times \mathbb{N}$$

This says that *sty* is some tuple consisting of a primary colour and a natural number. A possible value of *sty* is then (*green*,8). Note the difference between *sty* and *Styles* (defined above) – *Styles* is the *set* of all possible tuples whereas *sty* is one particular tuple. In fact we could have used *Styles* as the type of *sty*:

$$sty : \; Styles.$$

2.2.2 Functions and relations

Functions are black boxes which given an element from one set return an element of another. Most readers will have come across some mathematical functions; for example, *square*, the function which given a real number (that is any number not just integers) returns its square, e.g. *square*(1.5) = 2.25. The type of a function is shown using an arrow and the function, for example the type of *square* might be $\mathbb{R} \rightarrow \mathbb{R}$, that is it takes real numbers ($\mathbb{R}$) to real numbers.

Often functions take several parameters and this is denoted using the Cartesian product notation × which we saw earlier. For example:

  mix : Primary × Primary $\longrightarrow$ *Secondary*

says that *mix* is a function which given two primary colours returns a secondary colour. For example, if *mix* is standard colour mixing (for light rather than paint) we would have *mix*(*red,green*) = *yellow*.

If the sets involved are finite we can write out the function in full. For example, *mix* can be defined in full by:

mix = {	(*red,red*) $\mapsto$ *red,*	(*red,blue*) $\mapsto$ *magenta,*	(*red,green*) $\mapsto$ *yellow,*
	(*blue,red*) $\mapsto$ *magenta,*	(*blue,blue*) $\mapsto$ *blue,*	(*blue,green*) $\mapsto$ *cyan,*
	(*green,red*) $\mapsto$ *yellow,*	(*green,blue*) $\mapsto$ *cyan,*	(*green,green*) $\mapsto$ *green*
}			

Note that it is necessary to specify both *mix*(*red,blue*) and *mix*(*blue,red*) as in general these need not be the same. For example, subtraction (–) is a function of type $\Omega \times \Omega \rightarrow \Omega$, but $3 - 2$ is not the same as $2 - 3$.

In fact, expressing functions in full is the exception: usually they are described using some formula. For example, the function *hypot* might return the length of the hypotenuse of a right–angled triangle given the length of its two sides using Pythagoras' formula:

  hypot: $\mathbb{R} \times \mathbb{R} \rightarrow \mathbb{R}$
  hypot(*a,b*) = $\sqrt{a^2 + b^2}$

Notice that the first line gives the type of *hypot* and the second line its definition. Note also that *a* and *b* represent variables in the above definition whereas in a statement like *mix*(*blue,green*) = *cyan*, the colour names were constants. Specific notations have rules for distinguishing these, but for this chapter I hope it will always be clear from context.

Functions may not be defined for all values, in which case they are said to be *partial* as opposed to a *total* function which is defined for all values of the given type. However, a function must always give the same answer. So if we considered the set of all people, *mother* would be a reasonable function as everyone (new IVF developments notwithstanding) has a mother. However, *daughter* would not be a function as not only does not everyone have a daughter (which would simply make the function partial), but also some people have more than one daughter so there is not a single result.

Obviously one wants to deal with relationships like *daughter* and there are two effectively equivalent constructs for this. The first, in the spirit of inverted pyramids, is to have a function *daughters* which returns a *set*, so that the result of *daughter* is the set of daughters of a person. If the person has no daughters the set is empty. For example,

> *daughters(Alan)*   =   { *Esther, Ruth* }
> *daughters(Janet)* =   {}

That is, Alan has two daughters, Esther and Ruth, Janet has none.

The other way to deal with the problem is using a *relation*. We could have the relation *daughter_of(c,p)* which is true precisely when *c* is the daughter of *p*. For example, using the same family relations as above, both *daughter_of(Esther,Alan)* and *daughter_of(Ruth,Alan)* would be true, but *daughter_of(Janet,Alan), daughter_of(Ruth,Janet)* and *daughter_of(Alan,Esther)* would all be false. The type of a relation is sometimes written using a double ended arrow:

> *daughter_of* : *Person* $\leftrightarrow$ *Person*

We have already seen a function yielding a set, that is daughters. Its type can be written using the power set construction:

> *daughters* : *Person* $\longrightarrow$ $\mathbb{P}$ *Person*

and yes, you guessed it, you can have sets of functions, functions returning functions, sets of functions returning sets, ad infinitum!

2.2.3 States and operations

The most common use of formalism within computer science is to define the possible states of a system and the operations which can change that state. In other areas of computer science the part of the state which involves the user interface is often ignored. For interface design and analysis, we want to talk about everything that concerns the interaction.

As an example, consider what you would need in the state of a simple calculator. This of course depends very much on the particular calculator, but would at least include: the number displayed, the current running total, the operation about to be performed and something to say whether the next digit will be added to the end of the current number or replace it. Did you think of the last two? The operation pending is needed because after typing "1", "+", "2" the calculator needs to remember that it must add 1 to 2 if you type "=" next. The last part, the "typing" flag is needed to tell whether typing a "7" next will lead to "27" being displayed (to be added to 1) or whether the "2" will be replaced by "7".

The state is changed by each user action. A specification will say precisely how each part of the state is changed by each operation. For example, the rule for typing a digit would be something like:

type_digit(d) **if** typing flag is true
          then add d to the end of the number displayed
    if it is false
          then clear the number displayed and set it to d

A typical trace of operations might proceed as follows:

user action	running total	display	operation	typing?
< *start* >	1	?	+	yes
type_digit(7)	1	27	+	yes
=	28	28	none	no
–	28	28	–	no
type_digit(3)	28	3	–	yes

Notice how the effect of typing the "7" and the "3" are different because of the typing flag.

The state of the calculator is a tuple, for example, the state just after typing the "7" is:

(28, 28, +, yes)

The set of all states is therefore a Cartesian product:

CalculatorStates = $\mathbb{Z} \times \mathbb{Z} \times$ Operation $\times$ *Flag*

and an operation can be regarded as a function from states to states:

type_digit(7) : *CalculatorStates* $\longrightarrow$ *CalculatorStates*

This function says how the states changes when the operation is performed.

Often some parts of the state can be thought of as the underlying application whereas other parts are to do with the process of interaction. For example, the running total is obviously what one really wants out of the calculator, whereas the typing flag is part of the ephemera of interaction. Often the bits describing the interaction are the most complicated – in order to make something that is simple for the user, the system has to be complex.

When the system gets more complicated we don't want to have to write the full state in one go. For example, a CAD package may have the following state:

$$CADstates = MenuState \times Selection \times Drawing \times Notes$$

The components may be named, so if *cstate* is a particular state of the CAD system, we may be able to refer to *cstate.menu*, *cstate.sel*, *cstate.draw* and *cstate.note*. The various sets *MenuState* etc. refer to possibly complex sets representing parts of the state. For example, *Selection* would have information regarding the currently selected object in the drawing, and *Drawing* would record all the shapes and lines which have been drawn. These would each be complicated sets in their own right. A full specification notation makes it easy to define these sets one by one and hence build up the whole specification. In the next chapter, Z's structuring mechanism *schemas* are used to build a complete specification.

In this example too we can see that some parts of the state, *cstate.draw* and *cstate.note* correspond to the underlying application and the rest *cstate.menu* and *cstate.sel* are the state of the interaction.

Note, however, that this distinction is an area where authors of HCI papers using formalism often appear confused. They begin to talk (correctly) about the changes that happen to the system in terms of transitions between states. However, at some point they want to refer to the interaction component, but do so by talking of it as a *subset* of the states. That is, the states are classified into interaction states and application states. They basically say something like the following:

$$Istates \quad \subset \quad CADstates$$
$$Astates \quad \subset \quad CADstates$$

This is entirely wrong – it is the components of the states which can be classified. Think what they are saying: the set of states represents possible snapshots of the system at any moment in time. To classify the states would be to say that at some moment the system had only interaction state or only application state. The latter is bad enough, but if the former were true what would have become of all your lovely drawing! Certainly the human–computer dialogue at any moment may be concentrating more on surface interaction (e.g., menu manipulation) or deep interaction (e.g., invoking a structural analysis), but the other components of the state are also present even if unchanged.

Unfortunately, this is not simply a matter of the authors knowing what they want but having trouble translating it accurately into the formal notation. Personally, that wouldn't bother me too much so long as the intent is clear – and to be honest I've seen far worse in papers on software engineering where formal methods are supposed to be the central focus! However, there are occasionally points where the errors represent a deeper confusion, not just about the mathematics, but in the authors' general thinking. I have several times seen pictures similar to Figure 2.1, which exactly captures this idea that some of the states (the black ones) are solely to do with the underlying application and others (the white ones) are to do solely with interaction.

application states   interaction states

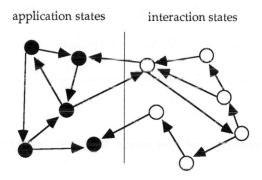

Figure 2.1 The WRONG way of thinking about state!

The confusion arises because at any moment of time one may be able to divide up the state of the system into an interaction part and an application part, which is in a sense looking at a "subset" of the components. But this process is selection of components and is a process of abstraction. If one wants to talk generically about the relationship between the state of the system and the "interaction state" one needs an abstraction function to obtain the relevant portion.

iabs: CADstate → MenuState × Selection

This difference between abstraction (only looking at some aspects of things) and selection (only looking a some things) can be subtle, but is important in both our formal and informal thinking.

2.2.4 Specialist notations

So far we have been talking about standard mathematics and the specification in the next chapter will be in Z, a general–purpose formalisms. However, there are also several special–purpose notations which can be useful for interface design. Notice the specifications only considered either single states of the system or simple transitions between states. It is slightly more complex to talk about sequences of actions – not impossible, for example one can use sequences of states to represent the history of an interaction, but certainly more difficult. The dialogue notations discussed at the end of this chapter are aimed at the specification of the possible sequences of user actions. However, they specify precisely what a system does, but are not suited to describing *constraints* on the temporal behaviour.

Various forms of temporal and modal logics are better suited to this and allow one to make statements like: "it is always true that when the user presses the "print" button the document will eventually be printed". In temporal logic one can write this as:

$$\textbf{0} \text{ user presses ' print'} \implies \Diamond \text{ document is printed}$$

The symbols o and ◊ are read "always" and "eventually" respectively. Note that "eventually" means precisely what it says, not instantly, not even necessarily today, but ... eventually. However, there are stronger statements that can be made! C. W. Johnson (1992) has made extensive use of temporal logic in specifying and prototyping safety critical process control interfaces.

Special purpose interface notations usually involve some sort of notation to talk about sequence of actions, but more often of the dialogue notation rather than the temporal logic style. In addition, such notations may allow the interface to be defined in terms of semi–autonomous agents (Abowd, 1990, 1991). This corresponds more closely to the object–oriented style of many interfaces, but has the disadvantage of being more program–like.

I have been particularly involved in two areas where current notations seem particularly weak. The first is in expressing properties such as the dragging of an icon across a screen with a mouse. In the style of specification used above, this would have to be expressed as lots of little mouse movement events which each change the state by a little, and hence change the display. This description using small scale events does not adequately reflect the fluid feel that such an action has for the user. This is an example of a status–status mapping within the interface, which reflects the variation of certain phenomena *between* events. Effective notations to describe both event and status phenomena is a current area of research (Dix, 1992).

The second area is in the description of asynchronous groupware. In synchronous groupware the effects of one user's operations are usually assumed to be instantly visible (if they happen to be on screen) to other users. However, when network delays are considered there are always small discrepancies between the state of the system at different users' machines. In addition, some cooperating users may have machines which are not permanently connected at all, communicating by email or floppy disk transfer. Extensions to temporal logic are being formulated to deal with such distributed applications (Dix 1994).

2.3 Generic models of interaction

We found ourselves in the last section beginning to discuss formal properties of multi–user systems at quite an abstract level. We moved from the discussion of shared spreadsheets to formulations of properties which could apply to any system. The models we will look at in this section are designed specifically for that purpose.

2.3.1 The PIE model

The simplest such model is the PIE model which was developed at York nearly ten years ago (Dix and Runciman, 1985). The letters used to denote various parts of the model are retained for historical reasons (if I changed them the model would no longer be a PIE). However, I won't bother to quote all the full names which go with the acronym as they now serve only to confuse.

The PIE model is based on a black–box model of an interactive system. That is, it does not look at the internal workings or structure of the computer, merely at what goes in (user inputs) and what comes out (the display and other outputs such as printed documents) (see Figure 2.2).

Whereas the specification of the calculator was constructed out of various components, the PIE model does not look inside the systems state and simply demands that there is some set *E* of states. Similarly, it does not say what the display is like, merely that there is some set *D* of legal displays. The function giving the current display from the current state is called *display* (happily not all the names are obscure). The display is intended to cover any form of immediate output whether visual or aural.

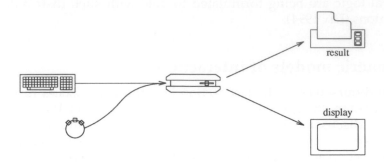

result

display

Figure 2.2 Inputs and outputs of single–user system

The model distinguishes the display from the results of the interaction; these are the outputs which persist beyond the interaction, for example the printed form of a document. However, this is in a sense potential rather than actual, as there is always assumed to be a result that you would get if you stopped the interaction now. The set of such potential results is called R and is obtained from the current state E by the function *result*.

These functions can be given mathematical types:

> *display:* $E \rightarrow D$
> *result:* $E \rightarrow R$

The user's inputs are called commands. The model can be used at various levels of granularity; for example, the commands may be individual keystrokes, or may be similar to the operations on the spreadsheet. In the case of a spreadsheet the set of commands C would be something like:

> $C = \{$ *move_left, move_right, ..., insert_col,*
>   *set_formula(*'A1+B2'*), set_formula(*'57'*), ...* $\}$

Notice that operations like *set_formula* which required extra parameters are transformed so that each instance is a separate command. At the keystroke level the set of commands might be:

> $C = \{$ 'a', 'b', ..., '0', '1', ..., *Ctrl_A, Ctrl_B, ...* $\}$

The current state of the system is a function of the history of all commands which have ever been entered. This command history is called P and the function is called I.

$$P = \textbf{seq}\ C$$
$$I: P \rightarrow E$$

This gives all the elements of the PIE model, depicted graphically in Figure 2.3 – which looks rather like the original illustration.

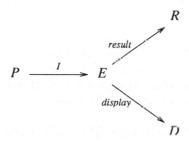

Figure 2.3 The PIE model

One does not normally think of the state as being generated from the history of user operations and specifications are not usually written this way. Instead, one considers the state transition which results from individual operations. The two views of interaction are useful in describing different properties, and so we also define the state transition function *doit* which says how a sequence of commands alters the state:

doit: $E \times \textbf{seq}\ C \rightarrow E$

Given the transition function for individual commands one can easily generate the transitions for longer sequences. For example, if *a* and *b* are two commands, we can work out the effect of $\langle a, b \rangle$ on a state *s* by:

doit(*s,* $\langle a, b \rangle$) = *doit*(*doit*(*s, a*) *b*)

The PIE model has been used to analyse a range of properties. One of the first was the meaning of WYSIWYG – "what you see is what you get", and the structure of the model was to some extent oriented towards this, representing the display – what you see, and the result – what you get. Several variants formalizing aspects of this have been produced and details can be found in Dix (1991). The basic flavour of these properties is that there must be some relationship allowing you to infer the current result from the display. The simplest is to demand the existence of a function *predict* such that:

$$predict: D \rightarrow R$$

$$\forall \ s \in E \ \bullet \ predict\,(\ display\,(\,s\,)\,) = result(s)$$

Let's consider what this says in detail. The first line says that *predict* is a function which from a display will give you a result. The second line uses $\forall$ (the universal quantifier), which is read as "for all". It says that if you consider any state s, take the display of that state and then apply the *predict* function to that display, then the result you get is exactly the same as if you had applied the *result* function directly.

In a very simple drawing package, a tracing of the screen would be exactly the same as the printed drawing. The process of drawing is effectively the *predict* function – you can predict the exact form of the printed output from the display.

This particular formulation is rather strong as it says that you can *completely* determine the result from the current display. This would not allow the printing of off–screen information. For example, imagine the drawing package had a larger drawing than would fit on a screen, with scrollbars to move about it. At any moment, the display would only show a part of the drawing and hence one could not predict all of the printed form from the *current* display. In reality, one would simply scroll back and forth over the picture in order to see it all. Variants of this predictability property can capture this sort of behaviour, but are slightly more complex.

Examining the limitations of formal properties, as we did above, not only reveals problems with the formulation of the mathematics, but also exposes real usability issues. For example, one of the early attempts to extend the predictability property asked whether it was possible to predict the result from *all* the possible displays which had that result. This was meant to mimic the user's ability to scroll over all of a document or drawing. However, an attempt to prove this over very simple systems exposed a class of interface problems. In general, you not only need to know what displays are possible, but which part of the document they referred to. This problem we called *aliasing* – you can't tell the identity of something from its content – and it arises in a wide variety of contexts. For example, many early text editors did not have a status line giving the current location. So, in a large file of numerical data it was very easy to get lost. Although most modern editors have scrollbars which show the location, these are severely limited for very large documents. There are typically only a few hundred pixels on the scrollbar, so, if the document has more lines than this, the scrollbar only gives a general idea of where in the document you are. Similar problems arise when, for example, two copies of a document are made – if the name of document is not very salient it is easy to change the wrong one!

Another set of properties concern *reachability*, that is what you can do with the system and how hard (or impossible) it is to get from one state to another. Undo is a special case of this as it concerns how one gets to the previous state in an interaction.

2.3.2 Undo

It is widely agreed that user interfaces ought to include some sort of undo facility. This not only allows recovery from errors, but gives the user confidence to explore new parts of the system. There have been several models of undo including various forms of redo (Archer et al., 1984; Vitter, 1984; Yang, 1988). However, we will only look at fairly simple undo.

The basic requirement for an undo command is that it reverses the effect of the previous command. In other words, if c is a command, then the sequence c followed by *undo* has no effect. This can easily be formalized in the PIE model:

$$\forall\ s\ \epsilon\ E\ \bullet\ doit(\ s, \langle\ c\ , undo\ \rangle\ ) = s$$

That is, whatever state, s, you start in performing c and then *undo* leaves you in the original state.

Of course, for undo to be useful it must work on all commands. Thimbleby (1990) tells the sad story of a paint program. It had an undo button which worked for all simple cases (where it wasn't really necessary). But, when one day he accidentally performed an area fill which wiped out the whole picture, he found that the undo button was disabled.

This suggests that the above formula should be true of *any* command at all. This at once raises the issue of whether the *undo* command itself is included – that is, is undo undoable? The purist would argue that for consistency's sake all commands should be equal. Indeed, if one accidentally hit the undo button surely one would like to be able to undo it. Furthermore, the undo button on many systems appears to function in this way: if you hit it a second time it restores the system to the state before the first undo. Or does it? Let's look a little more closely.

Assume our system does indeed obey the undo property for all commands *including* undo itself. Consider an arbitrary start state, call it s_0 and any two commands, say a and b. If we issue a from state s_0 we would get to some new state of the system, call it s_a whereas if we had issued b we would have got to a state s_b. However, from either state the *undo* command should return us to state s_0. This situation is shown in Figure 2.4. Notice that whichever way you go round the lozenge you get back to s_0. The top and bottom path around it represent different possible traces of user behaviour. But, what now happens if the user enters a second *undo*? Looking at the top of the lozenge, corresponding to the trace where the user entered *a*, the rule that *undo* followed by *undo* has no effect would suggest that the resulting state (denoted by "?") is s_a. However, if we look at the bottom of the lozenge, we would conclude that the state is s_b. So if our system satisfies the undo property states s_a and s_b must be identical. However, the commands *a* and *b* were not special, so whatever commands the user enters in state s_0 it always ends up in the same state (call it s_1). Of course, s_0 was also an arbitrary start state, so the system always does the same thing no matter what command the user enters. Given that one of those commands, namely *undo*, always returns one to the previous state, this implies that the system is either a flip–flop, with only two states (rather boring) or has only one state (i.e., it does nothing at all – even more boring).

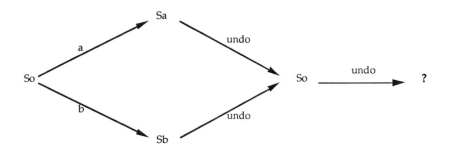

Figure 2.4 Undoing undo

Perhaps you feel you've been hoodwinked by the formal argument. Surely the above is just a limitation in the formalization of the problem. The diagram represented two possible ways the system could be used, whereas of course in reality only one could happen. Let's say it was the top path, the user does *a* followed by two *undo*s. Now when the user performs the second *undo*, surely you might say, the system knows the user did the action *a* and can thus redo it? But, if this were the case, then the system would have to explicitly remember that *a* had been done – and this knowledge would have to be in the state – just as your memories are in the internal "state" of your brain. However, if the system were remembering the *a* after the first *undo*, it could not be in the same state as it was at the start (s_0). So, either the first *undo* doesn't forget the *a* properly, or the second one can't remember it in order to redo it! The formal argument is really just a more precise and conclusive version of this argument.

The nice thing about the formal argument is that, once you have overcome the hurdle of the formalism itself, it is particularly easy to discuss different potential sequences of actions which get quite involved when expressed textually.

So, in short, we can conclude that *no* reasonable system can *ever* have an undo command that works uniformly for all commands including itself. This is an extremely general and powerful result. It means that one can stop trying to endlessly fix and refix algorithms which attempt to obtain this impossible goal. Instead, one can concentrate one's efforts on developing forms of undo which are both achievable and useful.

If this is so, then what about those systems which appear to have undoable undo? In fact, if you look carefully "appear" is the right word. The way they work is more or less as follows. Imagine the system without an undo command. It has some system state associated with it. When the undo command is added to the system the state is made more complex and effectively contains *two* (different) copies of the original state. These correspond to the current state and the last state. All the undo command does is to swop these two copies. However, the effect of a normal command is effectively to push out the old previous state and make a new current state. The undo command does not reverse this process.

Notice that in this explanation there is a difference between the state of the system that you normally think of, and the full state of the system when we take the undo command into account. The undo command reverses the effects on the former, not the latter. Like version control and other history or auditing mechanisms undo is best thought of as a meta–command that operates on a completely different level.

As well as being able to study single–user undo it is also possible to look at the meaning of undo in a multi–user context. One problem is the meaning of undo when the user (say Alison) who issues the undo command is not the same user (say Brian) who issued the last command. Should Alison's undo operate on Brian's command – called *global undo*, or on her own last command – called *local undo*. In most circumstances it is clearly local undo which the users will expect. However, there may be some form of interference between commands, so it is not clear when local undo is meaningful. A formal analysis of multi–user undo (Abowd and Dix, 1992) has exposed precisely those circumstances when local undo is possible and also shown that there are circumstances when there is no sensible meaning to it. This impasse acted as a spur to look more closely at what undo is *for*, and hence a complete re–evaluation at an informal as well as a formal level of what facilities ought to be offered for undo.

The example of undo shows how useful formal models can be as tools for understanding. The specification we originally gave for undo sounded good enough, but was inconsistent. If we had tried to build a system having such an undo, we would either fail, or *think* we had succeeded. In the former case, we might keep fruitlessly trying to build a system with a single universally applicable undo button. In the latter, we might delude ourselves into thinking this was what we had, only to discover (after selling the system!) that there were cases where it failed.

2.4 Dialogue analysis

The difficulty about proving properties of systems is that the state is very complex. For example, the state of a word processor will contain information such as:

Screen: edit screen
Text: "to be or not to be, ..."
Menu: file menu displayed
Cursor: at the 7th character line 12

To be able to prove things about such a state, we need to reason about numbers and text as well as mode indicators such as **Screen** and **Menu**. The number of possible texts and cursor positions is infinite, or even if we take into account system limits *very large*. This means we have to reason symbolically – heavy mathematics!

Dialogue descriptions usually limit themselves to the finite attributes of the state– those which have a major effect on the allowable sequences of user actions. They are thus instantly more amenable to automated analysis (we can sometimes simply try all cases). Furthermore, dialogue descriptions are often used as part of design anyway, thus we may be able to take an existing product of the design process and obtain instant added value.

I said earlier that all formalisms abstract away some details in order to emphasize and make precise others. Dialogue notations abstract away most of the details of the system state in order to emphasize the user's actions on the system and the order in which they can occur.

Even within dialogue notations there is some variation of level of abstraction. Some deal with low–level user events such as mouse clicks and keystrokes, others deal with more abstract events such as "enter login name". Also some dialogue notations do capture some aspects of the state, especially those which are intended for prototyping. However, in the latter notations the state description is usually clearly separable from the "real" dialogue description. More normally the effects of user's actions on the system state is denoted by textual annotations or by the use of meaningful names.

2.4.1 Notations

There are a large number of different dialogue notations. Some use diagrammatic representations of the dialogue (see below) and others use textual representations (such as the use of grammars or production rules).

Of the diagrammatic techniques, *state transition network* (STNs) are most heavily used. (But even they come in several variants.) We will base our discussion primarily on STNs, but other notations could equally be used.

State transition nets consist of two elements:

circles – denoting the states of the dialogue
arcs – between the circles, denoting the user actions/events

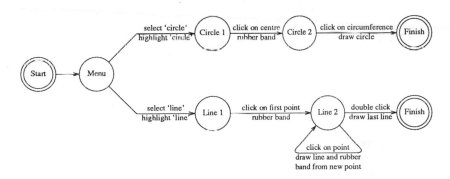

Figure 2.5 State transition network for menu–driven drawing tool

Figure 2.5 shows a STN describing a portion of the dialogue of a simple drawing tool. The arcs are also labelled with the feedback or system response resulting from the user's actions. Note how cramped the arcs get – obviously a lot is happening at each event.

The STN for a full system would usually be enormous. To manage the complexity, STNs are often described hierarchically. For example, Figure 2.5 shows the higher level dialogue for the drawing tool, selecting between several sub–menus. The menu in Figure 2.5 corresponds to the graphics sub–menu. Each of the sub–menus would have similar STNs describing them.

The hierarchical decomposition in this diagram is of states. Single states in the high–level diagram correspond to an entire low–level STN. There are other possibilities for hierarchical decomposition; for

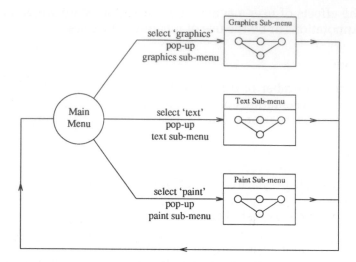

Figure 2.6 Hierarchical state transition network for complete drawing tool

example, augmented transition networks allow both user actions and system responses to be decomposed into further STNs.

2.4.2 Why do people use dialogue notations?

One advantage of performing formal analysis on dialogue descriptions is that they often "come for free", a natural product of the design process. There are several reasons for this which we'll look at in turn.

UIMS

If we use a User Interface Management System (UIMS) or User Interface Development Environment (UIDE) this will usually include a formal description of the dialogue. This may be in the form of production rules, a grammar or even some graphical representation. Some of these representations, especially production rules, do not completely separate the dialogue from the underlying state. However, the conversion required is certainly far less work than generating the description from scratch *and* is guaranteed to be consistent with the actual system.

Paper specification

A second reason for the use of dialogue descriptions is simply as a paper specification method, just as one might use data–flow diagrams for information systems or entity–relationship diagrams for database design. Several years ago I was working in a data processing department producing information systems under a forms–based transaction processing (TP) environment.

Programming a TP system is similar to many window systems, basically a stimulus–response model. Your program gets a screen full of data and must decide what to do with it. When it has processed that screen, it sends a fresh template to the user and then goes on to service a *different* terminal. Because of this form of programming, one cannot implicitly encode the dialogue within the program structure. So, for example, it is quite difficult to ensure that the user can only delete a record after it has been displayed.

To ease the problem of writing (relatively) complex dialogues under this regime, the author used flowcharts to describe the interaction with each user. Figure 2.6 shows a flowchart for a delete sub–dialogue similar to those used.

Note two things, despite surface similarities, there are important differences both from normal program flowcharts and from STNs.

First, note that a flowchart of the program implementing this dialogue would (because of the stimulus–response model) be tree-like. It would have to explicitly store the dialogue state and generally being totally incomprehensible *without* the corresponding dialogue description. Furthermore, the sorts of things one puts in the boxes of a dialogue flowchart are different from what goes into program flowcharts. For example, reading a record could be a complex activity, say searching through a file until the matching record is found. However, from the dialogue viewpoint this corresponds to a single system action.

Note also that although superficially like an STN, with boxes connected by arrows, the emphasis is rather different. The boxes represent system processes or user interactions; that is, the notation is event/process oriented rather than state oriented.

In a different vein, formal notations are often criticized for the amount of work required. However, the author's experience counters this. The author used these diagrams and converted them, mechanically, but by hand, into COBOL programs. Using this method I was able to produce, within days, systems which had previously taken months to complete. Furthermore, changes could be accomplished within hours (no mean feat within such an environment!). Although it might be nice to think this was due to superior programming skills (!), this could in no way account for an order of magnitude difference in productivity.

That is, the adoption of a kind of formal notation did not waste valuable time, but instead made phenomenal time savings.

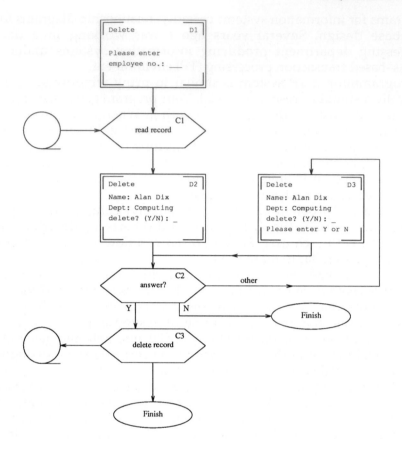

Figure **2.7** Flow chart of deletion sub–dialogue

Prototyping

Dialogue descriptions can be used to drive prototyping tools or simulators. This is rather like the use with UIMS, but usually with a less extensive environment. One example of this is Heather Alexander's SPI notation (Specification Prototyping and Interaction) (Alexander, 1987). This uses a variant of CSP for the dialogue description and then has tools which allow one to "run" the dialogue seeing the possible interaction paths.

Another support tool is Hyperdoc developed by Harold Thimbleby (Thimbleby, 1993), shown in Figure 2.8. The screen shows part of the description for a JVC video–recorder. The top half of the screen is a drawing of the interface. The buttons on the drawing are active – the simulation runs when they are pressed. On the bottom left, we can see part of the dialogue description. This describes the transitions from the state "playPause". For example, if the user presses the "Operate" button, the state will change to "offTapeIn".

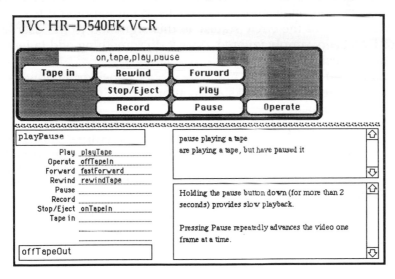

Figure 2.8 Hyperdoc

In fact, this tool does more than simply simulate the dialogue, it can perform several forms of dialogue analysis.

2.4.3 Dialogue properties

Given a dialogue description, we can begin to look at what properties it satisfies. There are several dialogue properties which are to do with local dialogue actions from a single state:

- *Completeness* – look at each state, is there an arc coming from that state for each possible user action? If not, what is the effect on the system if the user performs this action? This is a good way of checking for "unforeseen circumstances".

- *Determinism* – is the behaviour uniquely defined for each user action. In a simple STN this corresponds to checking that there is at most one arc labelled with each user action from a particular state. Non–determinism can be deliberate, corresponding to an application decision. However, it can be a mistake, and this is especially easy in complex hierarchical STNs, production rules systems etc. Automatic tools can help check for this.

- *Consistency* – does the same user action have a similar effect in different states? If not are these dialogue *modes* visibly different?

If we look back to Figure 2.4, we can check it for completeness. The action "select–line" is not mentioned in either of the line states, but this is deliberate. The line option is assumed to be on a pop–up menu and so cannot occur except from the menu state. The remaining actions are then single and double clicks. What happens if we double click in either of the circle states? Is this signalled to the user as an error by a beep, simply ignored, does it do something odd (a feature!) or does it crash the program?

Another set of properties are more global, considering how easy or difficult it is to get from one state to another, and often encompassing whole trains of actions.

- *Reachability* – can you get anywhere from anywhere? That is, imagine you are at a particular dialogue state and you want to get to a different state. Is there a sequence of user actions which is guaranteed to get you there? In addition, we may want to ask just how complicated and long that sequence is.

- *Reversibility* – can you get to the previous state? Imagine you have just done an action, but wished you hadn't. This is a special case of reachability, but one which we expect to be especially easy – we all make mistakes. Note this is *not* undo – returning to a previous dialogue state does not in general reverse the semantic effect.

- *Dangerous states* – there are some states you don't want to get to. Does the system make it difficult to perform actions which take you to these dangerous states?

As an example, we can check the reversibility of the drawing tool (Figures 2.5 and 2.6). Imagine we want to reverse the effect of "select 'line'" from the graphics Menu state. We can perform three actions:

click – double click – select "graphics"

These return us to the graphics pop–up menu. However, these will leave a vestigial circle on the display. That is, in this case, as we warned, reversing the dialogue is *not* undo.

Note also that this reachability for dialogue states is equivalent to the definition for full system states, but weaker. A system cannot be reachable in the PIE sense if it is not reachable at the dialogue level, but, like undo, dialogue reachability does not guarantee full reachability.

In graph theoretic terms, dialogue reachability is called strong connectivity and the Hyperdoc tool, described previously, is able to perform this analysis for the designer.

2.4.4 Example – digital watch

User's documentation

A digital watch has a very limited interface – 3 buttons. These must control the watch display (time/calendar) a stopwatch mode and an alarm.

We only consider one of the buttons, button "A", which is used to move between the four main modes: time/calendar, stopwatch, alarm setting and time setting.

Figure 2.9 shows a portion of the user instructions. It is a simple state transition network.

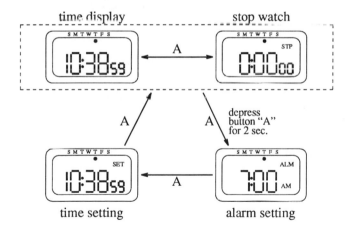

Figure 2.9 Instructions for digital watch

We can analyse this network. The time and alarm setting modes are dangerous states: we don't want to set the time by accident. These states are guarded – you have to hold the button down for two seconds. This button is very small and it is difficult to hold it down by accident.

What about completeness? The idea of holding the button down suggests that we ought to distinguish the actions of depressing and releasing button "A". So, what do these actions do in the different modes?

Although the STN is incomplete this is acceptable for the user instructions so long as undocumented sequences of actions do not have a disastrous effect. However, the designer must investigate all possibilities to check this.

Designer's documentation

Extensive experimentation eventually revealed the complete STN for the watch, shown in Figure 2.10. This includes for each state the effect of the three actions:

- depress A
- release A
- wait two seconds

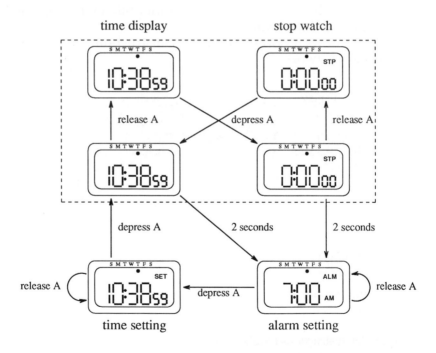

Figure 2.10 Design diagram for digital watch

Notice that this required the addition of two meta–stable versions of the time/calendar state and the stopwatch state. This is the sort of diagram that the designer would need to analyse and to pass on to the implementor.

The diagram looks fairly complex – and we've only looked at one button!

2.4.5 Example – dangerous states

One of the word processors being used to prepare this document exhibits dangerous states. It has two main modes, the main mode where you edit the text, and a menu and help screen from where you perform filing operations. You switch between these modes with the "F1" key. In addition, from the menu you can exit the word processor by hitting the "F2" key. These modes and the exit are shown in Figure 2.11.

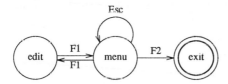

Figure 2.11 Main modes of text editor

If the text has been altered it is automatically saved upon exit. However, if you have altered the text, but then decide to abandon your edits, this automatic save can be turned off by hitting the escape key in the Menu mode. Subsequent edits will reset this and the text will be again be saved. Of course, not saving altered text is dangerous (but may be required). In order to expose this behaviour the diagram must be redrawn with the states duplicated to differentiate exit with and without save . We therefore get the diagram in Figure 2.12, in which the dangerous states have been hatched.

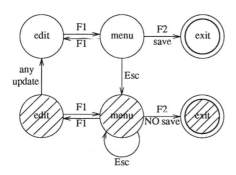

Figure 2.12 Revised STN with dangerous states

This multiplying of states is a *semantic* distinction, but can be recorded in the dialogue. We can then ask at a dialogue level whether or not it is easy to get into the dangerous states by accident. The user spends most of the time in the edit state, so the most dangerous sequence is "F1–Esc–F2" – exit with *no* save. This is rather close to the sequence "F1–F2" – exit *with* save, but is this mistake easy to make?

If we decided it was, we can insert a guard, such as a dialogue box asking for confirmation. In fact, the word processor has no such guard.

The dialogue is *not* as is sometimes claimed independent of presentation. There are various lexical and presentation issues which impinge on the dialogue. In particular, the layout of keys on a keyboard or menu items on a screen affects the sort of lexical errors which occur. For example, the author's old computer had the function keys on a separate keypad. One could not accidentally hit "Esc" in the middle of the sequence "F1–F2". However, the author's current keyboard layout is as in Figure 2.13 – disaster!

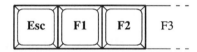

Figure 2.13 Dangerous function key layout

2.5 Summary

Because it forces you to be explicit, using a formal specification forces the designer to clarify design issues. Details which might be missed or ignored are made explicit and salient. We saw that even when discussing a simple four function calculator and it will also be apparent in the next chapter. This does not mean that one is swamped in a sea of detail. The ability to work at different levels of abstraction means that you can choose which aspects require this precise treatment. However, having selected the appropriate abstraction, the formalism does not allow you to fudge issues!

Generic models are designed to allow particularly high–level analysis. In our example, we saw how a formal analysis showed that certain types of undo command are impossible. It would be virtually impossible to come to this conclusion without a formal analysis. Even many failed attempts at designing and programming such an undo system would not convince one of its impossibility as the complexity of the task would suggest that there were still alternatives to try.

However, note that the result of this analysis is an improved understanding of undo which can then be communicated without necessarily using full formalism.

We saw that formal modelling techniques, although powerful and useful, require a high level of formal expertise. The generation of informal understanding is one way that the benefits of formal work can distributed. However, in order to "give away" the benefits of this work to the typical human–factors practitioner less maths–intensive forms of analysis are also required.

Dialogue notations of various forms are often used during the interface design process. We have seen how simplified forms of the usability properties can be tested on dialogue descriptions, sometimes with automatic support. Furthermore, the dangerous states example showed how the dialogue description can form a focus for information from both the semantic level (what is dangerous) and the lexical level (what slips are easy to make).

Diagrammatic dialogue notations are not less formal because they are graphical. They simply are formal about different things. Even a drawing of a proposed screen design is formal in that one can check the eventual system against this "specification": are the specified fields present, are they positioned as shown? Similarly, an hierarchical task analysis, as in Chapter 7, makes very precise and formal statements about the performance of a task using a system. Any form of specification involves some formal parts about which it makes precise statements, some informal parts perhaps in the form of textual comments, and some things about which it says nothing. The important question is not whether or not you should use formal methods – instead one needs to look at the methods being used and ask whether you know which aspects are formal, and if so whether they are being formal about the right things. And if not – well, perhaps you should try some of the ideas in this chapter!

Further reading

General

Dix, A. J., Finlay, J. E., Abowd, G., and Beale, R. (1993). *Human-Computer Interaction*. London: Prentice Hall.
The material in this paper draws extensively from Chapters 8 and 9 of this book, which also expands upon several of the areas.

Formal models of interaction and specification

Dix, A. J. (1991). *Formal methods for interactive systems*. London: Academic Press.

This covers the PIEmodel and many extensions and other models, including those on which status/event analysis is based.

Harrison, M.D. and Thimbleby, H.W., (eds) (1990). *Formal Methods in Human Computer Interaction*. Cambridge: Cambridge University Press,.

An edited collection covering a range of formal techniques.

Thimbleby, H. W. (1990). *User Interface Design*. New York: ACM Press, Addison-Wesley.

A wide–ranging book which some extensive explicit formal material, and employing a formal approach to problems in much of its informal material.

Dix, A. J. and Runciman, C. (1985). Abstract models of interactive systems. In *HCI '85: People and Computers I: Designing the Interface*, P. Johnson, and S. Cook (eds), pp. 13–22. Cambridge: Cambridge University Press.

The original PIE paper.

Sufrin, B. (1982). Formal specification of a display editor. *Science of Computer Programming* 1, 157–202.

A classic paper describing the formal specification of a display based text editor.

Dix, A. J. (1992). Beyond the interface. In *Engineering for Human-Computer Interaction*, J. Larson, and C. Unger, (eds), pp. 171–190. Amsterdam, North-Holland.

Describes some aspects of status/event analysis relating status/event phenomena to the timescales over which they operate and the concept of *pace*. See also Chapter 9 of Dix et al. (1993) for status–event timeline diagrams and Chapter 10 of Dix (1991) for its formal roots.

Undo

In case the reader's appetite for the fascinating area of undo has been whetted here are a few papers to read. In addition, see Chapter 2 and 4 of Dix (1991) and Chapter 12 of Thimbleby (1990).

Abowd, G. D. and Dix, A. J. (1992). Giving undo attention. *Interacting with Computers* 4(3), 317–342.

A formal analysis of undo in the context of group editing.

Archer, Jr., J., Conway, R. and Schneider, F.B. (1984). User recovery and reversal in interactive systems. *ACM Transactions on Programming Languages* 6(1), 1–19.

A classic paper analysing different forms of undo.

Vitter, J. S. (1984). US&R: A new framework for redoing. *IEEE Software* 1(4), 39–52.

Takes undo and redo to its extreme!

Yang, Y. (1988). Undo support models. *International Journal of Man-Machine Studies* 28(5), pp. 457–481.

Informal analysis and review.

Dialogue

As well as the following, see Chapter 8 of (Dix et al., 1993) which describes dialogue properties in more detail and any book on UIMS.

Alexander, H. (1987). *Formally-based Tools and Techniques for Human-Computer Dialogues*. London: Ellis Horwood.
Describes her SPI notation which is both quite powerful and very easy to read.

Thimbleby, H. W. (1993). Combining systems and manuals. In J. L. Alty, D. Diaper and S. Guest (eds),*HCI '93: People and Computers VIII*,   pp. 479-488. Cambridge: Cambridge University Press.
Describes the Hyperdoc tool, which supports simulation, dialogue analysis and automatic documentation.

Chapter 3

The software engineering of interactive systems

Roger Took

3.1 Introduction: The role of abstraction in development

Effective and efficient construction of interactive systems needs firstly a precise and abstract specification of the *functionality* of the required system. Secondly it needs a rigorous *development method* by which to turn this specification into a concrete implementation. This at least is the software engineering perspective on interactive system construction. This view takes account of the *end* user of the system firstly in an initial *requirements* phase which discovers the functionality (*What* does the user want the system essentially to do?). The user is secondly consulted (it is to be hoped) during development when details of the presentation and behaviour of the system (*How* does the user want the system to do it?) are worked out.

There are a number of perceived benefits to this engineering approach. If pursued rigorously, then the client user is guaranteed to get what was asked for, in the sense that fundamental to the approach is the *preservation*, through to the concrete implementation, of properties expressed abstractly. Perhaps more importantly, however, a rigorous software engineering approach distinguishes clearly between *essential* properties on the one hand, and, on the other, *design options*, among which the designer and/or user is free to choose according to taste or usability.

Abstraction has two further benefits. Firstly, an abstract formulation of the requirements of an interactive system is, ideally, *tractable*, such that the consequences and any inconsistencies of an initial design can be explored and exposed before committing to an implementation. Further, it may be possible to express, at a similar level of abstraction, *general* properties which *a priori* or through experience should hold of *all* interactive systems. This perspective is taken in the previous chapter. Secondly, an abstract formulation is the ideal raw material for an *architectural* design, that is, an organization of the system into a structure of logical components which satisfies the original requirements but which may be more *rational*, such that it optimizes software *reuse*.

The perspective of this chapter is towards abstraction both as a means of rationalizing requirements, and as a way of reconciling the rigorous (and hence mechanical) development advocated by software engineering with the more creative, user–oriented aspects of system design. The first part of the chapter examines the variety of ways of *abstractly* designing and organising interactive applications. The second part of the chapter then examines various options for practical architectures, that is, architectures in which components are *implementations*.

The chapter uses a simple game as a prototypical interactive system. Its abstractions are expressed in the formal notation Z (Spivey, 1989), for which all necessary explanation is given as required. It is important to recognize that Z here is just the *medium* for the message. There are a number of other classes of formal notation, each with advantages and disadvantages in expressiveness and power. Z is chosen here since its meaning is fairly intuitive, and it can express relatively clearly the *structuring* of a specification.

3.2 An example

As an example throughout this chapter I will use a game called *Min*, which is a simplified variant of the well known game of *Nim* (Berlekamp et al., 1982). The task will be to construct an interactive computer–based version of *Min*. This illustrates all the relevant issues in building interactive systems from some specific requirements, with the minimum of extraneous detail. The standard rules for *Min* from which we start are the following:

> *Min is a game for two players. Seven matches are laid on a table. Each player, in turn, picks up either one or two matches. The winner is the player to pick up the last match.*

An obvious prototype for our target system is one in which the computer supplies a bare representation for the matches, and a means for the players to remove them. For example this could be a graphical picture of the matches, and removal could be by clicking the mouse cursor over match images:

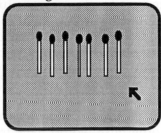

This is hardly computer *support* for the game, since players must still remember whose turn it is, restrain themselves from taking more than two matches, and recognize when and by whom the game has been won. We at least require an interactive computer-based version of *Min* to support this functionality.

Note how these requirements for *Min* typify interactive systems in general. There is a *state* which must be maintained throughout the interaction (the set of matches and the current player). There are *operations* which update the state (each player can *take* one or two matches from the set). There are *constraints* on the use of the operations which must be enforced (each player takes in *turn*; no more than *two* matches can be taken). There are *functions* which must be *evaluated* (has the current state of the game been *won*? If so, *which* player has won?). There is, finally, an implicit *enquiry* on the internal state which generates an output *presentation* (the match images) which we require to be reused as an input medium. This last requirement for *direct manipulation* (Shneiderman, 1982) is pragmatic rather than essential, since we could have satisfied the other requirements with an indirect command–line system where users explicitly enquire of the internal state using a query operation such as state?. Interaction might then proceed (system output is in bold):

```
Player1> take 2
Player2> take 2
Player1> state?
There are 3 matches left.
Player1> take 1
Player2> take 2
Player2 has won!
```

We first of all examine how we might express these requirements precisely, concisely, and abstractly.

3.3 Abstract architectures

We think of an architecture as a logical structure of components. The key quality of an architectural component is *reuse*. If a component cannot be reused in another context, then there is little point in distinguishing it. On the other hand, by virtue of its generality, a reusable component can *factor* properties from a range of different contexts. For example, a User Interface Management System (UIMS) is reusable to provide interfaces for a range of applications, and (in theory) it can incorporate general user interface properties and constraints that otherwise would have to be reimplemented in each application.

An architectural component can either be *inherited* or *addressed*. Classes of general user interface tools, for example dialogue boxes, buttons, or menus, may be inherited into more specialized tools for a particular application. On the other hand, a window manager may provide constructs (windows) and primitives (text, lines and circles etc.) which are addressed or *called* by the application. Architectures built with inheritance links are also called *is_a* structures, and their components are *types* or *classes*. Architectures built with addressing links are also called *has_a* structures, and their components are objects or procedures.

3.3.1 Is_a structures

Is_a structures are essentially *acyclic*, and so are in the shape of trees or hierarchies. For example, in considering how to build *Min*, we might first abstract a class representing *any* game, and place this at the top of our hierarchy. We might then *specialize* this into a number of separate *subclasses* for one–player games, two–player games etc., and then make *Min* a subclass of two–player games:

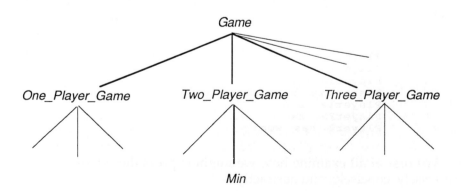

We say that *Min is_a Two_Player_Game,* which *is_a Game.* This is because *Min inherits* all the attributes of the class of *Two_Player_Games,* which in turn inherits all the attributes of the class of *Games.* The benefit of this organization is that inherited attributes do not have to be redefined in the subclasses.

The great difficulty of building such a hierarchy is that there are almost always alternative classification schemes. For example, we could consider classes of individual games as distinct from team games, or games that involve skill as distinct from games that involve chance. There are a number of rules of thumb. If two classes share a number of attributes, then it is rational to abstract those attributes into a superclass. If a class has only one subclass, then there would seem little point in distinguishing it from that subclass.

We go on to consider the representation of a class as a *state space,* using *Min* as an example.

3.3.2 State and state space

The critical feature of state is that it contains *values* that are *identifiable* via *names* or *attributes.* These names *persist over changes* to their values, and we keep track of, and update, the values through their names. Thus the names in this case are *variables.* We can model state abstractly using a *name–value* mapping or function. The natural use of the word *state* is ambiguous here: we should carefully distinguish between a *particular* state, which records the current values of the named attributes of some entity at a particular point in time, and the state of a system in *general,* which we can more precisely call the *state space* of a system. The state space is the set of *all possible* name–value mappings. It is called a space because we can regard each variable name as identifying a *dimension,* and each mapping (i.e. each state or instance) as equivalent to a *coordinate point* in the space defined by the dimensions.

The formal notation Z takes this model of state as fundamental, and packages variable names in a *schema,* which has a box–like syntax and can itself be named. Schemas generally have two parts. The upper part, or *signature,* records the set of variables and the types or ranges of values that they can be bound to. The lower part is a *predicate* (i.e. a *truth–valued* expression) which states *logical constraints* over variables in the signature. The schema itself is thus a *state space,* and represents that subset of the possible values of the variables for which the predicate is **true.** The predicate may be empty (i.e. always **true**). For example, the state space for our architectural component that represents games in general can be expressed as the predicate–less schema:

Game_State _____

player: one | *two*
won: **true** | **false**
_____

In *Game_State* we model the current player state by a variable *player* for which we enumerate the special values *one* and *two*. We could generalize this for any number of players by declaring *player* to be of type **N** (i.e. a natural number), but the extra machinery obscures the issue. In any particular *Game_State*, also, it may be **true** or **false** that the game has been *won*. Thus the state space of *Game_State* is two–dimensional (it has two variables), and has four points (each dimension has only two values). This can be illustrated:

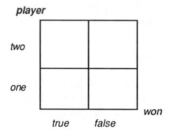

Clearly, as we might wish, *Game_State* records the essential elements of a game state, that is, whose turn it is, and whether the game has been won.

Thus we identify class, state space and schema, and take a particular state to be an *instance* of a schema. Note that in a fully *object–oriented* language, the attributes of a class include the *operations* possible within the class. In Z, however, operations are expressed *over* schemas.

3.3.3 State change

Z models operations as *state transitions*. That is, an operation in Z acts on a state in some schema state space, and results in a new state somewhere in the *same* state space. The operation itself is conceived to be the set of *all possible* such state transitions, or in other words a state ↔ state *relation*. Z defines operations using schemas in which *primed* (') variables refer to the resultant state *after* the operation, and unprimed variables to the state *before,* and in which the predicate expresses some relationship between the previous and resultant states. If a schema name is *included* in another schema, it is understood that the first schema's signature and predicate are added to the signature and predicate respectively of the including schema. As a shorthand, Z provides a symbol Δ which when prefixed to an included schema name, means that *two* copies of the schema are included, one with its variables primed and the other unprimed.

Thus a fundamental operation *Turn* on *Game_State*s can be defined as the schema:

```
Turn
    Λ Game_State

    ¬ won
    player' ≠ player
```

Preconditions and partiality

Preconditions of Z operations are any clauses (lines) in the predicate (lines in the predicate are implicitly logically *and*-ed) which are expressed purely in the *unprimed* language. So a precondition of the *Turn* operation above is that the previous *Game_State* should not already have been won (¬*won*). By this means we ensure that a game stops as soon as it is won, since then no further *Turns* can be taken. Note that preconditions limit the *domain* of the operation (i.e. the set of previous states in which the operation is possible). In this case we say that the operation is *partial*. Thus *Turn* is partial over its domain of (*player, won*) pairs – it is *impossible* when *won* is **true**.

Postconditions and determinism

Postconditions of Z operations are any clauses that are expressed using the primed language, or a mixture of primed and unprimed language. Thus the *postcondition player'* ≠ *player* ensures that play alternates between the two players. However, we do not provide a postcondition for *won'*. That is, we do not say at this level of abstraction whether the game is *won* as a result of the *Turn* operation. This is as it should be, since in effect *winning* will be a decision necessarily based on the particular semantics (rules) of whatever game we are using *Game_State* to build, which it would clearly be premature to specify here in advance. Thus while we are sure what the resultant *player* state will be, given its previous state (it is *determined* by this operation), the resultant state of *won* may be *either* **true** or **false**. Therefore the operation *Turn* is *non-deterministic*.

3.3.4 Initialization

A characteristic of interactive systems is that there is some start state or states. Conventionally in Z the start state is specified by an initialization *operation*. This has *Init* in its name, and is understood to take place at the beginning of interaction. In other respects it is a standard Z operation, except that it makes no reference to *previous* state (i.e. it does not use unprimed variables). A *Game_State* initialization is:

$$
\begin{array}{|l}
\hline
\textit{Init\_Game\_State} \\\\
\hline
\Delta\,\textit{Game\_State} \\\\
\hline
\neg\,\textit{won}' \\\\
\textit{player}' = \textit{one} \\\\
\hline
\end{array}
$$

Thus initially the game has not been *won*, and it is *player one*'s turn.

3.3.5 Inheritance

So far we have defined a general class *Game_State* that factors the essential attributes of games from all the possible particular games that we might wish to define. In order to use this component in a specification *architecture*, these attributes must be *inherited* into some more specific component that adds either language to its signature or properties to its predicate. For example, in order now to create the particular game of *Min*, we can define a state–space schema *Min_State* by inheriting and adding to the *Game_State* schema:

$$
\begin{array}{|l}
\hline
\textit{Min\_State} \\\\
\hline
\textit{Game\_State} \\\\
\textit{matches} : \ \mathbf{N} \\\\
\hline
\end{array}
$$

In this case we add extra language (*matches*) to the signature, but no further properties to the predicate.

The initial state of *Min* is one in which (according to our informal requirements) there are 7 *matches*, in addition to the initial attribute values of all games inherited from *Init_Game_State*:

```
Init_Min_State _____

  Init_Game_State
  Δ Min_State
_____

  matches' = 7
```

In the same way, in order to construct the essential interactive *Min* operation which allows each player in turn to take some number of matches from *matches*, we inherit and specialize the general *Game_State* operation *Turn*. Thus we define an operation *Take* which is *parameterized* by the number of matches to be taken (in Z, a variable suffixed with *?* is understood to be an *input* parameter):

```
Take _____

  Turn
  Δ Min_State
  number?:  N
_____

  1 ≤ number? ≤ 2
  matches' = matches – number?
  matches' = 0 ↔ won'
```

The rule that only one or two matches can be taken in each turn is incorporated here as a precondition for *Take* (its first clause). The *effect* of *Take* is given in the last two clauses as a postcondition: *matches* is reduced by *number?*, and if as a result *matches'* is zero, then the game has been *won*. Note that specifying exactly when the game is *won* tightens the inherited non–deterministic *Turn* to be deterministic. That is, for any previous *Min_State*, *Take* now specifies only one possible resultant *Min_State*.

Any interactive system can be specified as consisting fundamentally of a single operation like this. In order to cope with the apparent multiplicity of, say, a graphical desktop, this basic operation may have to be multiply parameterised. Essentially, these parameters will specify a *selection* of the graphical (and hence internal) state, and some *update* factors of that component of the state.

3.3.6 Operation design

Whenever an operation is parameterized, there are design options. That is, we always have a choice of providing *more* operations with *fewer* parameters, without in any way affecting the abstract state–transition capability of the system. A parameterized operation can be converted into a more specific operation by *pre–applying* it to one or more of its expected parameter values (technically, this is called *currying*). For example, we can create a more specific (parameterless) operation *Take_One* by specifying in advance that *number?* must be 1:

```
Take_One _____
  Take
  _____
  number? = 1
```

Clearly, in order to satisfy *Min*'s requirements we would also have to create another operation *Take_Two* in which *number?* was pre–set to 2.

Thus we have the design option to make two operations *Take_One* and *Take_Two* instead of the single *Take*. In the same way, we can use currying to decompose any monolithic operation into a number of more specialised operations. In the case of *Take_One* and *Take_Two* this has the advantage that the user cannot now enter an illegal *number?* of matches to take. However, this is only feasible since there are just two choices for the user at this stage. Other application operations may have parameters with many or an infinite number of values. We could model a word processor, for example, as a single operation *make_document* which took a string of characters (the text) as its parameter. It would certainly be infeasible to implement this as an infinite number of buttons each of which generated a different ready–written document!

These considerations on operation decomposition are especially important in deciding whether to use a dialogue box (a single operation with multiple parameters) or a series of icons or menu hierarchy (an equivalent *set* of operations with fewer or no parameters).

3.3.7 Has_a structures

Schemas or classes represent the set of all their possible instances. Thus they behave and can be used as a *type,* and variables can be declared of schema (class) type. In an object–oriented context, such variables are known as *objects.* That is, an object is identifiable by name, and can have a number of values over time, all of which are instances of the object's class.

The second important kind of structure is over objects, and is expressed in a relation which is variously called *has_a, part_of,* or *uses.* Consider a schema *Icon*, which is an abstract specification of any visual object. This has just a coordinate *position*, and an *area* represented as a set (**P** for *power set*) of coordinate points:

```
Icon _____
  position:  N × N
  area: P (N × N)
```

Now if we should wish to build a *Display* consisting of two distinct *copies* of *Icon*, we might naïvely expect to achieve this by multiply inheriting *Icon*:

```
Bad_Display _____
  Icon
  Icon
```

Since inheritance (schema inclusion) is simply the *union* of signatures and predicates, *Bad_Display* is identical to a schema that inherits *Icon* just once. Moreover, it is unlikely that we would consider *Icons* to be *Displays*, as the *is_a* relation would suggest. Instead we must *use Icon* as a type, and declare two *Icon objects* as *part_of* the *Display:*

```
Good_Display _____
  icon1:  Icon
  icon2 : Icon
```

The *Icon* objects are now distinguishable by their names. Building an instance of *Good_Display* means making two instances of *Icon*, and assigning them as initial values for the names *icon1* and *icon2*. Classes like *Good_Display* are sometimes called *aggregate* or *container* classes.

Has_a structures coexist with *is_a* structures in architectures, but may be modified dynamically, since this is a matter of *updating* values. In contrast, an *is_a* structure is difficult to modify once any instances have been made from it, since then the ancestry of the instances changes. A *has_a* structure is necessary wherever we wish to distinguish between copies of a class, but it is sometimes also useful to *use* (i.e. name), rather than inherit, a class, even once. On a larger scale, for example, we can model *channels of communication* between discrete software nodes using *has_a* (i.e. named) links. Thus an application might *have* a link to the window manager. This style of programming is sometimes called *delegation* (Lieberman, 1986; Stein, 1987). On a smaller scale, *has_a* structures model variables in a record, and procedure calls in a program.

3.4 Refinement

In standard software engineering practice, once an abstract specification has been formulated and verified, then it can be developed into a concrete implementation by a process of *refinement*. Refinement preserves the abstract properties, but allows further properties to be introduced for the convenience of the implementor or end user. Thus the user interface of an application is, ideally, a refinement of the abstract properties of the application. It is during refinement that there is most scope for user–oriented design.

As we have seen, the abstract properties may specify both the functionality of the system (i.e. its set of operations), and its state or *data*. Refinement is correspondingly split into orthogonal steps of *operation* refinement and *data* refinement (Morgan, 1987).

3.4.1 Operation refinement

We noted above that our abstract operation *Turn* was both partial and non–deterministic. These qualities point to two ways in which *operations* may be refined. As partiality results from a strong precondition (i.e. one that is not just **true**) which limits the *domain* of an operation (i.e. the set of states on which it can operate), we can *extend* the domain of an operation by logically *weakening* its precondition. The abstract specification of an operation specifies the result state(s) if the operation is applied to any state in its (limited) domain. So long as we implement at least this abstract state–transition relation, then we are free to extend this by defining the result of applying the operation to states *not* in its abstract domain. If I require a spanner to undo a particular nut, then I should be satisfied with an *adjustable* spanner, even though it is applicable to more nuts. We are also strictly free to implement any change whatever for states not in the abstract domain, as the operation is not abstractly defined on them. So if the spanner breaks when I attempt to undo a nut of a different size, then I have no grounds for complaint since I did not originally request this wider capability.

In *Min*, since we parameterize the abstract *Take* operation with *any number?* of matches to be taken, we allow the user to make an *error* by attempting to take too many matches. Abstractly we have only defined *Take* partially in the cases where a legal *number?* of matches is entered. A suitable refinement of *Take* in a concrete interactive system is to extend its domain to handle the entry of illegal *number?*s of matches, but in these cases to respond with an error message. Thus the concrete operation can become *total* over its domain, and so always behave sensibly.

However, we cannot achieve this precondition–weakening refinement using inheritance. This is because new properties are always logically *conjoined* (*and*–ed) with inherited properties, and conjunction only ever *strengthens*. So formally we must rewrite the operation. Both here and probably in implementation, this is in the form of a case statement which discriminates between legal and illegal invocation. We also make the error message an *output* variable *report!* (*!* is Z convention for output):

$$
\begin{array}{l}
\textit{Take+} \\\hline
\textit{Turn} \\
\Delta\,\textit{Min\_State} \\
\textit{number?: } \mathbf{N} \\
\textit{report!: String} \\\hline
\textit{number ? } > 2 \quad\quad \Rightarrow \textit{matches' = matches} \wedge \textit{report! = "Too many!"} \\
\textit{number? } < 1 \quad\quad \Rightarrow \textit{matches' = matches} \wedge \textit{report! = "Too few!"} \\
1 \leq \textit{number? } \leq 2 \quad \rightarrow \textit{matches' = matches - number?} \wedge \textit{report! = ""} \\
\textit{matches' - 0 } \Leftrightarrow \textit{won'}
\end{array}
$$

This refinement throws up error–handling design issues which are unclear from the requirements. What happens to the state of the system in the case of an error? Here we assume the state is unchanged (*matches'* = *matches*). What happens to the *player* who makes an error? Here, since we inherit *Turn* as before, the player loses his turn.

The second way in which we can refine an operation is to reduce its non–determinism. For example, if I do not specify whether or not the spanner is to *tighten* the nut, then, strictly speaking, I should be satisfied either with one that does tighten the nut, or with one that does not. This refinement is obviously only applicable to operations that are (in specification) non–deterministic. Non–determinism is reduced by *strengthening* the *postcondition*. This *can* be accomplished by inheritance. In fact, refinement by postcondition strengthening occurs between *Turn* and *Take*, since, as we noted, the conjunction of the predicate *matches'* = *0* ⇔ *won'* resolves the non–determinism over winning in *Turn*.

3.4.2 Data refinement

Data refinement allows us to *enrich* the representation of our abstract values (states). In the case of *Min*, even though we have named the state component *matches*, our abstract representation for this is simply as a number. By contrast, the standard implementation of *Min* uses *sets* of *actual* matches. Not only does this have the properties of sets, it has the (perhaps infinite) number of distinct empirical properties of real matches: weight, length, colour, material, combustibility, etc. Formally speaking, such data refinement adds *observations* of the abstract states in terms of *external* (already understood) sorts of things like grams, millimetres and colours.

In a computer–based interactive system, of course, the closest we can get to this sort of enrichment is to *image* matches on the display. Even here we may require a large number of properties to specify this visual representation. In Z, we can make this sort of data refinement easily by adding observations as extra variables in the signature:

$$
\begin{array}{|l}
\hline
\textit{Match\_Image} \underline{\hspace{9cm}} \\
\quad \textit{Icon} \\
\quad \textit{stem : Icon} \\
\quad \textit{head : Icon} \\
\hline
\quad \textit{position} = \textit{stem. position} \\
\quad \textit{area} = \textit{stem. area} \cup \textit{head.area} \\
\hline
\end{array}
$$

Thus when we observe a *Match_Image* we see that it is an *aggregate Icon* consisting of two sub–*Icons* representing the head and the stem of the match. We identify the position of the whole match with the position of its stem, and the area of the whole match is the union ($\cup$) of the areas of its component *Icons*. Clearly in order to fully specify a match image we would need many more observations on particular sizes, shapes and colours, and constraints between these, but space precludes this.

Now we can *use* a set of *Match_Images* to construct a *Display*:

$$
\begin{array}{|l}
\hline
\textit{Display} \underline{\hspace{9cm}} \\
\quad \textit{display : } \mathbf{P}\, \textit{Match\_Image} \\
\hline
\end{array}
$$

Before we express how this *Display* is a refinement of the abstract state, we need to establish some general rules for data refinement.

3.4.3 Access

In enriching our abstract representation by data refinement like this, we must ensure that the enriched concrete representation is adequately *distinct* to be able to *access* the abstract representation through it. For example, we would have to be sure that from each *Display* the user could access the *number* of *matches*, which is the essential measure of *Min*'s state. So it would not do to implement *Display* with some *Match_Images* off screen, or some distinct, say, in colour but not in position, so that one obscured others.

This requirement has been formally expressed (Jones, 1980) using a *retrieval function* from concrete to abstract values. Here we rename this function *access*:

$$access: C \rightarrow A$$

The strongest criterion here is that access should be *unambiguous*. This is conveyed just by its functional nature ($\rightarrow$). Thus each concrete state in C should represent just one abstract state in A. This outlaws the possibility of off–screen or overlapping *Match_Images*. Conventionally also, *access* is required to be surjective. That is, *all* abstract states in A must be accessible from the possible concrete states of C. For example, *Display* should be capable of representing all possible *Min* states. It is not usually a requirement that *access* be *total*. Thus we may allow some concrete displays to be uninterpretable as *Min* states (this would allow us to have start screens and help screens, for example). It is also not usually a requirement that *access* be *injective*. Thus two or more concrete states may represent the same abstract state. For example, the following two distinct *Displays* may represent, quite intuitively, the same *Min* state:

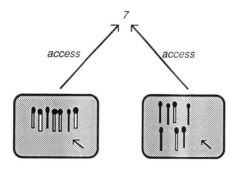

3.4.4 Homomorphism

Formally, if we refine the data values (states), then we must also refine the operations to handle these new types of values. Thus data refinement entails some operation refinement. If we expect to be able to access the abstract from the concrete *states*, then it is natural also to expect to access the abstract *operations* from whatever concrete operations we refine them into. For example if we implement some mouse action *act* which has the effect of deleting one *Match_Image* from a *Display*, then we understand that:

$$access\ (act) = Take\_One$$

The general property that must be fulfilled in refinement is called *homomorphism*: for any concrete operation *op* and concrete state *c*:

$$access\ (op\ (c)) = access\ (op)\ (access\ (c))$$

This is best illustrated using a diagram:

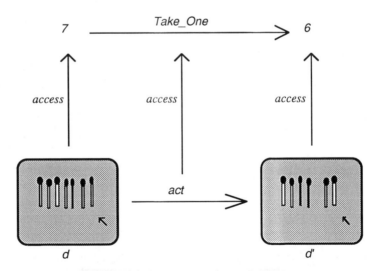

Here the concrete value *c* is the left–hand *Display d*, and the concrete operation (the bottom arrow) is *act*, so that:

$$act\ (d) = d'$$

Starting from *d* we can reach the resultant abstract state (here, *6*) by two routes. Either we can apply the bottom arrow followed by the right arrow *(access (act (d)) = 6)*, or we can *first* access the abstract state from *d* (i.e. along the left–hand arrow: *access (d) = 7*), and *then* apply the accessed abstract operation (the top arrow: *Take_One (7) = 6*). Thus in this instance, as required:

$$access\ (act\ (d)) = access\ (act)\ (access\ (d))$$

The homomorphism property requires that this equation hold for all interaction. The effect is that the abstract and concrete representations never become inconsistent. From the users' point of view, if they *understand* the concrete operations provided in the interface to be, for example, the abstract operations of *Min* (that is, *access* captures the users' conceptual model of the interface), then nothing in the behaviour of the system proves inconsistent with this view.

3.5 Practical architectures

In practical architectures we are principally concerned with *separating* components specific to a particular application from ready–implemented and reusable components. The more components we can take off the shelf and reuse the more efficient our software engineering of interactive systems.

The separation can occur on either of the *is_a* or *has_a* abstract architectures we have seen previously. Separation on *is_a* architectures results in libraries of reusable classes as distinct from application–specific classes which may be derived from them. Clearly here an object–oriented implementation is ideal. Separation on *has_a* architectures may occur at run time, and is typified by the *client–server* relationship between software objects.

3.5.1 Dialogue managers

Early attempts at separating out architectural services from an interactive application concentrated on abstraction of the *sequences* of operation invocations possible. Conventionally this has been called *dialogue*. There are clear cases where the sequence of operations needs to be fully determined (for example, a login sequence) as well as many examples where the user needs to be free to invoke an arbitrary sequence of operations. The essential semantic property that necessitates dialogue control is *partiality* in the application operations. That is, in some state some input may be in *error*, so that the user should ideally be prevented from submitting this input in the first place.

For example, the alternation of turns in a game is a dialogue constraint. We can make this explicit by specializing *Turn* into operations whose precondition specifies a particular player:

```
Player_One_Turn_____
    Turn
_____
    player = one
```

Thus *Player_One_Turn* is partial – it can only operate when it is *player one*'s turn, and as a result it becomes *player two*'s turn (a postcondition of *Turn*).

A *dialogue manager* is an architectural component which *executes* a dialogue specification, and so ensures that only permissible sequences of the application operations are invoked (Green, 1986). Since the dialogue manager typically makes *calls* on application operations, it represents a separation on a *has_a* structure.

Dialogues have typically been specified using *grammars* (Reisner, 1981), *state–transition automata* (Parnas, 1969), and *production systems* (Hopgood and Duce, 1980; Olsen, 1990). For example, if we have events *P1* and *P2* which invoke *Player_One_Turn* and the obvious *Player_Two_Turn* respectively, then we can construct a grammar which (recursively) accepts only the permissible sequences of these actions (assuming also the constraint that *P1* starts):

Game ::= P1 P2 Game

We could express exactly the same dialogue as a *state–transition* automaton:

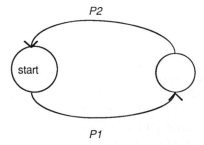

or as a production system (*turn1* and *turn2* are *flags* which can be raised (↑) or lowered (↓). A production (→) is only possible if all its flags are raised):

start		→	*turn1*↑	*turn2*↓
turn1	*P1*	→	*turn1*↓	*turn2*↑
turn2	*P2*	→	*turn1*↑	*turn2*↓

Dialogues which can be expressed in these notations are technically called *regular*. There are many common interactive dialogues, for example *help – return from help* sequences, that are not regular. Some UIMS have used extensions of these notations, for example pushdown automata (Olsen,1984) and recursive transition networks (Wasserman, 1985), to model more complex dialogues.

Finally, not all dialogues can be decided in isolation from the application. *Turn* manages a simple dialogue (rotation of players) that is clearly distinct from the semantics of any particular game. The dialogue which manages the first level syntax of an interactive system (for example, whether the user of a graphical user interface first selects operation icons and then operand objects, or vice versa) is similarly separable from particular applications, so long as the dialogue manager can distinguish between operation and operand icons. However, in many cases the dialogue is dependent on *application* state (for example, the constraint that a *Turn* cannot be taken if the game has been *won*). In this respect *Turn* cannot fully be separated from the application that determines the rules of a particular game. In these cases the dialogue specification must be developed within, or with knowledge of, the application semantics.

3.5.2 Model–view architectures

Model–View architectures (Szekely, 1987) allow us to separate an implementation of the abstract state (data) and operations on it, from an implementation of the display observation, or view, of that state. A distinguishing characteristic of such architectures is that the model (the abstract state) may have a number of different views, possibly even concurrently presented to the user. Ideally these views may be extended without changing the model.

Each view is in effect accomplished by a *view* function which projects the abstract model into some concrete representation. For example, in order to view the *Min* state as a set of *Match_Images*, we need the view function (what follows is a Z *global* schema):

---

view: **N** → **P** *Match_Image*

---

view (n) = matchset ⇔ #matchset = n

This function *view* implements the accessibility constraint that a *view* of some number *n* as a set *matchset* of *Match_Images* means that the size (#) of *matchset* is *n*. In order to generate a number of different views of the same model, we are free to specify either a number of different *view* functions, or a *view relation* which in effect is the inverse of the *access* function. For clarity here we define just one *view*.

In Model–view architectures this view function is incorporated in each of the *operations* on the model. This is sometimes called active values (Myers, 1987), or access–orientation (Stefik et al., 1986). Thus each time the abstract state changes as a result of an operation, the concrete display is updated also by *view*. We can extend *Take* in this way:

View_Take

Take
Δ Display

---

display' = view (matches')

Even though the model and the view are both updated by *View_Take*, this does not prevent *Min_State* and *Display* themselves from being implemented separately. This is separation on a *has_a* structure, since the operation makes a *call* on *view*.

One problem with this approach is that both the model and the view components may be application–specific, so that it may be difficult to provide a general reusable infrastructure to support the architecture. Systems conforming to the model–view paradigm, like Smalltalk's *MVC* (Krasner and Pope, 1988) and Coutaz' *PAC* (Coutaz, 1987), are generally more successful in defining a philosophy of design than in providing practical support.

3.5.3 Model–based architectures

An alternative class of interactive architectures, often now called *model–based* (Wiecha et al., 1990; Wilson et al., 1993; Szekely, 1993), *pre–packages* a set of abstract types with built–in views, and so relieves the designer from the need to build views. For example, numbers might have some fixed view as numerals or as some more graphic representation like scaled bars. These special types are intended to be used like the built–in types of a programming language. Indeed, a variant of the model–based approach is to pre–process the built–in types of a standard language like Pascal so that the interface is built automatically simply from the application program. This approach has been tried in Olsen's Mike and Mickey systems (Olsen, 1986, 1989). The benefit to the user interface designer is that visual presentation of the abstract application state is largely automatic. The disadvantage is obviously that the designer loses expressive freedom – it is unlikely, for example, that the built–in observation of numbers is as sets of matches!

We can incorporate a built–in view in *Min* as an *invariant* of the system class:

Concrete_Min_State

Min_State
Display

---
display = view (matches)

Contrast this with *View_Take*, in which the view is invoked during the *Take operation*.

Concrete_Min_State is a simple extension (in effect, a subtype) of *Min_State*. In an object–oriented setting this means that operations on *Min_States* can be reused on *Concrete_Min_States* without change. Thus in model–based architectures the separation occurs not between model and view states, but between model types or classes (with built–in views) and application–defined operations on these types. Thus this is more an *is_a* separation.

In some model–based systems, for example UIDE (Sukaviriya et al., 1993), dialogue may also be managed automatically by interpreting predicates on the state expressing *preconditions* of operations.

3.5.4 The problem of direct manipulation of semantic feedback

Direct manipulation of semantic feedback has been both the grail and the bane of interactive system development since the advent of the bitmapped screen. The debate about separability (Edmonds, 1992) hinges on the appropriate architectural rationalization of this capability. After all it is evidently *possible* to provide direct manipulation of semantic feedback. Consider the user interface to *Min* that we have illustrated above. The set of *Match_Images* constitutes the semantic feedback from the *Min* application (whose abstract semantics is expressed just in the number *matches*). We have reasonably assumed that the players may *take* matches by directly clicking with the mouse on their displayed image.

In the architectures that we have looked at so far, however, this may not be so easy to achieve. All of these have supported a *separation* between the application and the view or representation of this that is fed back to the user. We have noted that these views are typically *data refinements* that extend the abstract types with *observations* into more detailed types. Now under direct manipulation the input that arrives from the user is in terms of the observations, for example screen pixel coordinates. In order to *access* the semantic denotation of the input within the application, it must first be dereferenced against the display representation. The key problem of separation is *where* to perform this input interpretation.

We can illustrate this problem by first of all formulating a directly manipulable interactive system (in this case *Min*) as abstractly as we can. We already have reusable definitions of the *Concrete_Min_State* which includes the data refinement to the display. What we still need to define for direct manipulation are concrete operations using input that is *dependent* on this display representation. For simplicity, we choose to refine *Take_One*:

Concrete_Take_One _____

Δ *Concrete_Min_State*
Take_One
cursor?: $\mathbf{N} \times \mathbf{N}$

$\exists$ *match* $\in$ *display* •

         cursor? $\in$ *match.area* $\wedge$
         display' = *display* − *match*

Concrete_Take_One operates on the *Concrete_Min_State*, but now requires an input value *cursor?* which models directly manipulative mouse input as a coordinate pair ($\mathbf{N} \times \mathbf{N}$). We assume that a *Match_Image match* ($\in$ *display*) is *selected* when the *cursor?* is at one of the points in its *area*. The *Concrete_Take_One* schema says that the more abstract application operation *Take_One* is invoked only if there exists a *match* on the *display* that has been selected, and that in this case that *match* disappears from the *display*.

Thus *Concrete_Take_One* extends *Take_One* firstly with *Concrete_Min_State* to provide the data refinement required for semantic feedback, and secondly with the extra predicate to access the application state via the *display* and so provide direct manipulation. Note that this is now a slightly more *operational* definition of how the *display* is updated (in contrast to *view* above). There is an implicit obligation on us (which we do not discharge here) to show that this *display* update preserves the homomorphism property.

We wish not to implement this operation as a single lump of code but instead to make an architectural separation between an application component and a user interface component. The problem is *where* to evaluate the predicate in *Concrete_Take_One*. If this is evaluated in the application component, then the application must know about *Match_Images* and their positions. On the other hand, if the predicate is evaluated in the interface, then the semantic response of deleting the selected match (*display'* = *display* − *match*) is delegated to the user interface component. This is hardly satisfactory, since it means that the user interface becomes bound to *Min*'s semantics (we might want to reuse displays of matches in different applications). Nor can we solve this problem by simply taking out the display update clause from the predicate above and relying on the *view* constraint inherited from *Concrete_Min_State* that the set of *Match_Images* should always be of size *matches*. If we did this, then it is consistent for the user to click on one match, and have *another* disappear, which is hardly direct manipulation.

3.5.5 Toolkits

A common alternative solution is to break the requirement for *direct* manipulation, and provide intermediate toolkit objects that mediate user input. Toolkit objects differ from view objects in model–view architectures in that tools are pre–formed whereas views must often be built by the interface constructor. Toolkit objects differ from model–based objects in that the latter typically represent fairly low–level types and compositions of these, whereas tools can process higher levels of input. To illustrate toolkit objects, we might devise some *Button* type as a subtype of *Icon*:

```
Button
  Icon
  label: String
```

Then we might *use* two of these *Buttons* to specialise the *Concrete_Min_State*:

Concrete_Min_State + _____

Concrete_Min_State
B1, B2 : Button

B1.label = *"Take One"*
B2.label = *"Take Two"*

(We might also specify their position.) Now we can define a version of *Min* using *indirect* manipulation of its semantic feedback:

Indirect_Min _____

Turn
Δ *Concrete_Min_State* +
cursor? : $\mathbf{N} \times \mathbf{N}$

---
cursor? $\in$ *B1.area* $\Leftrightarrow$ *matches'* = *matches* − *1*
cursor? $\in$ *B2.area* $\Leftrightarrow$ *matches'* = *matches* − *2*

A possible display state in this interaction might be:

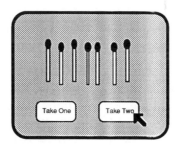

Here the semantic changes to the abstract *matches* are invoked by the user's clicking on one or other of the *Buttons*. However, now we do rely on the *view* constraint in *Concrete_Min_State*+ to update the *display*, but as a result we lose control over *which Match_Image* is deleted. Thus while we directly manipulate the *Buttons*, we only *indirectly* manipulate the *Match_Images*.

Such architectures are commonly provided by toolkits, which might consist of a number of types or classes of interactive objects such as icons, menus, dialogue boxes, etc. In an object–oriented setting these objects might be encapsulated with display–oriented operations such as highlighting or limited capability for user manipulation such as moving or sizing, and in order to invoke semantic actions they may either generate messages that the application must understand, or they *have* links to application operations. In the former case they act to *transpose* input from lower to higher (more abstract or logical) types for application consumption. A window manager can be seen as a single large toolkit object which filters user input in this way. Some of this input is trapped by the window manager and is interpreted to move, size or iconize windows. The rest of the input is despatched to applications on the basis of window ownership or current window.

3.5.6 Surface interaction

The architectural approach *surface interaction* has been presented in (Took, 1992), but here I give a new formulation. This architecture recognizes the need for direct manipulation of semantic feedback, and the difficulty of making the application and the interface completely independent in this case. Instead it seeks to package as much interactive presentation and behaviour into the *surface* without imposing any semantic bias there. The surface is currently implemented as *Presenter* (Took, 1990).

The surface maintains a structured set of *Icons*, which models the state of the user interface display. The surface receives all input, and dereferences it against the display model to determine which *Icon* is the target of the current input. The only semantic information which an *Icon* carries is a decision function as to whether the current input on the *Icon* is to be *reported* to the owning application, or is to result in default surface behaviour. This default behaviour, or *surface interaction*, consists of standard geometric manipulation of the *Icons* and editing of their content.

From the application's point of view, input is transposed and reported as *(event, Icon)* pairs – that is, the input event (of which there is a small set: *press, drag* and *release* events for each mouse button, a *tick* event, etc.), plus the *Icon* upon which the event occurred. Thus the application is insulated from low–level output device details such as pixel location. Having received an input report, the application may *preempt* surface interaction, and substitute instead some application–defined output response, known as *deep* interaction. This architecture can be crudely illustrated:

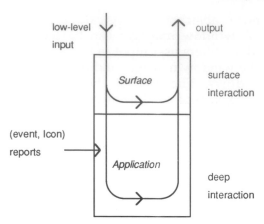

From a formal point of view, we would wish any interactive system running within this architecture to be a standard refinement of the application specification. The *Icons* on the surface may enrich (data refine) the abstract application representation, and surface interaction is a useful way of extending the domain of the abstract application operations. For example, using *Presenter* to implement *Min*, it would be possible to allow the user to *drag* matches around freely, without contravening the rules of the game.

However, the experience of the user interface constructor using surface interaction is not that of refining the application into an interface, but rather of *tailoring* the surface to fit the application. The key distinguishing feature of the surface interaction architecture is that the final interactive system is *not* a standard refinement of the surface. This is because the input reporting system which allows the application to *preempt* the default surface behaviour in effect *limits* the possible previous states of the surface operations, and semantic feedback from the application in effect *overrides* their possible result states.

Consider an interface to *Min* implemented under surface interaction:

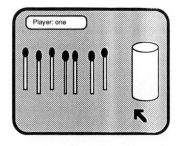

Here we use *Icons* to model each of the matches, and a message box to signal whose turn it is, and a dustbin. The intended interaction is that the user can pick up any match with the mouse, and drag it around the display. This behaviour is provided in the surface and requires no application involvement. We wish the application to become involved under two conditions. Firstly, if a player attempts to drag the dustbin, then he or she is prevented from doing so. Secondly, if a player drags a match into the dustbin, the match disappears, and is considered *taken*. We also assume, but will not implement here, that when a player clicks in the message box, a new turn is signalled.

We are interested here not in the details of this implementation, but in its architectural structure. The surface state consists of the set of *displayed Icons*, one of which may be *current*. Currentness is designated by mouse selection, which is handled at a lower level than we specify here:

Surface

displayed: **P** *Icon*
current: *Icon*

Surface interaction is by means of a set of operations on this state. These are available both to the end user, via mouse actions, and to the application program via messages to the surface. Surface interaction changes the state of the *Surface*, generally by affecting the *current Icon*. A precondition of any surface interaction is that the *current Icon* should be *displayed*:

Surface_Interaction

Δ *Surface*

current ∈ displayed

Consider a particular surface operation which *drags* an *Icon* from one *position* to another:

```
Surface_Drag _____

  Surface_Interaction
  distance?  N × N
_____

  current'.position = current.position + distance?
  current'.area = current.area
  displayed' = displayed
```

This moves the current *Icon* by updating its *position* by some input *distance?* (we assume that + here works on coordinate pairs). The *area* of *current* does not change, nor does the set of *displayed Icons*.

Now consider *tailoring Surface_Drag* in order to implement the *Min* interaction above. In order to *prevent* the user's being able to drag the dustbin, we must *restrict* the domain of *Surface_Drag* (i.e. *strengthen* its precondition). We assume that one of the *displayed Icons* represents the dustbin and has been so named:

```
Pre_Deep_Drag _____

  Surface_Drag
_____

  current ≠ dustbin
```

The predicate in *Pre_Deep_Drag* is a *precondition* (it uses no primed language), and allows the operation to go ahead only if the *current Icon* is not the *dustbin*.

The second form of tailoring *overrides* the postcondition of the operation. This occurs in our example when dragging a match into the dustbin deletes the match, which is not a standard surface result of dragging, but is particular to the *Min* application. Overriding cannot be expressed by logical extension since it involves *contradicting* previous conditions. For example here we would contradict the postcondition inherited from *Surface_Drag* that *displayed'* = *displayed*. We get around this in Z by inheriting *Pre_Deep_Drag*, but *hiding* (\) from it all clauses which use *displayed'*. This leaves us free to *redefine* the postcondition on *displayed'*, which we must therefore declare explicitly in the signature:

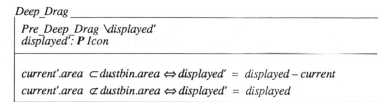

Thus *Deep_Drag* behaves like *Surface_Drag, except* if the user attempts to move the dustbin (a precondition inherited from *Pre_Deep_Drag)*, *or* if the *current Icon* ends up wholly within (⊂) the dustbin, which causes the *current Icon* to be deleted from the display.

With this surface interaction architecture we preserve the user's direct manipulation of the display objects, as well as semantic feedback from the application, without involving the application in more than the absolutely necessary details of the display representation and management.

3.6 Conclusions

This chapter seeks to clarify the organization and rationalization of user requirements into an abstract interactive system design, and the refinement of this design into a concrete usable system. This process is not just of interest to software engineers, since both the initial design and its refinement have a number of well–defined option spaces, whose choice could fundamentally affect the success of the finished system. The architectural perspective taken here emphasizes the reuse of software. Again this is not just a software engineering issue, since it affects the ease with which systems can be modified and rebuilt, possibly to user requirements.

Further reading

Woodcock, J. and Loomes, M. (1989). *Software Engineering Mathematics.* Pitman, London
A good and gentle introduction to Z, the mathematics behind it, and formal specification in general.

Bass, L. and Coutaz, J. (1991). *Developing Software for the User Interface*. The SEI Series in Software Engineering, New York: Addison–Wesley.

A good overview of the user interface software development process, with particular reference to the *Serpent* UIM. Interesting discussion on architectural issues, and many concrete examples in code and graphics.

Foley, J. D., Van Dam, A., Feiner, S. K., Hughes, J. F. and Phillips, R. L, (1994). *Introduction to Computer Graphics*. New York: Addison–Wesley.

Latest version of a definitive text on computer graphics. Some useful chapters on object hierarchies and interaction design, all in the context of sophisticated visualization techniques.

Olsen Jr., D. R. (1992). *User Interface Management Systems: Models and Algorithms*. San Mateo, CA: Morgan Kaufmann.

Largely concerned with software engineering issues in user interface construction and management. Many useful algorithms given, which are rarely presented elsewhere.

Larson, J. A. (1992). *Interactive Software: Tools for Building Interactive User Interfaces*. Yourdon Press.

Addresses both design and construction issues in user interface engineering, including analysis of users' conceptual models.

Gray, P. and Took, R. K. (eds) (1992). *Building Interactive Systems: Architectures and Tools*. Workshops in Computing Series. Berlin: Springer–Verlag.

A collection of papers on architectural and software engineering issues in the design of interactive systems.

Chapter 4

Applied experimental psychology

John McCarthy

4.1 Background

It is now broadly accepted that, in order to build a usable computer system, designers have to understand how users are likely to interact with it. This involves understanding how people process information, make decisions, allocate attention, control their actions, and so on. Applied experimental psychology is an approach to setting research goals and pursuing research projects which attempts to understand these processes in realistic contexts.

It is important to be clear, at this stage, that applied experimental psychology is not another school of psychology like social, developmental or cognitive. Neither is it an application domain like engineering, aviation, or human computer interaction. Rather, it is an approach to doing psychological research which can be applied in any of the schools of psychology or in any application domain.

My aim in this chapter is to introduce applied experimental psychology in such a way that you will appreciate its scope and limitations, and have some "feel" for the process of carrying out applied experiments. In this section, I will briefly introduce the approach and outline its historical roots. Section 4.2 will deal with the application of this approach in HCI. In Section 4.3, I will present a detailed description of a fairly recent applied experiment in HCI. This study is used, in Section 4.4, to clarify the process of planning and designing an applied experiment and, in Section 4.5, to facilitate discussion of some of the main features of applied experimental psychology. Finally I will discuss the strengths and limitations of the approach and its relations with other disciplines.

To paraphrase Kerlinger (1973), empirical research is the systematic, controlled, empirical and critical investigation of hypothetical propositions about presumed relations among phenomena or variables. After thinking about a problem, reflecting on past experience and observing relevant phenomena, the experimental psychologist is likely to formulate a hypothesis. A hypothesis is a tentative proposition about the relationship between two or more phenomena or variables. A variable is simply a property of some phenomenon that takes on different values. For example, one might hypothesize a relationship between menu size and search time in a menu–driven database system. Two types of variables are of particular interest in an experiment. The independent variable is the variable manipulated and controlled by the experimenter, menu size in this example. The dependent variable is the variable measured by the experimenter, search time in this example.

Much of the power of the basic laboratory experiment is due to the random allocation of subjects to experimental conditions. On the basis of probability, with random allocation, any variables other than the independent variable are equally distributed across conditions. Random allocation is not always possible or desirable in field experiments. The best the applied experimental psychologist can do, in such circumstances, is to measure and account for the contribution of variables other than the independent variable to the final results.

The purpose of an experiment is to examine the effect of manipulating an independent variable on one or more dependent variables. A causal connection is implied in such a design, but other designs are available. In the absence of evidence suggesting a causal relationship, a researcher might want to systematically investigate the relationship between two variables using a correlational design. Using such a design the researcher might be able to tell that two variables are related, and might be able to describe some aspects of the relationship, but would not be in a position to imply a causal direction. A strong positive correlation between the amount of time teenagers spend playing computer games and their examination results does not imply that one causes the other.

Within HCI, the challenge to experimental psychology is articulated most forcefully in critiques emerging from ethnography. Ethnography argues that experimental psychology is theory driven, insensitive to context, takes an impoverished approach to data, and is solely concerned with simple cause–effect relationships. However, in this chapter, I hope to demonstrate that applied experimental psychology is an approach to psychological research which is problem focused and context sensitive, which has a rich approach to data and attempts to deal with complex relationships.

The name "Applied Experimental Psychology" implies a bridging between two approaches to psychology which are often considered to be separate. Experimental psychology is considered to be a methodologically–driven and exclusively laboratory–based approach to studying human behaviour and experience. As such, it has been criticized as being irrelevant to people's everyday lives. Applied psychology, as the name suggests, is concerned precisely with the application of psychological knowledge to "real" world problems. Applied experimental psychology argues that the distinction between applied and experimental psychology is invalid (Broadbent, 1971). It argues that applied and theoretical research are part of a single process of understanding human functioning with respect to "practical problems which at any one time will point us towards some part of human life" (Broadbent, 1980). It is essentially pragmatic with respect to methodology and argues that research can be carried out in the laboratory or in the field.

Applied experimental psychology is rooted in the development of an empirical approach to psychology in the late 19th century. From the beginning, there was a philosophical and methodological debate out of which grew a number of approaches including applied experimental psychology. Differences in emphasis between two of the founding fathers of psychology, Wundt, who founded the first experimental psychology laboratory in 1879, and James, who established academic psychology in America, exemplify this debate.

Wundt's early research was geared towards making aspects of consciousness amenable to experimental manipulation and observation, just like the facts of physics, chemistry, and physiology. Whereas James appreciated the innovative features of Wundt's experimental psychology, he argued that ideas should be evaluated for their utility rather than for some illusory absolute truth. However, instead of trying to refine the methodology to incorporate utility, James reverted to philosophy. Applied experimental psychology did not emerge as a distinct approach until another experimental psychologist, Bartlett, revealed the limitations of the natural science methodology when applied to human behaviour and experience.

As an example, consider Bartlett's criticism of early memory experiments which used nonsense syllables. Nonsense syllables were used on the basis that, as they meant nothing to anybody, everybody started at the same level. Bartlett (1932) argued that nonsense syllables set up a mass of associations which vary more from person to person than those aroused by meaningful language. He asserted that it is impossible to rid stimuli of meaning, so long as they arouse any human response at all. Therefore, starting from the premise that stimuli were inevitably meaningful, Bartlett's experiments on memory used stories, not nonsense syllables, as stimuli. In today's methodological jargon, Bartlett concluded that the attempt to exclude contextual effects was futile and he opted instead for a context–sensitive approach to experimentation.

Bartlett's analysis showed that if it wanted to be an experimental science, psychology would have to be a far more complex experimental science than many of those which preceded it. Complex in the sense that it could not rely on simple cause–effect accounts, nor on the explanatory power of the stimulus, nor could it continue to pretend to do context–free experimentation. People had histories, opinions, attitudes, moods and so on, any or all of which could impinge on the response to the most apparently meaningless stimulus.

Bartlett's work, especially his approach to methodology, had important implications for the development of applied experimental psychology. After Bartlett, it was no longer possible to pretend that, when studying psychological processes in realistic contexts, all variables could be controlled. A more pragmatic approach in which some variables may be manipulated and controlled but others simply measured was required. These are the real strengths of applied experimental psychology: an honesty about the complexity of people, processes and situations and a willingness to work with that complexity rather than pretending that it doesn't exist.

Once psychology freed itself of the "shackles" of its physiological roots, the potential for an applied experimental psychology existed. But it took another ten years to blossom. That was when psychologists contributing to their country's war effort began to tackle real life problems in earnest.

The second world war was characterised by a dependence on human–machine systems. There was some concern at the time that the increasing complexity of machines would outstrip the capacities of human operators. This led to the systematic applied experimental analysis of the capacities and limitations of human information processing in human–machine systems, a research area which became known as Human Factors or Engineering Psychology (Wickens, 1992). Bartlett was again at the centre of these developments, playing a pivotal role in research carried out at the Cambridge Psychological Laboratory, where he was head at the time.

He directed research into the length of time a pilot or flight crew could sustain their performance, in a series of studies that became known as the Cambridge Cockpit studies. The Cambridge team was concerned with examining performance in the kind of detail which, at that time, required laboratory conditions. However, they also wanted to observe performance which was relatively realistic. In order to achieve both aims, they developed a piece of experimental equipment which was built around a Spitfire cockpit and into which was fitted instruments and controls which behaved in a highly realistic manner. This very early simulator became known as the Cambridge Cockpit. For the purposes of this chapter, one of the most salient features of these studies is the extent to which Bartlett and his team went to construct realistic laboratory–based experiments which could not possibly have been carried out in the field. Pilots' performance disintegrated with fatigue. Their management of the complex task of flying an aircraft deteriorated. From these experiments, Bartlett was able to characterise the form this deterioration took and the factors that accelerated or ameliorated it.

After the war, applied experimental psychology was also directed at activities such as commercial flying, where a major research interest was the importance of social and group factors in safe and efficient flight crew performance (see Foushee and Helmreich, 1989, for a review). For instance, in an experiment carried out by Foushee, Lauber, Baetge and Acomb (1986) at the request of the US Congress, the performance of fully qualified crews in highly realistic settings was examined. Following a number of accident investigations, Congress was concerned about the effects of pilot fatigue and jet–lag. The experimenters took real crews, one set of which was just reporting for work after at least a two day break ("pre–duty" condition) and the other set of which had just spent two days on duty ("post–duty" condition). Both crews were required to perform a set of flight exercises in a simulator. Due to the emphasis on operational realism, the experiment incorporated everything that airline pilots would experience on an actual flight. Some of the results were counterintuitive. Whereas post–duty crews were more fatigued than pre–duty crews, they were also rated as performing significantly better than pre–duty crews, particularly on operationally significant measures. These and other findings were interpreted as indicating that the time which the post–duty crew already had flying together allowed them to build up detailed knowledge of their individual strategies and styles which they then harnessed to produce a cohesive group performance.

With the growing appetite for research into complex systems and cooperative work within the HCI community (see, for example, McClumpha, 1992), I feel that I have been addressing the issue of the interaction between applied experimental psychology and HCI for the last few pages. However, lest anyone form the impression that applied experimental psychology is useful in complex systems alone, I will refer to some functions of applied experimental psychology in the mainstream areas of HCI in the next section.

4.2 Application in mainstream HCI

There are far too many applied psychology experiments in HCI for me to do justice to them in any attempt to be comprehensive or historical. Instead I will adopt a functional approach, giving one or two salient examples for each function discussed. Four functions for applied experimental psychology are suggested. They correspond to Landauer's (1987) four functions for cognitive psychology in HCI.

4.2.1 Existing knowledge and theory can be applied directly to design problems

The results of pure and applied experimental research into topics such as human memory, attentional limitations, skill development and action control have been used to inform design decisions on menu configuration, screen layout and interface concepts such as icons and metaphors. Landauer discusses some specific examples of the application of psychological knowledge from work in which he had direct involvement. One was a study in which Landauer and Nachbar (1985) applied some well known laws governing decision and motor selection time to menu design. The aim of this research was to find the optimal menu structure for accessing a large database.

Before applying any existing psychological knowledge, Landauer and Nachbar had to understand in detail the task to be performed by the user. In large menu–driven databases, users are presented with a series of choices designed to guide a hierarchical search of the database. Imagine a dictionary search interface of this type. One menu structure might present three choices on each menu: the words "apple to mother", "motor to trouble", and "under to zebra". If the user chose "apple to mother" the next screen would present a further subdivision: "apple to cap", "car to keep", and "key to mother". An alternative menu structure might present six choices per menu: the words "apple to far", "fat to mother", "motor to park", "past to trouble", "under to window", and "wine to zero". The designer is faced with a key question: how broad and deep should the menus be? Landauer and Nachbar judged that two laws from psychology, Hick's law on decision time and Fitts' law on movement time, were relevant to answering this question. They generated predictions using these laws and validated their conclusions by running some experiments in which menu breadth and depth were varied.

This general form of this research is as follows: analyse the task or problem; identify an appropriate psychological model to be applied to the current problem; attempt to apply the model; design and run experiments in the current context to test the validity of the model for this domain; and refine the model to fit the domain more precisely. Other good examples of this kind of work are: Grudin and Bernard's (1984) attempt to apply principles from the paired associate learning paradigm in psychology to command naming in HCI; and McKendree and Anderson's (1987) research on the application of ACT*, a human performance model developed by Anderson (1983), to the development of programming skills.

4.2.2 New psychological models, analyses and tools can be developed

In this context, Landauer refers to a class of human performance or interaction models developed directly from empirical research carried out within HCI (e.g. Card, Moran and Newell, 1983; Polson and Kieras, 1985). Sometimes, though not always, applied experimentation has been used in developing these models. More often, the validity and scope of these models has been tested using applied experiments. Much current work in the area of computer mediated communication is of this type. That is, experiments are run, using and testing some theoretical concepts from social and cognitive psychology, ethnography and conversation analysis, to develop models of computer–mediated interaction (e.g. Gale, 1990; Sellen, 1992; McCarthy, Miles and Monk, 1991). Sellen's study, described in detail in the next section, is an example.

In another domain, computer–assisted decision making and process control, Berry and Broadbent (e.g. Berry and Broadbent, 1990) have refined their account of different modes of learning, such as implicit and explicit, to take account of action and interaction. Sanderson who has also carried out some interesting research in process control (e.g. Sanderson, Haskell, and Flach, 1992), has developed a model of human performance in human–computer interaction, which incorporates task type and display type.

4.2.3 Psychological methods can be applied to the evaluation of designs, design alternatives and design principles

This is probably the area in which applied experimental psychology is most commonly used. Buxton has used applied experimentation to evaluate a range of interesting input devices (e.g. Kabbash, MacKenzie Buxton, 1993; Kurtenbach and Buxton, 1993). For example, Kurtenbach and Buxton report a series of experiments designed to investigate the limits of expert performance using hierarchic marking menus. A hierarchic marking menu uses hierarchic radial menus and zig–zag marks to select from the hierarchy. They found that different input devices and the breadth and depth of menus affected response times. Carroll and Carrithers (1984) used applied experimentation to evaluate the "training wheels" approach to designing for learning to use a computer system. Kraemer and Pinsonneault (1990) reviewed a number of applied experiments which evaluated the "usability" of group decision support systems.

The list is endless and that is a problem for applied experimental psychology, as many researchers and practitioners see this kind of evaluative comparison as the only role for applied experimentation in HCI. Landauer has argued that cognitive psychology should aspire to play a greater role in the creative and inventive side of HCI. I would also argue that applied experimental psychology has shown, in areas such as work psychology, that it can play a greater role in understanding social and political aspects of implementation and acceptance of new technology.

In both cases a major contribution of the applied experimental psychologist would be to point to the great variation in human behaviour and the concomitant possibility of measuring it. Applied experimental psychologists should always insist on the use of a large number of representative users, using the system to perform realistic tasks under realistic work conditions. Their respective approaches to accepting or minimizing variation is one of the features that often distinguishes the applied experimental psychologist, interested in behaviour in practice, from the pure experimental psychologist who is often more interested in reducing variation to show that a particular theoretical position is, in principle, valid. Similar contrasts between pure and applied experimentation exist in other disciplines. For example, a materials scientist may test a piece of plastic for deformation under loads, but the precise manner of failure of, say, plastic curtain tracks requires realistic experiments which would examine the effects of variables such as uneven dynamic loads, twist buckling and so on.

4.2.4 Design problems can inform basic psychological research

The process described in 4.2.1 above is not always wholly successful. For instance, Landauer argued that the basic research on paired associate learning failed to transfer fully to dialogue design. When this happens useful information is made available to both the pure and applied psychologist about the scope and generality of their findings in the real world.

Norman (1988) has developed an account of intentional behaviour based on his analysis of poorly designed systems and the problems people have with them. For example, he has looked in some detail at the difficulties people have in using "bathtub water controls". Although interested in manipulating the rate of flow and the temperature of the water, people are often forced to use two physical devices, one of which controls the rate of flow of hot water and the other of which controls the rate of flow of cold water. With this system there is no direct mapping between "quickly filling a tub with warm water" and the "bathtub water controls", creating what Norman calls a "gulf of execution" between the person's goals and the physical devices. To bridge this gap people engage in a number of processes including: intention formation, action specification, and action execution. The goal of "quickly filling a tub with warm water" is first expressed in intentional terms which are constrained by the person's understanding of the physical devices. Then the precise actions required to achieve the goal given the device constraints are specified, that is, the required changes in the physical variables are specified (e.g. a decision to bring both hot and cold water taps to the point where there is an equal and relatively fast rate of flow). Finally, the person interacts with the physical devices to execute the appropriate action sequence. Of course, this is not always a straightforward linear process and is subject to continuous feedback based on the person's perception of the state of the system (e.g. the perceived temperature of water in the tub).

In a complementary research programme, Reason (1990) has expanded understanding of basic psychological mechanisms, such as similarity matching and frequency gambling, through his analysis of human error in complex human–machine systems. He has found that when people act in situations which are incompletely cognitively specified, where it is not clear what actions should be undertaken to achieve desired goals, they tend to execute actions which have previously worked for them in similar contexts and actions which they frequently execute anyway. Reason cites many cases in which this response pattern is evident and argues that it is a sufficiently strong pattern to merit the status of a "workable generalization" about human information handling, which should be taken into account in the design of complex and particularly safety critical systems and in training people who operate such systems.

Having reviewed, in brief, the contribution of applied experimental psychology to HCI, I will examine a particular example in detail in the next section.

4.3 An example

In this section I will describe a piece of applied experimental psychology in detail. As I describe the experiment I will explain some of the technical terms or experimental jargon. However, I will not consider the broader issues at this stage. In later sections, I will use aspects of this study to illustrate the process and some of the main features of applied experimental psychology.

The research I have chosen is a study of video–mediated communication carried out by Abigail Sellen (1992) at the University of Toronto. I have chosen it for a number of reasons. It is an example of the applied experimental approach in an area of HCI where critics of the experimental approach, such as ethnographers, say it should not be used, that is the relatively social domain of computer–mediated communication. It is a laboratory–based study. These critics also argue that little of use can be learned from laboratory studies. I could have avoided this issue by choosing a field experiment, such as those performed by Johannson and Aronsson (1980). However, I believe that the question of the utility of laboratory based studies needs to be tackled directly. Being a study which looks at design options before they have been embodied in full scale systems, it draws attention to the relatively broad range of roles experimental method can play in the full design process. It is not just an evaluation technology. Being a study in computer–mediated communication, it is directly relevant to current concerns in HCI.

Alternative examples of applied experimental psychology can be found in Johannson's research into the effects of new technology, wherein she designed experiments in the field using the conditions and circumstances that already existed, or in Hollingshead, McGrath and O'Connor's (1993) longitudinal analyses of group performance using communication technology. However, Sellen's study is particularly appropriate for this chapter as the motivation for this study, the design and running of the experiment, and the analysis and application of the results are all indicative of a sound applied experimental psychology approach to HCI design. Moreover, it embodies many of the compromises that the applied experimental psychologist often has to make. For example: (i) in order to compare relatively realistic communication systems, Sellen sacrifices some of the control normally associated with psychological experimentation; (ii) as her interest is in realistic social behaviour, she encourages relatively unconstrained communication – but, as she needs some consistency across groups to be able to compare responses in different conditions, she asks all groups to perform the same task.

What was the problem addressed in Sellen's research? Sellen's study was part of a large research programme concerned with the technological support of cooperative work. Within this study, Sellen was interested in understanding and evaluating various ways of supporting multi–party conferencing. Specifically, she was interested in evaluating forms of mediated communication, which differently affect eye contact, in terms of the quality of communication they support.

People who are in different parts of a building, a continent or the world use electronic multi–party conferencing to enable them to communicate in a more or less face–to–face manner without having to leave their offices. But electronic multi–party conferencing constrains the interactions between people who use it to support their communication, and many of those who have tried to use it have experienced these constraints as problems. For instance, it has been reported that electronic multi–party conferencing is characterized by long pauses due to floor control problems. People also have some difficulty ascertaining who is speaking to whom. These may sound like trivial problems but they can make communication extremely difficult if not impossible, thus rendering the technology unusable.

Sellen was interested in the relationship between different types of communications systems, the independent variable, and patterns of communication, the dependent variable. Having analysed the literature on mediated communication and reflected on her own experience with both video configurations, Sellen proposed four hypotheses. In summary, these hypotheses proposed that "Same Room" or face–to–face conversations would have the highest number of turns per session, the shortest turn time, the most equal distribution of turns per participant, and most simultaneous speech.

Sellen operationalised the independent variable, communication system, by setting up three different systems of communication in her experiment: Same Room, PIP, and Hydra. Picture–in–Picture (PIP) is a video system which divides the screen into quadrants each of which is occupied by one participant in the "conversation". As Sellen points out, when a number of participants occupy a single screen, they are limited in their ability to direct their gaze, establish eye contact, be aware of who is visually attending to them, hold parallel conversations and so on. Hydra is a prototype system designed specifically to overcome some of these limitations. Hydra uses a number of cameras, monitors and speakers to support multi–party conferencing. So, for instance, Hydra would simulate a four–way round table meeting by placing a camera, monitor and speaker in the place that would otherwise be held by each remote participant. Each person is presented with a unique view of each remote participant, and that view and its accompanying voice emanates from a distinct location in space. This means that when person A turns to look at the camera representing person B, B sees this as person A looking directly at him. Thus the problems listed above which are encountered with PIP systems should at least be ameliorated with Hydra.

Sellen operationalized the dependent variable, pattern of communication, in terms of measures of the number of turns per session, turn time, distribution of turns per participant and simultaneous speech. Before carrying out her experiment, Sellen trawled the literature on communication in general and mediated communication in particular to better understand any differences which might exist between Same Room, PIP and Hydra conversations. This led her to consider the literature on gaze and mutual gaze in particular. She found that gaze serves a number of specific functions from conversational management and information "overload" management to communicating emotion. It is at least plausible to suggest that the absence of mutual gaze in some video–links is a serious deficiency, which would be likely to lead to the kinds of problems experienced by people using these systems: floor control problems due to reduced ability to manage the conversation with gaze, and increased irritation due to the inability to indicate using gaze readiness or unwillingness to receive more information. At the very least it would seem that we have to develop a new set of communication skills and techniques when gaze is not available. This can be very demanding. Sellen used her analysis of the function of gaze as the basis for the conceptual framework within which she positioned her experiment.

The participants consisted of twelve groups of four adults, most of whom did not know each other previously. They were asked to take part in a set of three informal debates, each of which lasted for about sixteen minutes. Subjects were randomly assigned to a team of two to argue for or against the motion. Topics for debate were introduced using newspaper clippings. They were the right to smoke in public, mandatory drug testing and censorship in the news. Each group discussed all three topics, one in each condition. The conditions were Same Room, Picture–In–Picture and Hydra.

Sellen analysed the speech generated by participants in the conversations. Basically she converted the speech into on/off patterns and used those patterns to measure a number of phenomena which would allow her to test her hypotheses. For example, she counted the number of turns per session, measured the turn duration, and computed the distribution of turns. She also carried out a detailed analysis of simultaneous speech. Having counted or measured each of these variables, she carried out statistical analyses to determine whether the differences observed were statistically significant. For instance, she found that "number of turns per session" was distributed as follows: Same Room, 62.6; PIP, 64.1; Hydra, 68.7. Statistical analysis revealed that these differences were not significant, and therefore the null hypothesis, that is the proposition that there is no systematic difference in turns per session between the three conditions, could not be rejected.

In contrast, she found that there was a statistically significant difference between the three conditions in terms of the percentage of simultaneous speech (Same Room, 9.7; PIP, 7.1; Hydra, 5.4), and therefore the null hypothesis that there was no systematic difference in the percentage of simultaneous speech between the three conditions could be rejected. In applied experimental psychology, it is necessary to go beyond statistical significance and to also consider practical significance. There are at least two aspects of these results which suggest that they are of some practical significance. The first is that there is almost twice as much simultaneous speech in "Same Room" as in Hydra. This suggests that Hydra may not be a sufficiently robust communication technology to tolerate simultaneous speech. Therefore it is likely to impose an unwanted or unnatural constraint on those using it. The second significant aspect of the results is that 9.7% overlap is relatively high, that is, for one tenth of the time more than one person is speaking. It cannot be overemphasised that statistically significant differences are not always practically significant.

Sellen's overall conclusion from her analysis of these data was that mediating conversation with video technology had no discernible effect on the number of turns taken, the average turn length, or the distribution of turns among speakers. However mediation did have significant effects on the amount of simultaneous speech that occurred and in the time between switching speakers. More simultaneous speech could be taken to indicate floor control problems or a high degree of interactivity and spontaneity. Analyses of bids for floor control and speaker switching reveals that subjects were more reluctant to bid for floor control in the Video Mediated conditions, despite the fact that there was no real difference in the probability of bids for the floor being effective in Same Room and Video Mediated conditions. Sellen argued from this that the lower level of simultaneous speech in Video Mediated conditions was due to a kind of opportunism or politeness, that is, waiting for a pause or for the other speaker to finish before bidding to take the floor. This suggests a psychologically significant difference between Same Room and Video Mediated conditions: different patterns of interaction and possibly different conversational conventions, which are likely to require different social skills. Overall there were no behavioural differences between PIP and Hydra, though questionnaire data tends to show a preference among subjects for Hydra.

Sellen concluded that the study provides some useful data on differences between multi–party conferencing systems, which may be of use in design, but that more detailed and sometimes qualitative analysis would be required to explore these differences further. In terms of the value of applied experimental psychology to HCI, Sellen's study demonstrates the value of generating and testing clear, explicit hypotheses. As consumers of her study, we are aware of the following:

(i)   her interpretation of relevant literature as expressed in a series of hypotheses
(ii)   the method she has employed to test these hypotheses
(iii)   the resulting data
(iv)   her interpretation of these data and their value to design.

This experiment posed a set of researchable questions, answered some of them, and suggests how the others might be answered in future work. More than that, it answered them using a methodology which promotes a professional distance between the data and the interpretation. Sellen offers her interpretation but enables the reader to reach other conclusions by separating data and interpretation and making her own process of moving from data to interpretation explicit.

In the following sections, I will use Sellen's study to clarify some of the major steps involved in planning and designing an applied experiment and to elucidate some of the main features of this approach.

4.4 The process of applied experimental psychology

Planning and designing applied experiments involves resolving tensions between experimental control and precision on the one hand and performance in a realistic context on the other. In dealing with these tensions Sellen employed relatively realistic tasks and encouraged relatively unconstrained performance. In future work, I would suggest that the balance could be tilted even further in favour of the realistic context. For example, Sellen measured performance on three tasks each of sixteen minutes' duration. A better design would have incorporated a longitudinal dimension, that is performance would have been examined over days. Of course the way to maximise "realism" or what is know in experimental jargon as "ecological validity" would be to have carried out this experiment in a real office in real working conditions. This is not always possible and the developmental nature of the technology might have made it impossible here.

Design and planning are the foundations of good applied experimental psychology without which experiments fail or are meaningless. In this section I will outline the main steps in planning and designing an applied experiment.

Step 1 Identifying the problem to be investigated

Research for the applied experimental psychologist usually, but not always, starts with a problem that needs to be investigated. This contrasts with the approach taken by the pure researcher whose research is more often geared towards filling gaps in the existing theoretical literature. For Sellen, the problem centred on the difficulty of supporting rich interactional routines, such as gaze and mutual gaze, in mediated interaction, and the possibility of providing this support using different video configurations.

Step 2 Gathering information about the problem

Before running any experiment, the applied experimental psychologist engages in a process of information gathering. Sellen gathered information by reviewing and analysing literatures on communication in general, and gaze and mediated communication in particular. She would have observed people using mediated communication systems and also used mediated communication systems herself to get first-hand experience with the problem. This kind of information gathering helps to clarify the nature of the problem, informs later decisions about subjects and tasks, and helps in identifying a specific aim for the project. The point is that experimental hypotheses and measures do not come out of thin air. They are grounded in the experience of the experimenter and a large body of previous literature.

Step 3 Specifying the aim of the project

Identifying a project aim serves to bound and define the problem under investigation, and involves specifying the question or questions that the research project seeks to answer. Sellen's study sets out to answer questions about differences in the nature of communication supported by three communication systems: Same Room, PIP and Hydra. Thus her aim was to identify characteristics of the conversations that take place when people interact with each other in the Same Room or in different rooms using PIP and Hydra.

Step 4 Designing the experiment

There are many technical arguments in favour of different experimental designs which I don't have the space to explore here. However there are some general features of applied experimentation which need to be borne in mind. As we are interested in behaviour in practice rather than behaviour in principle, the experimental context should be as realistic as possible. This impinges on experimental design, in particular with respect to the duration of the experiment. Furthermore, Sellen, aware of the extent to which individuals differ, employed a within–subjects design. This means that each subject is exposed to each experimental condition, an approach that is to be recommended whenever possible.

Step 5 Specifying the hypotheses and variables

Once the project aim is clearly stated the hypotheses and variables are relatively easy to specify. However, great care needs to be taken with operationalizing or deciding how to measure the dependent variables. The nature or quality of communication can be measured in many different ways, and the ways in which they are operationalized can determine the success of the experiment.

Experimentalists often choose trivial dependent variables simply because they are available and easy to measure. The dependent variable chosen should be meaningful and make a contribution to understanding the phenomenon under investigation. As an approach, applied experimental psychology reminds the researcher that the dependent variables should point towards some part of human life. But it offers no techniques to ensure that the experimenter chooses meaningful dependent variables.

There is a strong and robust literature in mediated communication, dating back to studies in the 1950s, which indicates that mediation is unlikely to affect gross performance unless the tasks are very sensitive but often affects the underlying processes which generate that gross performance (see reviews by Williams, 1977, and Chapanis, 1986). Cognizant of these studies, Sellen avoids the trap of choosing trivial dependent variables by focusing on the process and pattern of communication.

McCarthy and Monk (1994) present a detailed discussion of some of the arguments surrounding the selection of dependent measures in mediated communication experiments. This paper pays particular attention to process–related dependent variables such as the establishment and maintenance of common ground, explicit and implicit topic references, and the use of first and second person pronouns. Following consideration of the efficacy of task and process–related dependent variables, McCarthy and Monk argue that experimenters should be concerned with three issues when choosing dependent variables: sensitivity, relevance and practicality. They concluded that process–related dependent variables score well on each of these dimensions.

Step 6 Selecting realistic tasks

In applied experimentation the tasks should be as realistic as possible. This is one of the main characteristics that distinguishes applied from pure experimental psychologists. Remember Bartlett's arguments in favour of using stories, not nonsense syllables, in memory research. Sellen's tasks would receive a middling score in this respect. Whereas they are not at the nonsense syllable end of the continuum, they are a little away from being real tasks in real working contexts. Furthermore, the early literature on mediated communication suggests an important distinction between cooperative and conflictful tasks (see Williams, 1977 and Chapanis, 1986, for reviews) and more recent work by Kraut and colleagues (e.g., Chalfonte, Fish and Kraut, 1991) suggests important interactions between medium of communication and task type.

Step 7 Finding subjects

Landauer (1987) argues that psychologists should insist on using large, representative pools of subjects. This is particularly true for the applied experimental psychologist who is interested in understanding behaviour in practice. To be representative, subjects should vary in age, computer experience, gender, occupational background and so on. There are many ways of collecting representative samples. See Leach (1991) for a detailed discussion of sampling.

4.5 Features of applied experimental psychology

In this section I will use Sellen's study to reveal some of the main features of applied experimental psychology.

4.5.1 Hypothetico–deductive

Applied experimental psychology employs the hypothetico–deductive approach, that is the applied experimental psychologist runs an experiment specifically to test a hypothesis or hypotheses. As we can see from Sellen's work, hypotheses don't come out of thin air. The psychologist uses the existing literature, relevant observations in situations which are similar to the one being studied, personal experience, and informal comparisons and analysis to inform the process of generating hypotheses. The applied experimental psychologist also attends to the practicality of various solutions or suggestions that are likely to emerge from testing different hypotheses. If a putative hypothesis is of theoretical interest only and is not likely to lead to some useful suggestions, even in the longer term, it is unlikely to be tested.

Critics of the hypothetico–deductive approach argue that one of its weaknesses is that hypotheses render the data collection process selective. Of course they do. For instance, Sellen's focus was on phenomena specified in her hypotheses. This is not to say that she would not have learned from other phenomena she observed during the study, just that testing the hypotheses resulting from those observations is another day's work. Starting from the position that all perception is selective and constructive, I believe that data selection on the basis of hypotheses is a strength and not a weakness. Even if there is no explicit hypothesis, it is not possible for the researcher to attend to all or even all relevant events and actions. Having an explicit hypothesis means that at least some of those preconceptions and assumptions which inform the selective perception and attention of the experimenter are placed in the public domain.

4.5.2 Simple cause–effect relationships in a complex world

It has been argued that pure experimental psychology examines simple cause–effect relationships of the form "if *p* then *q*". Applied experimental psychology, in contrast, is multivariate. It is concerned with relationships of the form: if $p1, p2,... pn$, then q; or if $p1$, then q, under conditions $r, s,$ and t. Thus Foushee, Lauber, Baetge, and Acomb (1986) looked at the interaction of crew composition, length of shift, difficulty of task and so on, on both performance effectiveness and the process of coordination within the cockpit. Perhaps Sellen's failure to find significant differences on some of the dimensions measured is due to her relatively simple hypotheses. If she had used a set of tasks which differed from each other in some fundamental way, she might have found the different communication systems suited different tasks. Complexity is also acknowledged in the emergence of process variables in psychological research.

4.5.3 Sterile laboratory tasks or real life tasks

One of the main arguments made against pure experimental psychology is that it is not sensitive to the effects of context. Thus it is argued that "pure" experimentation admits no material difference (literally a difference that matters) between the laboratory and the outside world. In contrast, applied experimental psychology strives for ecological validity. It often involves people performing real tasks in real workplaces or at the very least in high fidelity simulations under reasonably realistic work conditions. Excellent examples of this work are available in work psychology, which is carried out in the field and where naturally occurring groups are used for comparison. Some approximations in the CMC area have implicated task context as a significant variable in determining the appropriate configuration of media in a CMC system. For example, Kraut's work has demonstrated the importance of a video link when trying to communicate complex ideas.

There are some research questions which simply have to be answered in the laboratory. For instance, it would hardly be safe and ethical to vary the design of an aviation instrument such that half of the tested flights carried version one and the other half carried version two, when one is expected to be more effective than the other. That kind of study can only be safely done in the laboratory. However, it is important that the task and simulated instrumentation used in the laboratory be as close as possible to the "real life" task if the results are to generalize to performance in flight.

4.5.4 Theory–driven and problem–driven research

Pure experimental psychology tends to be theory driven. It is concerned mainly with identifying variables and hypotheses which will help test the validity of a theory or help choose between two or more theories in a particular context. In contrast, applied experimental psychology is interested in both theory and problem. It is as concerned with solving real life problems as it is with refining theory. Sellen, when discussing her motivation for carrying out this research at all writes: "While there are many interesting theoretical issues that arise, there are also practical issues motivating this work" (p. 49). Sellen's study is informed by existing theory and research but is driven by the need to solve a problem concerning the suitability of various media configurations for supporting different forms of communication. Other studies in CMC (e.g. Chalfonte et al., 1991) are geared towards providing some guidelines on the suitability of different media for different tasks. They contribute to a body of theory but that is not their primary purpose.

Of course, there is an overarching theoretical perspective or world view which guides the interpretation of the data. I want to say a few words about the psychological approach to interpretation now.

4.5.5 Interpretation

Data can be interpreted at a number of levels. Sociologists interpret at the level of society. Most psychologists interpret their data at the level of the individual, though of course that individual could be an individual interacting with others or acting in a context.

Even if, as many sociologists and psychologists claim, our discourse on human–computer interaction, work, communication and so on is socially constructed, there is nonetheless a system or an organism doing the construing. Part of the role of the psychologist is to explore the very process of construing, that is, how or why different individuals even from within the same culture may construe work or words differently. Why, for instance, people conform to the wishes, rules, or conventions of the group much but not all of the time.

Relating this to CMC: psychologists construe communication at an interpersonal as well as a social level. At the interpersonal level, information–processing models are appropriate. For example, Herb Clark and his colleagues (Clark and Schaefer, 1989) have attempted to understand the process of grounding in communication. Grounding is the process whereby participants in a conversation try to ensure that others have understood their utterances well enough for current purposes. It involves beliefs about what is likely to be understood by a partner given existing common ground, anticipation of the kind of response a partner is likely to make if they understand an utterance, interpretation of utterances and responses, etc. A number of CMC researchers have found this interpersonal and broadly cognitive approach very useful in interpreting CMC data. It is useful in that it helps us to construct an understanding of one dimension of one aspect of the communication process.

4.6 Discussion

Applied experimental psychology is an approach to understanding human behaviour and experience in "real life" contexts. It promotes the view that experimental psychology has a lot to offer in developing this understanding but it also acknowledges that experimental psychology does not have all the answers either in terms of theory or method. The applied experimental psychologist is not an ideologue driven either by theory or method. The applied experimental psychologist is more of a pragmatist who, realizing that behaviour in real life contexts is extremely complex, expects to have to use a broad range of methods and conceptual approaches to come to a satisfactory conclusion. In practice many of these methods and concepts originate in disciplines other than psychology. Much of the conceptual background for Sellen's work is in the conversation analytic approach. Thus one of the primary strengths of applied experimental psychology in HCI and other complex domains is that it is philosophically well disposed to inter–disciplinary work.

Applied experimental psychology brings particular strengths to any inter–disciplinary endeavour, one of which is hypothesis testing. This can be a highly context–sensitive practice. Moreover, any applied science needs to test hypotheses at some stage in the process. Otherwise we return to the grand rational arguments and untested theories of pre–scientific philosophy. Applied experimental psychology has developed expertise at simulating essential aspects of a complex context in laboratory conditions. This is particularly useful on those occasions when it is necessary to explore aspects of performance in a laboratory, especially when it would be unsafe or unethical to try to do so *in vivo*. Applied experimental psychology is also very comfortable with and indeed encourages experimentation in the field when that is possible.

Applied experimental psychology also brings characteristic weaknesses to any inter–disciplinary endeavour. I have already identified potential weaknesses with regard to choosing meaningful dependent variables and controlling random variance. There may also be a gap between the real world events, issues, and problems that generate applied experimental research and the hypotheses that are tested therein. The real world events and situations embody many possible hypotheses. Within psychology, a fairly informal analysis of the situation often characterized by a phase of exploratory observation precedes the selection of relevant hypotheses. While not bad when compared to a solely theory–driven approach or simple guesswork, it could be better. Systematic observation has been used in certain areas of psychology (e.g. developmental and social) and in ethnography. I am sure systematic observation could be profitably applied in the hypothesis generation phase of applied experimental psychology.

While applied experimental psychology deliberately avoids becoming theory–driven, it would benefit from a more formal approach to expressing or encapsulating its results. Within HCI, cognitive or formal interaction models could be used to perform this function.

I am not suggesting that the applied experimental psychologist would do ethnography or cognitive modelling. Rather that applied experimental psychology could benefit from developing its natural predisposition to inter–disciplinary work.

Further reading

Barber, P. (1988). *Applied Cognitive Psychology: An Information Processing Framework*. London: Routledge.
A fairly brief and readable introduction to aspects of cognitive psychology with applicability as the central focus. Chapter 1 deals specifically with the application of psychology, and particularly the relationship between theory and practice. Chapter 2 outlines the information processing approach which is adopted throughout the book. This is a particularly appropriate approach with which to start exploring the interface between applied experimental psychology and HCI. The remaining chapters deal with specific application domains such as mental workload, reading and design for action.

Landauer, T. K. (1987). Relations between cognitive psychology and computer system design. In J. M. Carroll (ed.) *Interfacing Thought: Cognitive Aspects of Human Computer Interaction*, pp. 1–25. Cambridge Mass: Bradford Books (MIT Press).
A thought–provoking discussion of the relationship between cognitive psychology and HCI. It provides a useful classification of the ways in which cognitive psychology and HCI interact. It points out some of the reasons why this interaction has not yet delivered its full potential in either direction yet, and suggests some ways in which the situation might be improved. Most of what is said also applies to applied experimental psychology and HCI.

Leach, J. (1991). *Running Applied Psychology Experiments*. Milton Keynes: Open University Press.
An extremely useful handbook for the researcher interested in doing applied experimental psychology. Part One examines the relationship between applied and pure psychology. Part Two goes into great detail on how to plan and run an applied experiment. Chapter 4 has a discussion of sampling, which was not covered in sufficient detail in this chapter. At times Leach makes too much of the link between applied and field studies. It should be clear from what I have already written that I believe that applied experiments can be run in both field and laboratory.

McCarthy J. C., and Monk, A. F. (1994). Measuring the quality of computer mediated communication. *Behaviour and Information Technology*, 13, 311–319.
This article provides a fairly detailed consideration of the issues surrounding experimental design and the selection of dependent variables in computer–mediated communication. Whereas the examples given are taken from a specific domain, familiarity with the general issues discussed would profit anybody doing or reading applied experimental psychology in any domain.

Wickens, C. D. (1992). *Engineering Psychology and Human Performance*. New York: Harper Collins.
This book has a similar approach to Barber (1988) above, but it is far more detailed and comprehensive. You should probably tackle it only if your appetite for applied experimental psychology has been whetted after reading Barber. It is not a book you will read from cover to cover, but it does contain quite detailed discussions of the application of psychology to complex systems such as process control and aviation. Probably not so strong on ordinary everyday interactions, such as your interactions with your own computer.

Chapter 5

An introduction to cognitive modelling in human–computer interaction

Andrew Howes

5.1 Introduction

In *The Long Dark Tea Time of the Soul*, Douglas Adams writes about airport designers: "They have sought ... wherever possible to expose the plumbing on the grounds that it is functional, and conceal the location of the departure gates, presumably on the grounds that they are not." Computer interfaces, like airports, are systems in which multiple constraints impose themselves on design solutions. One of these constraints is that a computer interface should be functional with respect to the psychology of the user.

Understanding the psychology of users involves predicting user performance at the computer interface. A cognitive model is a mechanism for making such predictions. In Human–Computer Interaction (HCI) cognitive models have been proposed that predict a range of phenomena. For example, there are models that predict whether one interface will take longer to learn than another (Task–Action Grammar, TAG; Payne and Green, 1986), and models that predict how long an expert will take to execute a particular sequence of actions (GOMS; Card, Moran and Newell, 1983).

Cognitive modelling is a relatively new discipline that grew from the concerns of experimental cognitive psychology and was facilitated by methodologies developed in artificial intelligence and linguistics. The hope is that the success of experimental psychologists in discovering a wide range of regularities about human behaviour could be capitalized on to construct precisely specified computational models to predict human behaviour.

Researchers developing cognitive models have two long–term aims. One is theoretical: to further our understanding of human problem solving and learning. Human–Computer interaction involves tasks that go beyond the traditional puzzle tasks used in the study of cognitive science. Unlike the eight–puzzle, tic–tac–toe, or checkers, HCI involves real–world problems that require significant amounts of diverse knowledge for decision making. Solutions are learnt using a mixture of instruction, manuals and exploration. Further, the skills that are acquired are highly interactive, requiring much back–and–forth information flow between the user and the device (Draper, 1986). All of these factors make HCI a rich domain for the study of cognitive science.

The second aim is applied: to help HCI practitioners understand how users will interact with computers. The practitioners may be designers, interested in shaping new interfaces; purchasers, interested in determining how easy an interface will be to learn; or educators, interested in constructing tools to support learning (Howes and Payne, 1990c). Cognitive models have had some success in impacting these concerns, notably in Project Ernestine (Gray, John and Atwood, 1992), and in motivating Cognitive–Walkthroughs (Polson, Lewis, Rieman and Wharton, 1992), but these examples are still few in number. In general the application of cognitive modelling to design is a research goal that has yet to see fruition (Bellotti, 1990; Gugerty, 1993). Further, success is predicated on a better computational understanding of psychology and on a better understanding of ways of delivering the psychology embodied in cognitive models to designers (Long, 1989; Barnard, 1990). For these reasons, this chapter introduces the reader to the foundations of cognitive modelling in the broader cognitive science. It does not discuss the applicability of cognitive modelling to design.[1]

5.2 Cognitive modelling in HCI: foundations

Cognitive science is about pursuing computational theories of the problem–solving and learning processes that underlie human behaviour. Theory construction involves many different types of description. In this paper I will focus on five types: behaviour, knowledge, representation and algorithm, cognitive architectural, and learning. The following paragraphs describe these.

A behaviour–level description of a user can be given simply by listing the user's *behavioural properties*. Behavioural properties must be determined by the results provided by experimental cognitive psychology (see Chapter 4). These results can be used as the highest–level specification of what a cognitive model is to simulate. The specification determines the functions that the model is supposed to

---

[1] For a review of the use of cognitive models in design see Gugerty (1993).

compute, or what Newell (1990) calls the *response functions*. A model computes functions (in the mathematical sense) of its environment. What these functions are, how long they take to perform, and in what contexts they are learnt, are the properties of the user that are being modelled.

Behaviour–level descriptions involve very little theorizing and will only support predictions of user performance in very specific contexts of device and user population. Deeper levels of explanation are required to provide more general predictions. The next level used in cognitive science is the *knowledge level* (Newell, 1990). Behavioural properties can be explained by analysing the knowledge that users need in order to perform their goals. Newell illustrates the knowledge level with a hypothetical situation in which an observer Y can see a person X looking at a number of blocks on a table. Block A is on top of block B, and block C sits by itself. If observer Y is to ask person X, "Which block is on top of B?" then observer Y can hypothesize that X will answer, "A". This hypothesis is formed purely on the basis of the knowledge and goals that observer Y believes X has. Similarly, as observers, cognitive scientists hypothesize the content of the knowledge that users bring to bear whilst using computer systems. Many HCI models are explicitly knowledge–level models. Young and Whittington (1990) describe the use of knowledge analysis in HCI, and Young, Howes and Whittington (1990) give a knowledge–level analysis of the interactive properties of human–computer interaction. I will refer to a model as knowing that it should respond J to stimulus K if it reliably responds J given K.

A description at the knowledge level specifies only *content*. However, knowledge must be represented in some way if it is to be used, and a process or algorithm must be defined to compute responses based on the knowledge. One way to represent knowledge is with logic. For the blocks world example above, it is possible to write down a set of predicates that represent the relationships of blocks A, B and C, and further predicates that support the inference of facts about the situation, such as whether block C has anything on top of it. Logic is a particularly well defined representation, but it is only one of many representational languages. Moreover, logic has many features that make it implausible as a model of human cognition, and indeed researchers in cognitive science have proposed a number of more plausible representational languages. A representation is judged to be more cognitively plausible if it encourages the computation of plausible response functions and inhibits the computation of others, i.e. if it exhibits the right behavioural properties. A number of cognitive models, for example

Task–Action Grammar (Payne and Green, 1986), are models of the representational languages in which people encode knowledge of how to use computers.

Whether it is by instruction, exploration or reading manuals, knowledge must be learnt. An important property of human learning is that it involves *generalization*. During training, whether it is under the guidance of a tutor, or self–motivated exploration, users experience *examples* of how to achieve goals with the device. From just a handful of examples people can abstract general knowledge that allows them to achieve a very wide range of goals.

One approach to modelling human generalization is Analysis–Based Learning (ABL; Lewis, 1988). This is a class of techniques, the best known examples of which are explanation–based learning (Dejong and Mooney, 1986), explanation–based generalization (Mitchell, 1986), and PUPS (Anderson, 1987). ABL techniques generalise on the basis of just one or two examples. In human–computer interaction the *analysis* is an understanding of how user actions achieve system responses. The analysis will facilitate generalization by providing the necessary structural information for the learner to construct an analogy from goals with known methods to new goals. I will refer to a model as having *learnt* new knowledge if given some stimulus it reliably changes its behaviour to produce one response rather than another.

Learning is one of the most important functions of a model of the human *cognitive architecture* (Pylyshyn, 1984; Newell, 1990; Anderson, 1987). The cognitive architecture brings together knowledge, representation, and learning to produce behaviour. It is a fixed set of mechanisms for acquiring and processing knowledge in order to achieve goals, often referred to as the programming language of the mind. There are a number of hypothesized models of the human cognitive architecture that range from network architectures such as CI (Kintsch, 1988) to rule–based architectures such as Soar (Newell, 1990), ACT–R (Anderson, 1993), and ICS (Barnard, 1987). Some architectures, such as Soar, CI and ACT–R, are computationally implemented. Each architecture has its own distinctive learning mechanism (e.g. chunking in Soar). Through the application of these learning mechanisms the models are able to acquire knowledge that allows them to achieve new goals in new situations. Put another way, fixed architectural mechanisms cause learning transitions at the knowledge level.

Individual models vary in all of the aspects of a cognitive system described above. Some models do no learning at all, but use many types of knowledge. Others do lots of learning, but only for a limited range of knowledge types. Some are implemented in architectures and others are not. They all cover different ranges of behavioural properties. Rather than reviewing each model in its own terms, this chapter views the modelling literature from the perspective of the foundations of cognitive science, and to this end describes a computer user in terms of: behaviour, knowledge, representation and algorithm, cognitive architecture, and learning. In this way the chapter puts to the background the importance of the constellations of behaviours and techniques that any particular model exhibits and instead, wherever possible, foregrounds the theoretical insights to which modelling has contributed.

5.3 Behaviour

Needless to say, people exhibit many behaviours. Cognitive modellers have focused on capturing those that determine the learnability and usability of an interface. The *learnability* of an interface is a measure of how long it takes people to learn, and of factors such as whether the device can be learnt without instruction, or without a manual. The *usability* of an interface is a measure of the ease of use once learning is in some sense complete. It includes factors such as the amount of time taken to perform tasks and the number of slips or accidental mistakes that users make. The following paragraphs give an overview of some of the aspects of human behaviour that relate to device learnability and usability. Only the briefest sketch of these behavioural properties (BP) is given; there are many more than are listed, and much more detailed descriptions could be given of those that are covered.[2]

BP1 Users perform tasks in predictable amounts of time

Device procedures take predictable amounts of time for users to perform. For example, using values taken from Lewis and Rieman (1993), the time taken to enter one keystroke on a standard keyboard is 0.28 seconds. The range is from 0.07 seconds to over 1 second for a inexperienced typist. Random sequences take longer than plain text. Response to a brief light takes from 0.05 seconds for a bright light to 0.2 seconds for a dim one. For more details, see John (1989) and Rumelhart and Norman (1982).

---

[2] To help the reader, I have grouped together a number of experimental results into each description of a behavioural property. Grouping the experiments in this way has necessarily entailed the use of theoretical intuitions that would not be appropriate in a purer description of behaviour.

BP2 Users find consistent interfaces easier to learn and use

A consistent interface is easier to learn than an inconsistent one. There are many aspects of consistency. For example, two commands can be said to be syntactically consistent if both put the action specifier before the object specifier (e.g. the Unix commands, "rm data_file", and "mail karen", are syntactically consistent with each other). There are many empirical results in HCI that indicate that having consistent mappings between tasks and actions improves the learnability and usability of a device (e.g. Barnard, Hammond, Morton, Long and Clark, 1981; Payne and Green, 1989).

BP3 Users find display–based interfaces easier to learn

In general, display–based devices are much easier to learn than command–oriented devices that have a similar functionality. The shift from command–oriented interfaces to highly display–based, window interfaces in the 1980s saw a radical improvement in the ease with which people could learn to interact with machines.

BP4 Expert users have limited recall of display–based methods

In addition to the effects of display–based devices on novice performance, displays also appear to affect expert performance. For example there are empirical results indicating that expert users may not be able to recall command names away from the display (Payne, 1991; Mayes, Draper, McGregor, and Oatley, 1988), nor the precise effects of commands (Payne, 1991), nor even the sequence in which commands should be performed (Duff, 1989).

BP5 Users become dependent upon locations

People become dependent on the location of items on the display. For example a hi–fi user, who knows where the "CD" button is, will able to change the mode to "CD" without having to search for the required button–label. The locational dependence of user behaviour has been demonstrated by Lee (1993), Lansdale (1991), Teitelbaum and Granda (1983) and by Nygren, Lind, Johnson and Sandblad (1992).

BP6 Users follow superficial cues when learning new methods

If novice users are given novel task descriptions then they will tend to prefer selecting menu items that appear, literally, in the task description (Englebeck, 1986).

BP7 Users learn by exploring, receiving instruction and reading manuals

Frequently users find themselves in situations where they do not know how to achieve a goal with the device. In such a situation they may explore. Sometimes they will be fortunate and successful, other times not. Often the space of possible explorations is large enough to make exploration very expensive, other times the device is sufficiently well designed that exploration is an efficient learning strategy (see Carroll and Rosson, 1987). However, users will not always explore, sometimes they will refuse to try options out, commenting "I'm scared I'll break it". Other times they will have access to advice from an instructor or colleague, and failing all of these then they may well read a manual. Whichever learning mode is preferred all are modes that can in principle be modelled. All involve their own learnability issues independent of the device but are also affected by its learnability. Even an instructor finds it hard to teach a novice to use a badly designed interface, and the representations used in teaching will affect later performance (Bibby and Payne, 1993).

BP8 Expert users make slips

Slips are a phenomenon of behaviour that do not appear whilst the user is learning to use a device, but instead start to emerge once they might be considered expert. Slips are not mistakes. Reason (1979) defines them as "actions not as planned", and Norman (1981) as "the error that occurs when a person does an action that is not intended." Green, Payne, Gilmore and Mepham (1985) state, "Everyday observation suggests that some computer systems entice their users into slips more often than others. (Try counting how often you hear a 'dear me, I'm always doing that.' Add points for vehemence.)"

BP9 Users require confirmation of their actions

Users need feedback from a device in order to inform them of discrepancies between what changes they intended to make to the device and what changes they actually did make. Appropriately designed feedback can be used to mitigate the effects of errors and badly designed feedback can actually be the cause of errors. For example, Payne (1990) reports observations of users of MacDraw, an application that supports the construction of simple line diagrams (consisting of squares, circles, rectangles, etc.) with a set of tools that are selected from a menu. Each tool is represented by an icon picturing the shape that the tool will create (e.g. a square or a circle).

Selecting one of these involves moving the mouse pointer over the icon and clicking the mouse button (where "click" means press and release the button). Unfortunately, midway through this interaction, when a user has pressed the button but not yet released it, the device offers feedback; it flashes the icon. Payne has observed that many novice users take this to mean that the tool has been selected and they then drag the mouse off the icon before releasing the button. In fact, if the button is not released over the icon then the tool will not be selected.

BP10 Users generate new solutions to new problems (sometimes)

This is such an obvious point that it may hardly seem worth stating but it should not be forgotten that computer applications are tools for solving larger problems than say drawing squares or deleting words. Computer applications are very powerful tools and they very often facilitate more than one solution to a particular problem. For example Lee and Barnard (1993) have studied the composition of different strategies in editing bibliographic references with a wordprocessor. The task was to go through a document replacing short–hand references such as "CAR83" with the full reference: "Card, Moran and Newell, 1983". Achieving the task involved looking up the short–hand in the Reference section at the end of the document. Lee and Barnard found that for the Microsoft Word5 wordprocessor many solutions can be constructed out of the building blocks provided by the device commands. Subjects who had not used Word 5 before were told how to use the scrollbar, Find <text>, split window, and Go To <page–number> commands, and then asked to replace the short–hand references. The authors found that the subjects achieved this task in a variety of ways: (1) using the scrollbar to move back and forth between the Reference section and the main body of the text; (2) using the Find <text> command to move back and forth; (3) using the split window command to display both sections of the text at once; and (4) remembering the relevant page numbers and using the Go To <page–number> command to swap between them. These four solutions are not all equally efficient, but whilst some users will find the most efficient, others will stick with the first that they happen upon. Sometimes the most useful or efficient solutions are given by manuals, instruction or colleagues; other times users will have to work out for themselves how to make the best use of an interface.

5.4 Knowledge level

According to the above analysis, user behaviour exhibits regularities that range from performing tasks in predictable amounts of time to finding display–based interfaces easier to learn. Some of these regularities are very specific and others very general. They cover a wide spectrum of skills from the beginner to the expert. The question for cognitive modelling is: how might it be possible to give an explanation in which all of these properties are all the result of a single set of mechanisms working together in service of a user's goals? To answer this question we need descriptions at deeper levels. The first that we shall examine is the knowledge level.

The knowledge–level description given in this section will be presented in the terms of the problem–space hypothesis of Allen Newell (Newell, 1980). According to Newell, cognitive behaviour can be analysed as a goal–directed sequence of operator applications that move a problem solver from an initial state to the goal state. A goal may be a task on the scale of writing a thesis, or on the smaller scale of selecting a particular menu item in a wordprocessor; an operator may be an external action, such as pressing a mouse button, or an internal action, such as specifying a subgoal. I will refer to a sequence of operators that achieves a goal as a method.

Viewed from the perspective of the problem space, a cognitive model is an engine for simulating the sequence of operators that a user would produce for a particular interface and goal. A cognitive model is given a goal and put in a state, and it will output an operator. This operator constitutes its prediction of what a user would do in the same circumstances. However, which operator it outputs is dependent upon a number of circumstances other than the immediate goal and state, including knowledge that it may have learnt or been given. Many types of knowledge are used to guide the selection of operators. The following paragraphs describe seven *knowledge types* (KT) that range from knowledge of the goal to knowledge of other methods, and from essential knowledge types to those that are used only as a last resort. Again only brief sketches are given.

KT1 Goals

The goal is the task, either state or process, that the model is currently attempting to achieve. All of the cognitive models analysed in this paper are goal–directed, which means that the selection of the next operator is dependent upon the current goal.[3]

Many, but not all, cognitive models support the specification of *goal–hierarchies*. Goal–hierarchies are a key aspect of cognitive science that date back to the work of Miller, Galanter and Pribram (1960). They have been justified recently in Anderson (1993). The hierarchy consists of a root, top–level, goal which has a number of subgoals, each of which may itself have subgoals. The goal most recently added to the hierarchy is the current–goal and it is this that guides the selection of an operator. As an operator is only sensitive to the current–goal and not all those above it in the hierarchy, the specification of how to achieve a particular goal can be used in many contexts. Many cognitive models are built around goal–hierarchies, including: GOMS (Card, Moran and Newell, 1983), TAG (Payne and Green, 1986), and BNF (Reisner, 1981).

These models do, however, vary in the content of their goals. For example, in Payne and Green's Task–Action Grammar (TAG) goals are limited to what they call *simple–tasks*. To qualify as a simple–task, a goal must not require the execution of complex control structures such as loop mechanisms. This constrains the applicability of TAG to modelling phenomena that derive from the lowest–level goal to operator mappings that users engage in, such as copy text T1 to location L1, but not copy text T1 to location L1 three times. In contrast goal specifications in GOMS are relatively unrestricted. GOMS goals can cover the full range of routine skill from moving the cursor to writing a letter.

Another analysis of the content of users' goals is given by Howes and Young (1991). They suggest that users determine *communication requirements*, information that a user believes the device needs in order for it to perform the desired task. Howes and Young observe that the assumptions users make about a device's communication requirements are often incorrect. Mismatches are often due to modes in the device. For example, when users first use a command–oriented interface they can be observed typing words into the command line and then waiting. They seem to expect the device to perform the command as soon as the last character of the last word is typed. They do not know that the device requires confirmation that the command is complete, and that this is to be communicated to the device with a Return character.

---

[3] The Task Analysis techniques described in Chapter 7 are relevant to the analysis of goals.

KT2 Display–based knowledge sources

After the goal, one of the most important sources of knowledge for the user is the content of the device display. Three of the behavioural properties listed above make direct reference to the use of display–based devices: BP3 (users find display–based devices easier to learn), BP4 (expert users have limited recall of display–based methods), and BP5 (users become dependent upon locations). These behavioural properties suggest that display–based devices affect both novice and expert performance.

For the novice (see BP3), display–based devices constrain the set of choices from which they must select. Command–oriented interfaces, such as the Unix Cshell, do not present the user with such rich sources of knowledge. For example, invoking a syntax checker might be achieved by typing "syntax", or, "syn", or "grammar", or "grammar–checker", "gram", or "grm" depending on the naming convention used. If the user does not know the right term then a number of guesses will be made before the correct word is found or the user may give up and consult a manual. In contrast, achieving the same task with a display such as the "Tools" menu in MS Word results in the user finding the correct choice much sooner. The MS Word Tools menu contains the items, "Spelling, Grammar, Thesaurus, Hyphenation, Word Count, Renumber, Sort, Calculate, Repaginate Now, Preferences, Commands". Given the "syntax checking" task and the Tools menu most users will select "Grammar". Even if there are ambiguous names on a menu then at least the choice set will be bounded and will usually consist of only a few possibilities.

For the expert, display–based devices provide buttons or menu options with semantically meaningful labels. A consequence of this is that knowledge of command names does not have to be remembered (BP4). Put another way, knowledge that is "left in the environment" does not have to be stored in the users long–term memory.

Further, users do not have to remember the precise effects of commands (BP4) because the device display is updated as soon as the user issues a command. Assuming that changes made to an interface are undoable, this provides a rich environment for acting with very limited planning.

A number of cognitive models have been designed to take advantage of display–based knowledge sources. Larkin (1989) proposes a model of the use of "where things should be" knowledge in the domains of coffee making and algebra. Young and Simon (1987) propose a model of interleaved planning and activity. Howes and Payne (1990a) and Kitajima and Polson (1992) both propose models of an expert user's display–based method knowledge. Howes and Young (1991) propose an architecturally implemented model of the learning and performance of display–based methods. Green, Bellamy and Parker (1987) propose a model called Parsing–gnisrap of the interleaved processes of parsing and activity in the construction of computer programs. Payne (1990) proposes a model of display use based on a present/accept conversational analysis. All of these models differ in the exact representations and process mechanisms that they use. They will be reviewed more thoroughly in the next sections.

KT3 Knowledge of other methods

In contrast to display–based interfaces, command–oriented interfaces such as Unix or Emacs impose very little constraint on the sequence of operators that that can be executed. Whereas there may be only ten items on a menu, thousands of words can be typed on a command line (as in the syntax checker example above). In such circumstances it becomes much more important that the mappings between goals and their sequences of operators share *similarities*. For example operator sequences can share the same syntax. They may also share similar ways of constructing mnemonics. For example if a user knows that the operator sequence for communicating the command "remove" consists of typing the first two consonants of the command name, i.e. typing "rm", then the user may infer that the operator sequence for the command "prepare" is to type "pr". An interface which is consistent will be more learnable because users can draw on knowledge of other goals (BP2) in order to infer the operator sequences for new goals.

There are many ways in which interfaces can support the inference of one operator sequence on the basis of knowledge of another. As a second example consider the case of a user who knows that to change some mode in a device it is necessary to type "on"; the user might infer that to change the mode back, "off" should be typed. This inference would be based upon the knowledge that "on" and "off" are *congruent* names (Carroll, 1982). Another example of a congruent pair is "stop" and "go". A non–congruent pair is "on" and "stop".

This knowledge–level analysis of the use of similar operator sequences emphasizes predicting a user's behaviour on the basis of the knowledge that the user is believed to possess. However, as I have said, knowledge must be represented to be used. A more precise way of revealing the ways in which the action sequences share structural similarities is at the representation level. Models that take advantage of representational constraints (e.g. TAG, Payne and Green, 1986) are described further in Section 5.5. An alternative approach is to describe models of the learning processes that benefit from the use of similar operator sequences (e.g. EXPL, Lewis, 1988; Explor, Howes and Payne, 1990b; Rieman, Lewis, Young and Polson, 1994). These models are described further in Section 5.6.

KT4 Knowledge of recent history

Operators must be sequenced. The sequencing of action has long been studied in cognitive psychology (Lashley, 1951). Models (such as TAG, Payne and Green, 1986; GOMS, Card, Moran and Newell, 1983) use knowledge of all of the previous operators applied for the current instantiation of the current goal to contextualize the choice of the next operator. Other models use the external display to constrain sequence (TAL, Howes and Young, 1991; D–TAG, Howes and Payne, 1990a; CCT, Kieras and Polson, 1985).

One of the effects of users learning sequences of actions is that, when expert, they start to make slips (BP8). Green, Payne, Gilmore and Meopham (1985) offer an analysis of expert slips in HCI that is based on what users know about the structure of the recent history of operators and the similarities between various methods (KT3).

KT5 Long–term history

During exploration (BP7) users acquire episodic knowledge of their activity. This knowledge is used to guide further exploration. The knowledge may include knowledge of which operators have been applied to which states, which operators have led to failure, and which to success. Users who are attempting to achieve a new goal can be heard to say things such as, "I've tried under that menu option repeatedly, but I can't see anything useful."

Ayn (Howes, 1994, 1993) is a model of exploration that uses episodic knowledge of which operators it has previously tried. The model may not know exactly how to achieve its goal but it can use knowledge of what it has tried to help guide further exploration. This model will be described in more detail later in this chapter.

KT6 Knowledge of operator effects

In order to problem solve and construct new solutions to new problems (BP10) users must have some knowledge of the effects of interface commands. Effect knowledge will enable the construction of new solutions to new goals.

Users can have knowledge of the effects of many different levels of operator (Moran, 1983; Payne, 1987 and, 1989; Payne, Squibb and Howes, 1990). For example, Payne argues that users need to construct two different problem spaces: one for the task domain (e.g. text, words, documents) and one for the device (e.g. a particular wordprocessor). He points out that users may not know all the details of the effects of commands in the device space but still know what the overall effect of sequences of device commands are in the task space. For example, Payne, Squibb and Howes (1990) demonstrate that users may use the Apple Macintosh Copy/Paste buffer without knowing that the Copy operation puts a copy of the selected text in a buffer. When given a task that involves copying one piece of text to three different locations a user without knowledge of the device space effects will produce an action sequence that involves multiple invocations of the copy command (i.e. "select, copy, paste, select, copy, paste, select, copy, paste" instead of "select, copy, paste, paste, paste").

Other researchers have emphasized other aspects of the use of operator effect knowledge. For example, Young and Whittington (1990) describe a model that uses *means–ends analysis,* i.e. knowledge that gives the problem solver the ability to choose operators on the basis of their effectiveness at reducing the difference between the current and desired situations. In addition, Monk and Dix (1987) and Howes and Payne (1990a) focus on what Payne calls the device space and provide formal mechanisms for analysing the consistency of the effects caused by device actions.

KT7 Knowledge of other devices, everyday knowledge, conceptual knowledge

A number of knowledge sources are important in the way that they bind particular device applications into a broader context (e.g. Young, Howes and Whittington, 1990). For example, all computer applications rely, to some extent, on everyday lexical semantics in command names. Whilst an everyday meaning of "copy" may not fully capture the meaning of the Apple Macintosh's "Copy" function (Payne, Squibb and Howes, 1990) and whilst people may generate many different words to describe the same function, the expectation that users will gain from appropriately labelled commands is not unfounded. Learning a computer application will also be facilitated by knowledge of other applications (Kieras and Bovair, 1984; Payne, Squibb and Howes, 1990), and by knowledge of the conceptual structure of the device (Young, 1981).

Summary

I have described seven types of knowledge important to device users: (1) knowledge of goals; (2) knowledge of the display state; (3) knowledge of other methods; (4) knowledge of recent history; (5)

knowledge of long–term history; (6) knowledge of the effects of actions; and (7) knowledge from other domains. Where appropriate I have pointed out how the use of a particular type of knowledge goes toward explaining a particular behavioural property. There are many other types of knowledge that users draw on and far more precise specifications could be given, but the above list should serve as an introduction.

5.5 Representation and algorithm

Whatever knowledge a particular cognitive model is designed to utilize, a language must be defined for representing that knowledge. There are many variations in the representational languages used in cognitive modelling. For example, goals are represented in GOMS as natural language sentences, whereas in TAG (Payne and Green, 1986; Schiele and Green, 1990) they are represented by *attribute/value* pairs denoting the semantic content of the goal. The attribute/value representation adds formalism, and therefore constraint, to the description of methods. Different representational languages give models different predictive capabilities. Payne and Green argue that an attribute/value representation is appropriate for capturing interface consistencies.

I will use TAG as an example of the power of representational constraint in predicting user behaviour. TAG is a notation language for describing the knowledge that users need in order to execute a set of tasks with an interface. For example where *T* is a task such as changing the font in a wordprocessor *W*, a TAG would describe the set of rules that map *T* into the sequence of actions *A* that are required to execute *T* on *W*. Many rules of the form $T \rightarrow A$ would be required to describe the interface. However, if the action sequences for two or more tasks were consistent, e.g. if they all shared the same syntax, then the TAG notation would allow just one rule to be written for the whole range of consistent tasks. In this way the number of rules required to describe the knowledge used for a particular interface would be reduced with the consistency of the interface. Predictions of whether one interface would take longer to learn than another could then be made by counting the number of TAG rules required to describe each interface's knowledge requirement. The one with fewer rules would take less time to learn.

```
TASK DICTIONARY
   {Effect = remove, Filename = duck}
   {Effect = prepare, Filename = duck}
   {Effect = more, Filename = duck}
GRAMMAR FOR LANGUAGE 1
   Task[Effect, Filename]
                    → type[first–two–consonants[Effect], type[Filename]].
GRAMMAR FOR LANGUAGE 2
   Task [Effect, Filename] → do[Effect], type[Filename].
   do [Effect=more] → type["more"].
   do [Effect] → type[first–two–consonants[Effect]].
GRAMMAR FOR LANGUAGE 3
   Task [Effect=remove, Filename] → do[Effect], type[Filename].
   Task [Effect=prepare, Filename] → type[Filename], do[Effect].
   do [Effect=more] → type("more").
   do [Effect] → type[first–two–consonants[Effect]].
```

Figure 5.1 A simple example of Task–Action Grammar (TAG).

As an example consider Figure 5.1, which illustrates Task–Action Grammars for three languages. Each language consists of $T \to A$ mappings for three goals: deleting a file, preparing a file for printing, and showing a file on the display. The task are described using two attribute/value pairs in the task dictionary of Figure 5.1. We assume that the name of the commands are known. The names are: "remove" to delete the file, "prepare" to prepare the file for printing (e.g. number the pages), and "more" to show the file on the display. For these tasks language 1 has one syntax that applies to all tasks: first type the *first–two–consonants* of the Effect of the command, whether "prepare", "remove" or "more", and then type the value of Filename. In Figure 5.1, only a single rule is required to represent language 1. Language 2 uses the same first–two–consonants abbreviation for "remove" and "prepare" but requires that the full name of the "more" command be typed. In Figure 5.1, three rules are required to represent this language. In language 3, the "prepare" task involves typing the filename first, whereas the "remove" task involves typing the effect first. In Figure 5.1, this language requires four rules to represent it. Applying a simplified version of TAG's rule count metric the prediction would be that language 1 would be easier to learn than language 2 which would be easier to learn than language 3.[4]

Like many other models of cognition in HCI, TAG is a model of an idealized expert skill. This means that the knowledge in the rules is

---

[4] Obviously Figure 1 is a very simple example. The Task-Action Grammar notation embodies a number of other mechanisms for dealing with various aspects of the configural properties of a command language (Payne and Green, 1986; Howes and Payne, 1990).

sufficient to determine the next operator. These models encode rules of the form *Goal, State → Operator–sequence*, in which there must be a unique sequence of actions for every combination of goal and state. In contrast, learning and performance models such as CE+ (Polson and Lewis, 1990), TAL (Howes and Young, 1991), and Ayn (Howes, 1994) have to deal with situations in which there is insufficient knowledge to suggest a single operator at every decision point. In such circumstances these models must employ *decision heuristics* in order to determine an operator. Decision heuristics model the ways in which users determine an operator based on the available knowledge.

In the absence of goal–specific knowledge TAL, for example, employs the following decision heuristics: (1) assume that the performance of the current goal G is similar to some other goal G' that is known, and (2) if there is no knowledge of a similar goal G' then ask for advice from an external advisor.

In contrast, in the absence of goal–specific knowledge, the CE+ model employs a *label–following* decision heuristic. Label following (Englebeck, 1986) is a simple strategy that involves preferring commands with labels that are also words in the task description. Label following only works in experimental or tutorial situations where users are not generating their own goal descriptions: however, in these circumstances it is a valid and observed heuristic (BP6: users follow superficial cues when learning new methods).

Ayn (Howes, 1994) employs two decision heuristics to take advantage of an episodic memory of tried operators (KT7). If it does not know of an operator that will definitely lead to success, then when attempting to achieve a goal that has not been achieved before it prefers novel operators, and when attempting to achieve a goal that has been achieved before it prefers familiar operators. These heuristics serve to constrain Ayn's search of the menu structure in the times when it may have achieved a goal once or twice but not yet learnt exactly which operators lead to success.

5.6 Learning

Knowledge, however it is represented, must be learnt. One way of describing a learning system is to describe the knowledge *K* that it learns given some situation *S*. If a person presses a button labelled "Ahhh!" and immediately gets a painful electric shock, then we might predict that they will not press a button labelled "Ahhh!" again. We would make this prediction on the basis of the assumption that the person employed a *learning heuristic* ($S → K$) which says, "if there is a situation in which an event *E* is immediately followed by some other event E' then learn that E causes E'," meaning that an event is caused by the immediately previous event. This specification of when the new knowledge (E causes E') is learnt is independent of the architectural mechanism that actually achieves the learning. Learning heuristics differ from decision heuristics in that where decision heuristics make the best use of the knowledge available, learning heuristics add knowledge to long–term memory.

Recall that analysis–based learning involves learning by constructing an "understanding" of an example in terms of what the problem solver knows about the domain in which the example is an instance. In HCI users must explain how a sequence of applied operators caused the achievement of a goal, that is, how user actions cause observed system changes. One way of constructing an explanation is with learning heuristics. The learning heuristic is a very general statement about the domain of methods; it may not always be true but it is a useful way of generating hypotheses, and therefore candidate explanations. The explanation will facilitate the construction of new methods for new goals. An account of how users construct new methods will give us a mechanistic account of how they utilize knowledge type KT3 (knowledge of other methods) in operator selection.

An important example of a model that constructs an explanation based on learning heuristics is EXPL (Lewis, 1986, 1988). EXPL employs a set of causal learning heuristics in order to analyse methods. They are the identity heuristic, the loose–ends heuristic, and the previous–action heuristic. The *identity* heuristic is characterized as, "if something appears in a user action, and in a later system response, the user action is probably a cause of the system response." The *loose–ends* heuristic assumes that all user actions contribute to the goal: hence if there is a system response which contributes to the goal, and there is a prior user action which hasn't yet been related to the goal, then hypothesize that the user action caused the system response. The *previous–action* heuristic was used above to analyse the pressing of the "Ahhh!" button; it says that if an event follows an action immediately, it is plausible that the action caused the event.

As an example of EXPL's output consider Figure 5.2, which shows an analysis of a demonstration of an operation that involves cutting (deleting) a picture of a car from a document in a MacDraw–like device. Each event is given a number and is flagged with a symbol to indicate whether it is a user action "u" or a system response "s". The outcome of the demonstration is shown in line 8. Events 3 to 5 describe the use of a pull–down menu with options zcut and zmove. In Figure 5.2, causal links are shown in parentheses after the method

LEARNING HEURISTICS

i	=	identity
p	=	previous–event
l	=	loose–ends

ANALYSIS

1	s	begin
2	s	show (p 1) zedit (p 1) zcar (p 1) ztrain (p 1)
3	u	press zedit (i 2)
4	s	show (p 3) zcut (p 3) zmove (p 3)
5	u	release zcut (i 4)
6	s	remove (p 5) zcut (i 5) zmove (p 5)
7	u	click zcar (i 2)
8	s	remove (l 5) zcar (i 7)

Figure 5.2 An EXPL analysis of a demonstration of a cut operation (Lewis, 1986). User event are flagged "u", and system events are flagged "s".

component that they explain. Each link specifies the heuristic that generated it ("i", "p" or "l"), followed by the event to which it points. EXPL assigns causes to components of system events ("s" in Figure 5.2) using first the identity heuristic ("i"), then the loose–ends heuristic ("l") then, if both of these fail, the previous action heuristic ("p"). User actions ("u" in Figure 5.2) are assigned causes in terms of previous system responses, using only the identity heuristic. The purpose of assigning causes to user events is to establish prerequisite system states.

In the last system response, the outcome, of Figure 5.2 (line 8), EXPL asserts that the reason the system did something to the zcar object was user action 7 (by the identity heuristic), and the reason that it removed something from the display was user action 5 (by the loose–ends heuristic). This simple analysis determines two new rules: (1) if the goal involves a zcar then click on zcar, and (2) if the goal involves removing an object then "press zedit" and "release zcut". The analysis can be said to "deconstruct" the demonstration into its structural relations. It supports what Lewis (1988) calls *synthetic generalization*. For a new goal, synthetic generalization builds new methods by recombining relevant individual links that have been generated from the analysis of one or more previous examples.

Another model that uses learning heuristics is Explor (Howes and Payne, 1990b). Explor is similar to EXPL in that it uses an analysis–based learning mechanism but it uses a different set of heuristics to EXPL. Explor constructs analyses partly on the basis of EXPL–like causal heuristics and partly on the basis of knowledge that the model has of the procedural semantics of the commands being executed (Johnson–Laird, 1983). A description of the procedural semantics of a command represents the meaning of a command in terms of its effect on a representation of the world. It achieves this by encoding a routine that changes the representation. For example, the procedural semantics of the phrase "plus 3 4" would be a function that computes the result 7. The increased analytic power that Explor's procedural semantics provide allow the model to generalize from a much wider range of demonstrations.

There are a number of other models in the HCI literature that use versions of analysis–based learning to do generalization, for example CE+ (Polson and Lewis, 1990) and TAL (Howes and Young, 1991). CE+ combines EXPL with the CCT (Kieras and Polson, 1985) production system implementation of GOMS to give an integrated model of learning and performance. TAL combines synthetic generalization with *category generalization*, a technique whereby methods such as that for achieving a "remove" are generalized to the whole category of operation. That is, if the method for "remove" involves typing the first two consonants of the command then the mapping for "prepare" and "more" will be assumed to do the same.

5.7 Cognitive architecture

The cognitive architecture brings together knowledge, representation, and learning to produce behaviour. Models of the human cognitive architecture include: Soar (Newell, 1990), ACT–R (Anderson, 1993), ICS (Barnard, 1987), and CI (Kintsch, 1988). All of these architectures define mechanisms for storing (learning) and retrieving knowledge from a physically implemented long–term memory. However, they vary in the learning and processing constraints that they impose on the use of this memory. In Soar learning only occurs over impasses which occur when there is insufficient knowledge to solve a problem. Rules are formed to avoid the impasse using a *chunking* mechanism that directly supports analysis–based learning. In CI, learning consists of strengthening weights between nodes in a network. ICS is not computationally implemented but it does embody a novel constraint whereby concurrent activity emerges from the process of transforming descriptions in one representational form to descriptions in other representational forms. Cognition is thereby modelled as the information–flow between various encodings rather than as problem space search.

In HCI the role of architecture is twofold: (1) facilitating predictions that derive directly from architecture–level effects, and (2) facilitating the development of broader scope theories (Young, Green and Simon, 1989). Architecture–level phenomena include performance times (as are used in GOMS), the shift from controlled to automatic processing (including the emergence of performance slips: BP8), and the maintenance of goal hierarchies.

The need for broader scope theories of cognition was first championed by Newell (1973). Newell claims that there are enough observed empirical regularities in psychology, and that the most pressing problem is to explain how this set of regularities could possibly be explained by a single coherent theory. Newell (1990) illustrates his point with a review of the literature on expert skill for typing, pointing out that there are approximately 30 observed regularities in the literature. The development of models of the human cognitive architecture is a response to the need for integrated theories that explain sets of regularities on this scale. Both Anderson (1993) and Newell (1990) provide impressive examples of the range of tasks that can be explained from one theoretical perspective. However, the examples of architecturally implemented models that exist in HCI are still far from covering the desired scope (e.g. CCT, Kieras and Polson, 1985; TAL, Howes and Young, 1991). Moreover, a set of models does not collectively constitute a broad scope model purely by virtue of being encoded in the same architecture. Unfortunately individual models too often use their own private representational languages and their own private learning conventions. Much more work needs to be done pursuing breadth in cognitive modelling.

5.8 Discussion: future directions

The future research agenda for cognitive modelling in HCI lies in a number of directions. On the one hand, motivated by the practical needs of the HCI community, researchers will continue to propose new ways of delivering modelling techniques to practitioners (e.g. Green, 1990; Byrne, Wood, Sukaviriya, Foley and Kieras, 1994; Gray, John and Atwood, 1992). On the other, the construction of broader models that integrate the diverse set of descriptions that cognitive modelling has and will provide is required. Integration is necessary between cognitive models (such as TAG and EXPL), and in addition cognitive modelling requires a closer relationship with perceptual and motor–system modelling.

Constraints in the motor system can have significant consequences for the usability of a device. For example, Card, Mackinlay and Robertson (1990) have done extensive work involving the use of Fitt's Law to predict the usability of various mouse designs. Similarly constraints in the perceptual system affect the readability of displays (Tullis, 1986). An understanding of the relationship between cognitive, perceptual and motor–system constraints would support a better understanding of the trade–offs involved in design. For example, the placement of the addition, subtraction, multiplication and division symbols on a keypad should respect: (1) the expectations that users have about the order in which the symbols appear (+, –, *, /), and (2) the physical constraints imposed by the ways in which the fingers can efficiently move over the keypad.

Motivated by the need to more precise and reliable theory, researchers will continue to pursue new accounts of knowledge requirements, representation, learning, and architecture. Eventually, we may come to understand the ways in which the extensive range of behaviours that device users manifest are the product of a coherent set of mechanisms.

Acknowledgment

This work was supported by the UK Joint Council's Initative in Human–Computer Interaction and Cognitive Science.

Further reading

Anderson, J. (1993). *Rules of the Mind*. Hillsdale, NJ: Erlbaum.
This book introduces the ACT–R model of the human cognitive architecture, and describes the applied experiments and theoretical work that have been used to guide its construction. It is an excellent example of the techniques of cognitive science.

Card, S. K., Moran, T. P. and Newell, A. (1983). *The Psychology of Human–Computer Interaction*. Hillsdale, NJ: Erlbaum.
The original text for cognitive modelling in HCI. This book describes the GOMS model, the Model Human Processor, and the Keystroke Model.

Howes, A. (1994). A Model of the acquisition of menu knowledge through exploration. In B. Adelson, S. Dumais and J. Olson (eds) *Human Factors in Computing Systems CHI94*. Boston, MA. 445–451.
This paper is an example of one of the directions being pursued in recent cognitive modelling research. It introduces a model of how menu structures may be learnt through exploration.

Lewis, C. H. (1988). Why and how to learn why: Analysis–based generalization of procedures. *Cognitive Science*, **12**, 211–256.
This is an excellent analysis of the uses of a machine learning technique, called Analysis–Based Learning, in modelling the users of computer systems.

Lewis, C. H. and Rieman, J. (1993). *Task–Centered User Interface Design.*
Shareware book available via anonymous ftp from ftp.cs.colorado.edu. This is a practical introduction to how to design computer interfaces. Chapter 4 focuses on how to use Cognitive Walkthroughs, and formal techniques such as GOMS, in the design process.

Newell, A. (1990). *Unified Theories of Cognition.* Cambridge, MA: Harvard University Press.
This book gives both an excellent introduction to cognitive science and a detailed description of the Soar problem–solving architecture.

Payne, S. J. and Green, T. R. G. (1986). Task–action grammars: A model of the mental representation of task languages. *Human–Computer Interaction* 2, 93–133.
This paper describes a notation language for describing the knowledge that users need to perform simple computer tasks. Descriptions in the notation support predictions about the consistency of an interface design.

Chapter 6

Artifacts and scenarios: an engineering approach

John M. Carroll

Here is a perplexing contrast. In the world of science, everything is made as self–consciously explicit as it possibly can be. In the world of practice, many things of critical importance are never made explicit. Indeed, some have raised this to a principle of ineffability, claiming that the most important things *cannot* be made explicit (Heidegger, 1962). Design work on human–computer interaction is a case in point: lots of scrupulously detailed normal science, lots of implicitly detailed design work, and far too little contact between the two.

We need to develop a proactive understanding of the gap between science and practice in human–computer interaction (HCI). We need a framework for HCI science that allows us to express what we have learned in a way that is relevant and appropriate for using this knowledge in HCI design. One approach is to try to build science *in* the extant practice, to reify the practical ontology of design so that it can be used more deliberately, interrogated, improved, and applied.

6.1 Action science

The approach described in this chapter is a response to two goals: to contribute to the development of HCI as a scientific domain and to contribute to the development of design methodology for HCI artifacts. Our particular interest is to make progress on these two goals conjointly, that is, through the "same" activity on our part. Thus, we propose viewing HCI research as an "action science," a science that produces knowledge–in–implementation (Argyris, 1980; Torbert, 1976), and a view of HCI design practice as inquiry. In part this commitment rests on critiques of the alternatives: the historically disappointing "normal science" paradigm for HCI research (Carroll, 1989; Carroll and Campbell, 1986) and analytic–decomposition paradigm for HCI design (Carroll and Rosson, 1985).

More constructively, we can be encouraged by modest success at creating an inquiry–based approach to instructional design grounded in an action science of learning (Carroll, 1990). But it must be noted that though these orienting commitments may not clearly be the standard view of HCI, they are at least implicit in an increasing proportion of current discussion about HCI (e.g., Landauer, 1991; Wixon, Holtzblatt, and Knox, 1990; Ehn, 1988) and about computer science more broadly (e.g. Floyd, Zullighoven, Budde and Keil–Slawik, 1992; Gilb, 1988).

Historically, basic science and technology development have often had little mutual impact (e.g. Basalla, 1988; Kuhn, 1962; Multhauf, 1959). The complexity of modern science and technology have created the need for better integration, and one can cite impressive recent examples of action science, particularly in large industrial laboratories. A good example is the invention of the transistor (Jewkes, Sawers and Stillerman, 1958/1969, pages 317–319; Nelson, 1962; and Schon, 1983, pages 177–182).

The physics of the semiconductor effect was well enough understood to have allowed the development of the transistor as early as 1931. However, early work was hindered by pursuing too closely the analogy to vacuum tubes and by an oversimplified practical understanding of the semiconductor effect. In "n" (or negative) semiconductors, there are many more electrons (negative charge carriers) than holes (positive charge carriers), whereas in "p" (positive) semiconductors the majority carriers are holes and the minority carriers are electrons. However, the practical understanding tended to see n semiconductors as simply negative and p semiconductors as simply positive.

In the late 1940s, Bell Labs significantly stepped up work on semiconductors, including the establishment of a small group directed at building a semiconductor amplifier: a practical goal, but one with significant science dependencies and opportunities. The work of this group consisted of embodying various hypothesized mechanisms in prototype solid state amplifiers. Discrepancies in predicted performance were grist for further hypotheses and prototypes. The project culminated in the recognition that minority carrier current flow is a major effect in semiconductor devices, and the discovery of the transistor effect (minority flow induced by one point contact back through another).

It is moot, of course, whether a richer practical understanding of semiconductors, one that kept in view the dual nature of semiconductor current flow, might have allowed the development of the transistor in the early 1930s. But it is clear that technology development can be obstructed by incomplete practical understandings. HCI methods must promote balanced design analysis so that important factors (the HCI analogues of minority current flow) are not overlooked.

6.1.1 The state of the art: implicit technology evolution

Much contemporary technical activity in HCI can be framed as an implicit transaction between tasks and artifacts. The tasks people actually engage in (successfully or problematically) and those they wish to engage in (or perhaps merely to imagine) define requirements for future technology, including new HCI artifacts. These artifacts, in turn, open up new possibilities for human tasks, new ways to do familiar things, entirely new kinds of things to do. They also create new complexities of learning and performance, new interactions among tasks, and of course, new errors and other difficulties for people. The new tasks eventually devolve into requirements for further technology evolution, provoking further transaction.

Examples of this task–artifact cycle are pervasive, but particularly good ones inhere in the particularly momentous technological developments in the field. Consider the spreadsheet. The first electronic spreadsheet, VisiCalc, was brought to market in 1979. It clearly embodied a simple, yet powerful response to a set of extant tasks: table–based calculations. Placing the spreadsheet in an electronic medium permitted accurate calculation and convenient handling. But it did much more. It opened up important new possibilities for table–based calculation tasks. Electronic spreadsheets facilitated projective analyses (what–if reasoning about altered conditions and abductive reasoning from a desired result to conditions that could produce it). A person using a spreadsheet could easily alter values and recalculate. Indeed, spreadsheets even afforded a kind of ad hoc work integration: users could type a memo describing an analysis right into a spreadsheet cell (Mack and Nielsen, 1987).

This evolution of spreadsheet tasks can be viewed as successively altering requirements for spreadsheet systems. Thus, in the early 1980s Context MBA provided integrated support for windows, graphing, word processing, and file management, for example displaying the spreadsheet in one window and a graph of selected cells or a report in another. Lotus 1–2–3 introduced natural order recalculation (in which cell dependencies determine the order of recalculation), easing the overhead of what–if explorations. These advances, in turn, can be seen as encouraging further task evolution. For many people, the spreadsheet environment became a fulcrum for work: planning, communicating, accessing information, reporting, and presenting. It is now typical for spreadsheet systems to support multiple windows, to integrate support for text and graphics, to share data with other programs. Many spreadsheets offer a range of recalculation options to facilitate projective analysis; some offer a "solver" function that takes a specification of a desired result and suggests how to obtain it.

Several reactions to this bit of history are possible and appropriate. One might lament that the emergence of the spreadsheet (and of most other HCI technology and applications) relied so little on the institutionalized science base of HCI. More hypothetically, one could contend that earlier and more systematic user testing, keystroke models, participatory design, and so forth might have produced more usable spreadsheet systems at an earlier point in time. But we must also try to take the facts as they are, try to take seriously the cycle of transaction between tasks and artifacts as a potentially significant pattern in technology development.

Taking the task–artifact seriously raises many issues and possibilities. How can the evolutionary transactions between tasks and artifacts be better managed? How can we insure that evolutionary design does not optimize too locally (cf. Gould, 1990), producing technologies suitable *only* for some fleeting situation, or perhaps worse, filtering out lines of future development because they did not suit some fleeting circumstance? Can such an "implicit" design process be made (partially) explicit, more auditable, more public? How can we learn something from evolutionary design?

In analysing and designing systems and software we need better means to talk about how they may transform and/or be constrained by the contexts of human activity: this is the only way we can hope to attain control over the design of useful and usable systems. A direct approach is to explicitly envision and document typical and significant user activities early and continuingly in the development process. Such descriptions, often called "scenarios", support reasoning about situations of use, even before those situations are actually created.

6.1.2 The task–artifact framework

Designers do not merely envision and plan "artifacts", they create possibilities for human action and interaction. The task–artifact framework for HCI design supports a continuing focus on the activities and experiences of the people who will ultimately use the system throughout the development process (Carroll, Kellogg and Rosson, 1991; Carroll and Rosson, 1992; Carroll, Singley and Rosson, 1992). In this approach, design and analysis focuses on scenario–based descriptions of artifacts in use. These descriptions are used as scientific analyses, that is, for explanation and abstraction, but also as design rationale – that is, justification for aspects of a system being designed – to guide various practical activities that comprise the system lifecycle.

We seek to describe and envision the use of HCI systems, software and user interfaces at the level people construe their activities to themselves – the things they characteristically want to do and need to do, as well as the momentous events of interacting with a system (breakthrough insights and errors). This is the "basic level" (Rosch, Mervis, Gray, Johnson and Boyes–Braem, 1976) at which tasks are meaningful to the people who engage in them. Many task analysis schemes focus on a much lower level than this (e.g., the unit task of Card, Moran and Newell, 1983; see also chapters 5 and 7 in this volume).

We believe that a good inventory of basic tasks is the best design representation of an artifact, which is after all a tool to be used (Carroll and Rosson, 1990). Moreover, building such a representation has uniquely empowering design pragmatics: studies of actual design situations document the use of fairly detailed conjectures about what people will do with a system (e.g. Carroll, Thomas and Malhotra, 1979; Lammers, 1986; Rosson, Maass and Kellogg, 1988). Scenario descriptions of envisioned use make it more feasible for users and designers to communicate effectively about system requirements and design options (Ehn, 1988; Greenbaum and Kyng, 1991). Indeed, current practice requires a set of basic tasks for constructing task–oriented instruction and other user support (e.g. Carroll, 1990) and usability evaluation instruments (Roberts and Moran, 1983; Carroll, Singley and Rosson, 1992). In our approach, an inventory of basic tasks also serves as the fundamental rubric for our approach to artifact analysis.

Designed artifacts (hardware, software, applications, interfaces) can be interpreted as theories, as embodying myriad specific propositions about their users and the circumstances of their use (Carroll and Campbell, 1989; Carroll and Kellogg, 1989). For example, a self–instruction manual can be seen as embodying a range of assertions about what the learners know, what they do, what they experience, about the nature of the learning tasks and the contexts within which these tasks are carried out, etc. This view often surfaces in "design memoirs", for example Jef Raskin's (1994) recent reflections on the early development of the Macintosh user interface. These memoirs can play a proactive role in organizing subsequent design efforts by focusing attention on particular issues.

However, such memoirs casually conflate "designer intention" (which may or may not characterize the realized artifact) and "design analysis" (in which assertions are systematically grounded in general laws of psychology, specific usage data, or some other rationale). In our approach the psychological design rationale of an artifact–in–use is articulated in causal schemas (which we call "claims") relating properties of an artifact and specific psychological consequences for the user(s), under the scope of a basic task usage situation. An example claim is "including open–ended exercises in an instruction manual supports learning–by–exploration for situations in which the learner wonders what sorts of projects might be appropriate to work on."

Such a claim might have been enabled by the manual because the designer intended to do it. However, the claim is neither more nor less true of the artifact in virtue of this intention, and the relevance and truth of the claim *vis–à–vis* the artifact and its use can be investigated independent of mere intention. Our objective in constructing use–oriented design representations is to improve the chance that designers will more deliberately manage the usage consequences they embody in their work.

We view HCI work as a task–artifact cycle (Figure 6.1) in which designers respond to user requirements (in the sense of basic level tasks to be enabled or proscribed) by building artifacts, which in turn present or deny possibilities to their users. On the one hand, we seek to support a more thorough and deliberate enumeration and assessment of the basic tasks (versus designing to an overly–narrow or plainly mistaken set of use–scenarios), and on the other hand, to support a more thorough and deliberate enumeration and assessment of claims implicit in the design (versus creating unintended and undesirable psychological consequences for people). We are trying to nudge the design pattern of the spreadsheet towards that of the transistor.

With respect to the broad landscape of approaches in HCI, our approach is similar to contextualist (Wixon, Holtzblatt and Knox, 1990), participatory design (Ehn, 1988; Greenbaum and Kyng, 1990), and situated action (Suchman, 1987) approaches in that we conceive of computer systems and applications as rich and dynamic contexts for human activity. However, we are more concerned with developing analytic models for understanding and design. (See Chapters 8, 10 and 11 in this volume.)

Conversely, our approach is similar to modern, efficiency–oriented approaches (Card et al., 1983) in its concern with analytic models and methods, but different in taking the broader–scope perspective on user activity and experience. Our approach differs somewhat from all these approaches in its action science commitment, in integrating the development of HCI as a domain of study with its development as a domain of design practice. (See chapters 4 and 5 in this volume.)

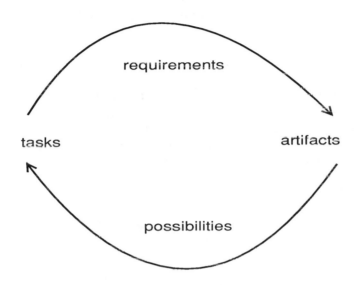

Figure 6.1 The task–artifact cycle: The tasks people engage in and those they wish to engage in define requirements for future technology. New artifacts, in turn, open up new possibilities (including new difficulties) which ultimately become understood as requirements for further technological developments.

This chapter surveys and illustrates a method in which scenarios provide an integration of task analysis and design envisionment – a basic level of design representation. Scenario representations can be elaborated as prototypes, through the use of storyboard, video and rapid prototyping tools. They are the minimal contexts for developing use–oriented design rationale: a given design decision can be evaluated and documented in terms of its specific consequences within particular scenarios. Scenarios and the elements of scenario–based design rationale can be generalized and abstracted using theories of human activity, enabling the cumulation and development of knowledge attained in the course of design. Thus, scenarios can provide a framework for a design–based science of human–computer interaction.

6.2 Scenario–based design: designing situations of use

To understand the consequences of computer technology for people, we need to be able to see computers as artifacts in human activity, as educational environments, as work tools, as media for communication. We can do this empirically, that is, we can learn from our experiences in deploying technology just what works and what does not work. We can also do this analytically: we can collect and consider user requirements, evaluate representations and prototypes, and build design rationales. Scenarios of use can be a key to all such analyses: traditionally, we tried to see computers as artifacts in human activity through functional specifications, but these provide a highly idealized view of use (e.g. features organized alphabetically, function by function) – not a view of how a user would engage the function and experience its effects.

The real use of systems can be concretely described by a set of user interaction scenarios obtained when people try to use a system. Figure 6.2 presents an observed example of an interaction scenario. An experienced procedural programmer is using a Smalltalk/V PMtutorial (Digitalk, 1989), working on an exercise to implement a new kind of text pane that displays its input in uppercase. This project focuses on concrete, albeit somewhat arcane, functionality; it involves learning about two key subtrees of the Smalltalk class hierarchy (Magnitude–Character and Window–SubPane–TextPane) and allows the programmer to implement a concrete and usable new Smalltalk object by extending existing system functionality with a minimum of coding. The programmer carries out the project by subclassing the TextPane class and specializing the code that processes character input from the keyboard. The scenario is a vivid and succinct description of a person learning something about Smalltalk; a comprehensive set of such scenarios would be a very concrete task analysis of the Smalltalk tutorial situation.

– A beginning Smalltalk programmer is working through a series of tutorial projects designed to provide initial familiarity with some central classes and methods. The programmer is trying to create a new kind of textpane that displays keyboard input in uppercase.

– The programmer searches for existing relevant functionality, simultaneously trying to define an approach to the project and to identify existing software resources for it. Eventually, the programmer locates the methods asUpperCase (in the Character class) and characterInput: (in the TextPane class). The sheer number of possibly relevant classes and methods necessitates considerable browsing In order to do this, and the programmer pursues several incorrect possibilities along the way (the programmer has trouble finding the Character class, later losing track of where it is while browsing in TextPane, and at first considers specializing the appendText: method of TextPane, which does not take a character argument).

– The programmer specializes TextPane by creating a new subclass UpperCasePane, copying down its characterInput: method, and altering one line of the code to transform the chacteracterInput: argument asUpperCase

– The programmer creates and tests an UpperCasePane. The programmer is satisfied with the result and decides to just move on to the next tutorial project.

Figure 6.2 A Smalltalk tutorial scenario "Creating UpperCasePane" A set of such scenarios – those suggested by the tutorial manual or system software and those observed or anticipated – comprises a use–oriented representation of the Smalltalk tutorial.

Even this single scenario is an obvious and immediate design resource: it highlights goals suggested by the appearance and behaviour of the system, what people try to do with the system, what procedures are adopted, not adopted, carried out successfully or erroneously, and what interpretations people make of what happens to them. One can use it to identify problem areas for further design work. For example, in Figure 6.2, the programmer has some difficulty navigating the Smalltalk class hierarchy – the tutorial could be improved by incorporating an indexing tool. A more subtle example, but an important one in the Smalltalk domain, is that the programmer in Figure 6.2 copied a method to a subclass instead of inheriting the functionality and merely implementing the specialization in the subclass.

6.2.1 Projecting scenarios in design.

We cannot rely only on observation to build a scenario representation. If we want scenarios to play a proactive role in guiding design and development, we need to be able to construct scenario representations for systems before any version is deployed in the field (Carroll and Rosson, 1990; Wexelblat, 1987). In this case we are representing anticipated use. We can do this in part by analogy: the new system may be similar to other contemporary systems or "descended" from earlier systems – the characteristic scenarios for these related existing systems can be observed and analysed. We can also make use of theories of human activity (Norman, 1986): that is, we can try to instantiate known categories of human activity in the envisioned context of the system we are developing. For example, people must orient to novel task situations, identifying and analyzing appropriate goals; later, they must evaluate their own actions to determine whether those goals were attained (e.g. Carroll and Rosson, 1992; Norman, 1986). In building a scenario representation for a system in development, we can envision possible goal orientation and evaluation situations. As we develop such scenarios, we can track specific impacts of our design decisions for these theoretical categories of human activity.

The novelty of this proposal resides simply in the suggestion that scenarios be systematized as working design representations, for it is well–known that scenarios are spontaneously and pervasively used in system development as practiced now – in requirements analysis, documentation and training, evaluation and so forth. Interaction scenarios are typical in contemporary functional specification documents (*officially* they are included as illustrations of the specification, but they often appear before any of the specification, and developers intimate that they are sometimes used in lieu of the specification). In sum, scenarios are already everywhere in the design process. Systematically developing and managing a set of scenarios as part of the working design representation can help integrate and leverage diverse, informal and currently uncoordinated uses. Indeed, the costs of doing more comprehensive scenario development might actually be less than the distributed costs of current practice.

6.2.2 Our experience

We have used scenario–based design representations in a variety of our recent projects designing tools and environments for Smalltalk instruction and programming (Carroll and Rosson, 1990, 1991; Rosson and Carroll, 1993, 1995; Singley and Carroll, 1995; Singley, Carroll and Alpert, 1991), for word processing instruction (Carroll, Kellogg and Rosson, 1991; Carroll and Rosson, 1992), and for a multimedia design history system (Carroll, 1994a). Our experience is admittedly tilted toward open–ended, construction domains, though one might expect that scenario–based methods would apply at least as well in relatively more circumscribed application domains (in which the core tasks are often literally enumerable). We have found that fewer than a dozen scenarios provides a useful and manageable design representation.

> – As the programmer completes a tutorial project, he or she is prompted as to the availability of a Smalltalk Guru post mortem for this project.

> – The programmer selects the post mortem and the Smalltalk Guru appears and explains that while the solution of copying down the superclass's the characterInput: method is correct, there is another approach in which the method code is maintained only with the superclass (in this case, TextPane). The Guru demonstrates how subclasses can specialize this functionality with a message send to the special variable "super," directing the Smalltalk interpreter to begin searching for the method code in the superclass. (The programmer whispers, "So that's how "super" gets used!")

> – At the end of the project–specific post mortem, the programmer is offered more general Guru assistance (for example, a discussion of inheritance), but decides to go on to the next project.

Figure 6.3 A Smalltalk Guru scenario, contrasting "copy down" and "reference to super" Scenarios can be written down, developed, and reasoned about before any system supporting them has been designed or implemented. The Guru "super" scenario is part of the design representation for the MoleHill intelligent tutor for Smalltalk (Singley and Carroll, 1995; Singley, Carroll and Alpert, 1991).

Figure 6.3 is one of the scenarios envisioned to drive the design of the Smalltalk Guru tool in our MoleHill intelligent tutoring system (Singley, Carroll and Alpert, 1991). The Guru tool provides guidance to the inclination people typically have for evaluating their own activity: just as the programmer finishes the project, the Guru offers suggestions about how to achieve a more modular code design, in this scenario exploiting Smalltalk's inheritance mechanism via the special variable "super". This example shows how empirical analysis of interaction scenarios for existing situations (for example, the Smalltalk tutorial situation illustrated in Figure 6.2) and abstractions from theories of human activity (the notion of an evaluation scenario) can provide proactive guidance in developing a scenario representation for a new system.

In our work, scenarios are more or less continually developed and reinterpreted. The scenario in Figure 6.3 is a development of the scenario in Figure 6.2, but it is not a final representation. It is merely a use–oriented view of the current design, a working representation. Different scenarios can conflict and "compete" in such a working design representation; the designer may resolve conflicts by synthesizing alternative scenarios, or by selecting one scenario over another. The competition among scenarios helps to force out greater clarity in the emerging vision of the system.

Developing scenarios through the coordinated use of direct empirical observation and abstractions from theories of human activity has the additional benefit of continually emphasizing to the designer the continuities among various design projects. System design is of course highly creative, but few systems are completely novel. Indeed, the history of technology is a history of cumulative development and evolution (Basalla, 1984). Nevertheless, it is easy in the context of design work to focus singularly on the project at hand and lose the benefit of whatever might have been done and learned before. Our deliberate development of the Guru scenario helped us to appreciate that the Guru was a sort of bug critic (e.g. Brown, Burton and de Kleer, 1982) and thus systematically related to other tutorial situations that had been designed and studied before. (This point is elaborated in the next section.)

6.3 Psychological design rationale: designing consequences for users

Representing the use of a system or application with a set of user interaction scenarios makes that use explicit, and in doing so orients design and analysis toward a broader view of computers. It can help designers and analysts to focus attention on the assumptions about people and their tasks that are implicit in systems and applications. But the scenarios themselves leave implicit the underlying causal relations of use: a scenario does not isolate just what it is about people or about a design that allows that scenario to occur.

6.3.1 Explaining scenarios

It can be valuable to make explicit a causal account or rationale for a scenario. Indeed, envisioning a "better" scenario for users may well require making explicit just what it was that needed to be improved in terms of specific consequences for users, how improvements were attempted in terms of managing or altering consequences, and what other consequences might have been entrained as side–effects. A direct approach to articulating why scenarios run as they do is to isolate individual causal schemas relating features of a situation of use and specific consequences for users:

IN <situation>, <a feature> CAUSES <"desirable" psychological consequence>
BUT MAY ALSO CAUSE < "undesirable" psychological consequence>

Figure 6.4 presents four such causal relationships, or "claims", implicit in the UpperCasePane scenario (of Figure 6.2). Thus, the Code Library Claim (a) asserts that the class hierarchy encourages standard design decompositions and reuse–oriented programming strategies. These are desirable consequences for the programmer working on the tutorial project. A downside, or undesirable consequence, of the large code library is that Smalltalk programmers may experience problems searching for code to reuse or making appropriate use of code. The Names Claim (b) observes that while descriptive class and method names may help programmers quickly identify relevant functionality, the names may also mislead. The Navigation Claim (c) is a hypothesis that searching the class library may cause the programmer to incidentally learn something about the functionality in the library, though the sheer size of the library may make it difficult to learn much, particularly if the programmer is frustrated in his or her search. Finally, the Programming Tools Claim (d) observes that the tool–rich, interpreted Smalltalk environment may support a very fluid and opportunistic style of code development; the downside is that programmers may not reflect enough on the designs they are generating.

A psychological design rationale such as this can be developed by asking questions to elaborate the events in a use scenario (Carroll and Rosson, 1990, 1992). Thus, for the UpperCasePane scenario (Figure 6.2), we might ask: Why did the programmer search for relevant functionality while still defining a strategy toward the project? Did anything about the situation make it especially difficult or easy to proceed in this way? What was the programmer thinking about while browsing for relevant classes and methods? Did the programmer have any particular difficulties with browsing; did he or she benefit from the browsing activity? Why did the programmer pursue several incorrect possibilities when searching for relevant functionality? Why was appendText: considered, and why was it finally rejected? Why did the programmer have trouble finding, and then later lose track of, Character class? Why did the programmer copy down the method code for characterInput:, instead of inheriting the functionality using "super"? How did the programmer decide to use

In the UpperCasePane scenario (Figure 6.2)

(a) Code Library Claim:
Existing code in the Smalltalk class hierachy causes prgrammers to reuse standard decompositions in designing new functionality (encourages the strategy of programming by assembling parts)
but may also cause search problems (because its so big) and nonoptimal solutions (reuse of inapproprite components

(b) Names Claim:
Descriptive class and method names cause programmers to rely on names in searching for functionality and planning reuse
but may also cause false alarms (by suggesting spurious connections)

(c) Navigation Claim:
Navigating the class hierachy causes unintentional learning about existing functionality
but may also cause confusion and frustration (since the class hierachy is so large)

(d) Programming Tools Claim:
Powerful programming tools cause browsing, opportunistic problem solving, and a rapid prototyping approach to code development but may also cause programmers to direct insufficient time and effort to code design

Figure 6.4 Some causal relations implicit in the UpperCasePane scenario. A causal account of specializing Smalltalk's TextPane includes possibilities for re-using code (a), opportunistic strategies (b), browsing (c), and the rich tool environment (d). (Claims (a), (b) and (c) correspond to (5j), (5k) and (5l) in Carroll and Rosson (1991), claim (d) corresponds to the Task Switching Claim in Singley and Carroll (1995).

Character's asUpperCase method? Why does the programmer test only one UpperCasePane, and test only the external behaviour of the pane?

The answers to such questions are a set of hypotheses about the underlying causal relations in the scenario, the analyst's hypotheses about why and how an observed (or envisioned) scenario of use could occur. The objective of raising these questions and articulating hypothesized causal relations is to open up a process of critique and refinement, to help designers interrogate and explain key scenarios in enough detail that they can be interpreted, revised, perhaps discarded as the design proceeds. It is important to emphasize that a psychological design rationale, such as the fragment in Figure 6.4, does not necessarily equate to the personal intentions of the designers. We know that the designers of Smalltalk actually did intend to promote code reuse (Pope, Goldberg and Deutsch, 1987), but it seems safe to assume that they did not intend to create search and reuse problems.

6.3.2 Using psychological design rationale

Psychological design rationale can be used as a working design representation throughout the design process. Just as in the case of scenarios, we want to use analyses of existing situations to help set the agenda for design work and to guide reasoning about particular possibilities.

The analysis in Figure 6.4 supported our work on MoleHill by clearly articulating what it is about situations like that depicted in Figure 6.2 that we should address in our design work. A general heuristic for using a psychological design rationale in this way is to envision alternate scenarios such that downside consequences of particular claims are obviated or mitigated, while upside consequences are enhanced or maintained. Thus the Guru scenario in Figure 6.3 mitigates the downside of the Programming Tools Claim while maintaining its upside. That is, the Guru project post mortem encourages reflection on code design, but does not constrain fluid and opportunistic programming activity prior to the post mortem.

Having placed on our design agenda the goal of encouraging attention and reflection on code design without diminishing flexibility and empowerment, we explored theories and techniques pertaining to reflective activity, and specific designs to promote such activity. Our object was to further elaborate the design of the Guru and its envisioned consequences for users. We studied LISP–CRITIC (Fischer, Lemke, Mastaglio and Morch, 1990), an experimental critiquing facility to which programmers may submit code fragments to get suggestions about how to make their code easier to read and maintain or more machine efficient. The system does not place any constraints on how programmers create the code submitted for critique, nor on whether or how they use its suggestions.

In our analysis, the psychological design rationale for LISP–CRITIC hinges on the possibility that a highly specific critique, delivered at the programmer's request and in the context of a current programming situation, can encourage programmers to reflect more on their work without undermining their preferred work style:

Situated Critique Claim:
a situated critique on specific code design problems – at the programmer's request – causes programmers to reflect more on their code without hampering opportunistic code development
but may also cause programmers to reflect on their work too narrowly (may improve a particular code fragment, but fail to teach a more general design lesson)

We had envisioned the Guru as providing a very similar sort of situated critique (though we wanted to address architectural issues, like inheritance – Figure 6.3).

This kind of scenario and its characteristic relations bears on the goal of helping programmers integrate their understanding of inheritance and the use of "super" in Smalltalk with their strategies for building code. We wished to create the upside consequences of the Annotated Demonstration Claim with the Guru, and believed that we could avoid the downside consequence since the Guru would only be a software tool initiated by the programmer. Figure 6.5 schematizes this pattern of deliberation.

We also investigated the theory and technique of "reflective practicum" (Schön, 1983) in which a teacher models expert performance for a student, while commenting on the process of producing such a performance and coaching the student on how to move toward achieving such a performance:

Annotated Demonstration Claim:
the teacher's self–consciously annotated demonstration of expert performance causes the student to integrate actions and concepts in a paradigmatic model
but may also cause the student to feel coerced (due to the power imbalance between teacher and student)

6.3.3 Our experience

Design reasoning is often quite local; designers address sets of requirements and then set aside tentative reasoning and partial results in order to explore other, hopefully converging, subproblems (Carroll, Thomas and Malhotra, 1979). This is precisely why it may be useful to create an explicit rationale: interim results and their backing can be preserved and deliberatively integrated into the overall design solution. Articulating the causal relations in LISP–CRITIC and reflective practicum situations guided us in combining their elements in the Smalltalk Guru . This is not to suggest that design reasoning can be reduced to a calculation, rather it is to admit that only when arguments are made explicit can they be evaluated.

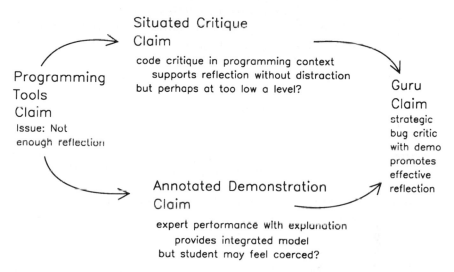

Situated Critique
Claim

code critique in programming context
supports reflection without distraction
but perhaps at too low a level?

Programming
Tools
Claim
Issue: Not
enough reflection

Guru
Claim
strategic
bug critic
with demo
promotes
effective
reflection

Annotated Demonstration
Claim

expert performance with explanation
provides integrated model
but student may feel coerced?

Figure 6.5 Design reasoning for the Smalltalk Guru. The Programming Tools Claim highlights the possibility that programmers may not direct enough time and effort to code design. Scenario analysis of the prior system LISP–CRITIC and of the theory and technique of Reflective Practicum brought to light a variety of issues and design ideas: providing critique within a current problem context, providing narrated demonstration of target skills to better link concepts and actions, allowing user–control of critique initiation and user–discretion as to consequent actions. Articulating the causal relations in these situations guided us in combining their elements in the Smalltalk Guru, a strategic bug critic with demonstration of programming process.

In our design work on instructional and programming tools, we have explored the usefulness of articulating the claims of a psychological design rationale (e.g., Carroll, Kellogg and Rosson, 1991; Carroll and Rosson, 1991, 1992; Carroll, Singley and Rosson, 1992; Singley and Carroll, 1995; Singley, Carroll and Alpert, 1991). We find that, like scenarios, these representations help us directly by creating auditable design claims about how an envisioned system will affect its users. We have also found that making a causal analysis of one scenario can often bring to light the need for considering and designing one or more other scenarios, thus helping to elaborate the overall design.

An obvious trade–off is that while articulating each individual claim of a psychological design rationale creates a more precise representation than a scenario, creating such a rationale is itself a more difficult design task. We have developed a heuristic for generating elaboration questions from which to develop psychological design rationales from scenarios, based on systematically interrogating the whys and hows of various phases of human activity (Carroll and Rosson, 1992), and have found also that having related rationales already in hand is a significant aid; nonetheless, developing a psychological design rationale is still a significant task. A practical compromise is to develop a full psychological design rationale only for key scenarios, or for cases where a scenario representation leaves open questions.

It is important to stress that psychological design rationales are heuristic explanations of human behaviour and experience. Their utility in system design derives from directly linking features of a designed situation with user activities and experiences. However, this can be an over–simplification: many of the causal relations between features of situations and consequences for people in those situations are not first–order, they derive from interactions and side–effects. Our hope is that when such interactions arise, we might improve our chances of noticing them and of beginning to fathom what's going on if we are keeping explicit account of what we expected would happen. If something is clearly working or failing, we have a basis for making credit/blame attributions, we have a starting point for systematically revisiting our decisions, and for understanding other situations that guided us to those decisions (Carroll, Singley and Rosson, 1992).

6.4 Current challenges: scenario–based abstraction and implementation

Two important current frontiers for scenario–based design methodology are (1) identifying abstractions to support the development of knowledge in the context of design work, and (2) creating tools to help verify and manage the alignment of scenario representations with detailed designs and implementations. The two are very interrelated since the best sorts of tools will be those that incorporate the appropriate abstractions.

6.4.1 Higher–order artifacts and situations

Our basic approach to abstraction has been to induce "types" from the observable tokens of the domains in which we do analysis and design. For example, earlier we discussed using the notions of goal orientation and evaluation situations from activity theory to help generate candidate scenarios. Goal orientation and evaluation are types of situations. Analogously, we can try to articulate types of claim relations. For example, the Situated Critique Claim is a special case of the a general claim in which the issues of whether the system or the programmer requests the code critique and the level at which the critique is couched is left open.

Artifacts can also be seen as instantiating genres, such as interfaces that incorporate direct manipulation (e.g. Newman, 1988) or programming environments that provide coordinated views of a "live" example (Carroll and Rosson, 1991), or prescriptive design models, such as the discovery–based, minimalist approach to instructional design (Carroll, 1990) or the drill–and–practice systems approach (Gagne and Briggs, 1979).

Such "second–order artifacts" (Carroll and Campbell, 1989) can be described by the typical and critical scenarios their exemplars "inherit", and by the claims embodied in these scenarios. For example, LISP–CRITIC – as noted above – is an example of a bug critic, a type of instructional artifact that includes many other tokens (e.g., Brown, Burton and deKleer, 1982). Carroll, Singley and Rosson (1992) showed how the MiTTS (Minimalist Tutorial and Tools for Smalltalk) tutorial package (Rosson, Carroll and Bellamy, 1990) inherits claims from both the minimalist model and the systems approach.

When we can view a scenario, a claim or an artifact–in–use as an instance of a type, we are in a position to generalize whatever we learn about that particular scenario, claim or artifact to the type. Thus, recognizing that the Smalltalk Guru is a kind of bug critic similar to LISP–CRITIC can serve two purposes: first, it can help us elaborate the design and the design rationale for the Guru, but second, it creates the possibility that things we subsequently learn about the Guru can be mapped back to LISP–CRITIC, or more generally to bug critics, as a specific hypothesis. Similarly, drawing upon general types of human activity – like orienting to goals or evaluating one's actions (Carroll and Rosson, 1990; Norman, 1986) – in generating scenarios to envision a system in design can also help us attribute things we learn about given scenarios of use for given systems to a more general analysis of human activity. Inductive generalization is the chief means for creating new knowledge, but it requires a framework for seeing a particular as an instance of a type. Some of our recent work has detailed how the framework of scenarios and psychological design rationale could leverage workaday usability testing as the empirical backbone of a design–based science of human–computer interaction (Carroll, Singley and Rosson, 1992).

6.4.2 The Scenario Browser

Traditional functional specifications are frequently inconsistent or incomplete with respect to the user's needs and predilections (this was one of the cataclysmic discoveries of the 1980s), but because they are organized function by function, they are at least easy to align with the detailed design and implementation of the system. An important practical question about scenario–based design, and more broadly about the move towards viewing design as the design of scenarios for human action, is whether it will increase the "gap" between specification and implementation. Our recent work on the Scenario Browser tool addresses this question by providing a software development environment in which the design and development of textual descriptions of human–system interaction are coordinated with the design and development of software that models the activity (Rosson and Carroll, 1993, 1995).

The technological key to the Scenario Browser is object–oriented programming systems and languages. In the object–oriented paradigm, computation is message sending interactions among highly encapsulated software objects. Thus, designing object–oriented software involves identifying key design objects and their "responsibilities" in these message–sending collaborations. Rosson and Alpert (1990) refer to this as the "intelligent object" metaphor: the software objects "know" about the tasks they will participate in. For example, a piece of mail knows how to format and send itself, and to what folder(s) it is related and how.

Since software objects are intelligent with respect to the tasks they participate in, the intelligent object metaphor has been embedded in a variety of scenario–based design methods. In these methods, task scenarios are analysed to create a problem domain model of objects and responsibilities – this model is the starting point for the software design (e.g. Wirfs–Brock, Wilkerson and Wiener, 1990). For example, the design of a bibliographic information system might have as part of its starting representation a story in which someone adds a citation to a personal database. The problem domain model will contain objects like the citation, a conference and an editor. This model becomes refined as the designer identifies appropriate abstractions among the objects and recognizes cross–scenario constraints governing their attributes and relations. The designer may realize that the conference location or the volume number of the proceedings should be modelled as distinct objects, or may recognize that authors and editors are both persons and both have names, etc.

Designing object–oriented software with the Scenario Browser involves developing textual sketches of the events and interactions that comprise the human task to be supported. These scenarios are then modelled in a persistent–object workspace. To a considerable extent, the initial model is a simulation of the scenario in which the physical objects are endowed with the task–specific intelligence they need to carry out their message–sending responsibilities. The Scenario Browser also coordinates the narrative and software views with various claim views in which the designer records arguments for various design decisions. Thus, as the designer creates the object models underlying a set of scenarios, the reasoning may be captured for later use by designers (for example, as they reinterpret and refine their metaphors) or by the users as they extend the original system by innovating new practices.

The Scenario Browser helps designers and analysts manage the myriad interconnections among user concerns, scenarios, claims, artifact features, types of applications, etc. Exploring and investigating these interconnections in the context of a design project is the real vision of an action science: knowledge relevant to action, provided in the context of action (see also Fischer, Lemke, McCall and Morch 1991).

6.5 Making use of the object of design

We must be heedful of a facile and historically mistaken view about the nature of technology evolution, that basic science regularly holds up a beacon to show the way forward (Basalla, 1988; Kuhn, 1962b; Multhauf, 1959) In the modern era, the need for science–based technology development has dramatically increased: technology is more complex and it evolves more quickly than ever before.

The opportunity for science–based technology development is also better than ever before. The notion of action science – science that seeks simultaneously to understand the world and to improve it — can be a key to this. As illustrated in the example of the transistor (among many others, Jewkes, Sawers and Stillerman, 1958/1969), this paradigm is already up and running in the contemporary physical sciences. The notion has been articulated for the social sciences (Argyris, 1980; Torbert, 1976) but there is a need for compelling exemplification.

Such work hinges on the simple argument that if we make the concepts and actions of HCI design work more explicit we will be better able to manage and to learn from it. We share many of the goals of software methodologists (e.g. Brooks, 1975; Floyd, Zullighoven, Budde and Keil–Slawik, 1992; Freeman, 1987; Gilb, 1988) since we assume that action science starts and ends with the real experiences and activities of the field: learning, using and designing computer systems and applications. But we want to pursue these interests in such a way as to construct explanations and generalizations about HCI tasks and artifacts; we want an action science of HCI.

Our work focuses on codifying, sharpening, and applying the concepts–in–action that already typify practice — the arguments developed for design decisions, either within the design process or as design memoir reflections on that process, and the scenarios embodying user concerns and requirements, either attributed as such to users or envisioned as possibilities to be enabled by new artifacts. We seek to refine these concepts–in–action, to make them better practical methods and better abstractions for action science.

The task–artifact cycle reifies the implicit structure of practical activity in the field. Effective application and development within this structure is the appropriate target for scientific abstractions and design methodology. This chapter has sketched a simple but extendable analytic method for managing usability and usefulness, by making use itself the object of design. In this method, user interaction scenarios are a concrete medium for describing existing situations and for projecting envisioned situations. A set of such scenarios is a broadly useful design representation; it is a resource for reasoning about what people will do and experience in a new situation; it is an auditable design claim about what will be delivered to the user. Such a representation can be further elaborated into a psychological design rationale, specifying causal relations among aspects of the designed situation and consequences for people in the situation.

This method attempts to leverage established practices in using scenarios to communicate with users about requirements, to illustrate functional specifications, and to manage usability testing and documentation development. Creating scenarios more systematically and earlier in the design process as planning and reasoning aids is only an incremental elaboration of current practice. If a designer or analyst finds that making more systematic use of scenario representations is truly valuable, he or she may be motivated to consider enhancing these with some causal annotation of why the scenarios run as they do. If this enhancement also seems valuable, he or she may consider developing a psychological design rationale for a project. Hopefully, the gentle gradient from current (somewhat casual) use of scenarios in design practice to the somewhat more systematic use we are developing will enhance the acceptability of the method.

In our own work we design things that we and others will use, but with a deliberate meta–focus on how we do that work. Thus, we know that the method can be used, since through its development it always has been used. Most generally, it helps in providing the designer with a framework for developing and interrogating ideas concretely and conceptually at the same time with seemingly little overhead. Using the task–artifact framework has diminished in us the tendency to fix problems *tout court* by helping us to more regularly focus on what is good about a current situation and to work through the implications a design move under consideration may have for those good aspects as well as for the more attention–getting problematic aspects (cf. Festinger, 1957).

The key to an HCI action science is to accommodate the background of current practice, adding to it a flexible range of options such that a modest assimilation of the framework is edifying but only modestly disruptive, and such that larger assimilations are no more than proportionately disruptive and perhaps more than proportionately edifying. In this way, designers can pursue projects and make recognizable progress with the confidence of familiarity. An action science of HCI that embraces and deliberately nurtures what rationality there is and can be in technology evolution could be an important vehicle for constructing rich understandings of human beings and their situations, and for designing appropriate tools and environments to delight and empower them.

Note

Parts of this chapter appeared earlier in J.M. Carroll and M.B. Rosson (1992). Getting around the task–artifact cycle: How to make claims and design by scenario. *ACM Transactions on Information Systems* **10**, 181–212; and in J. M. Carroll (1994) Making *use* a design representation. *Communications of the ACM*, 37, pp29–35.

Further reading

Carroll, J. M. ed. (1991). *Designing interaction: Psychology at the human–computer interface*. New York: Cambridge University Press.
This is a collection of papers that address the question of what role psychological science can play in human–computer interaction. The papers draw on a many psychological approaches, including cognitive science, German action theory, and activity theory.

Carroll, J. M. ed. (1995). *Scenario–based design: Envisioning work and technology in system development*. New York: John Wiley and Sons.
This is a collection of papers exploring and considering the role of user interaction scenarios as focal objects of design and analysis, not only in human–computer interaction, but in object–oriented software engineering as well.

Floyd, C., Zullighoven, H., Budde, R. and Keil–Slawik, R. (eds.) (1992). *Software development and reality construction*. New York: Springer–Verlag.
This is a collection of papers exploring broad implications of system development concepts and practices for the experiences and meanings of the people who use computer systems. Included are perspectives from linguists, philosophers, computer scientists and

psychologists – working within a considerable variety of intellectual traditions.

Greenbaum, J. and Kyng, M. (1991). *Design at work: Cooperative design of computer systems*. Hillsdale, NJ: Lawrence Erlbaum Associates.

This is a collection of papers describing a cooperative design perspective and approach developed at Aarhus University in Denmark. It includes papers on the nature of HCI, as well as on specific techniques for understanding work practices and for collaboratively designing new technology with users.

Moran, T. P. and Carroll, J. M. (1995). *Design rationale: Concepts, techniques, and use*. Hillsdale, NJ: Lawrence Erlbaum Associates.

This is a collection of papers describing various approaches to design rationale within human–computer interaction, and to some extent within software engineering.

Chapter 7

Task analysis as a framework for examining HCI tasks

Andrew Shepherd

7.1 What is task analysis?

Task analysis deals with issues associated with the performance of human beings interacting with tools, plant, equipment, other human beings, and the world at large. It has been used to examine systems failures, such as industrial accidents or failure to meet productivity targets, and it is used to help design solutions to problems, such as job–, interface, training and job–aid design. It is a practical discipline and must take account of the broader system in which the task is carried out. This requires sensitivity to the values of the people involved in the system and the pattern of events observed. Human factors implications in a system requiring an operator to be productive may be different to those in a system where the operator must avoid error. Task analysis should examine what people are required to do and the constraints that are placed on them. Another implication of the practical nature of task analysis is that a solution to the system's problem is of paramount concern; the costs involved in formally identifying the cause of these problems may be avoided if a solution can be found to negate the problem. For example, a satisfactory training solution to help people master a complex cognitive skill may be established by providing a set of conditions in which the skill may be practised, without requiring a full understanding of the psychology governing the skill in question.

Task analysis methods serve one or more of the following purposes: helping to define and establish the boundaries of problems; helping to collect information about a problem in a systematic fashion; organizing this information; modelling component processes in order to identify problem sources; and generating hypotheses to overcome the problem. It is rarely possible simply to categorize a particular task analysis method as serving one of these ends rather than another, because most task analysis methods were devised to solve real problems and tend, therefore, to involve bits of everything. There are several useful reviews of task analysis and the reader is referred to these for a fuller catalogue of task and job analysis methods (see Section 7.6). The present chapter is limited to general themes only. Firstly, it will outline some of the main directions different task analysis methods have adopted in the past, illustrating important principles. Secondly, it will describe the general analytical framework known as hierarchical task analysis, which has built on these earlier ideas. Thirdly, the application of these ideas to HCI will be discussed.

7.2 Approaches to task analysis

In examining the background to task analysis methods, we need to trace developments from early work study methods to methods which acknowledge the influence of less observable behaviour on performance. An important influence here is the trend in work technology and organization. In particular, we can see how early work study methods of the 1920s were important because a great deal of industry depended upon rapid and reliable manual skill. As the century progressed, different forms of work organization, made possible by increased automation, placed greater emphasis on cognitive skills. Equally, the psychological aspects of analysing work assumed greater prominence when it was increasingly recognised that the rate limiting factors in human work were often central psychological processes rather than physical or physiological constraints, such as muscular fatigue. More recently, with developments in information technology, new problems and opportunities prompt developments in task analysis methods, including both implications for automation and human–computer interaction.

7.2.1 Work study

An early approach to examining human work was Gilbreth's system of units to codify action, enabling work to be recorded in a convenient short–hand way (see Blum and Naylor, 1968, or most texts on industrial psychology). These descriptions of work could then be used to explore efficient ways in which tasks could be carried out. This approach recorded observable actions, although elements which could not be directly observed, such as 'searching' and 'inspection' were also inferred. The focus for these methods tended to be short–cycle repetitive tasks, such as assembly tasks, effective organization of which provided the greatest benefits for reducing work cycle times and, hence, profitability. From these beginnings work study emerged as a discipline in its own right as a set of ways of observing and organising the best ways of accomplishing tasks (see Currie, 1977). One set of objections to work study relates to the narrow criteria of success, namely focusing on meeting and exceeding production targets at the expense of wider criteria, such as adaptability, attention, cognition, occupational health and job satisfaction. As changes to work practices and technologies occurred, work study became inappropriate and new task analysis methods were needed. The move from manufacture involving short–cycle repetitive tasks through batch and continuous processing to wholly integrated manufacturing systems has been accompanied by placing requirements on human operators or controllers increasingly to monitor partially self–regulating systems, make decisions and plan strategies. These are all features with which work study was not designed to cope.

Table 7.1 Sample of a sensorimotor chart (adapted from Crossman, 1956), showing the analysis of a soldering task. The chart shows the progression of activities from first holding the iron and solder to cooling the joint. Each stage considers the action of each hand and the involvement of the brain. The kinetic and tactile feedback and the movement for each hand is recorded, as appropriate. Memory, decision–making and visual activity are also recorded as steps in the task progress.

Left hand	K	T	Mot	Mom	Dec	Vis 1	Vis 2	Mot	T	K	Right Hand	Notes
Holding iron											Holding solder	Solder one joint.
			—					—			—	Find next joint on list.
To joint			M 6 in					—			—	
Tip on wire		P						M 4 in			To joint	
H			H					P			Solder on tip	
H			H					H		Q	H	Wait for solder to melt then feed more on.
H			H					M 1 in			Feed solder	Avoid kinking and slipping. Stop when sufficient.
Remove iron			M 1 in					M 1 in			Remove solder	Watch joint till surface changes from bright to flimsy.
Wait cooling			—								—	Observe junction with wire. Decide whether good joint
			—								—	and either repeat or look for next joint.

Symbols used in Sensorimotor Process Chart

Perceptual activities

Plan	V
Control	≷
Check	∧
Initiate	O
Stop	●

Movement

Move	M
Position	P
Hold	H

Operation: sub-chassis soldering

7.2.2 Psychological perspectives

7.2.2.1 Sensorimotor charts

Crossman (1956) brought together elements of work study with a greater acknowledgement of human information processing. He produced the "sensorimotor" process chart, which recorded cycles of skill in terms of the relationship between observable actions, as with the earlier work–study approaches, and psychological processes such as perception, planning and memory. An illustration of this approach is given in Table 7.1. The analyst examines the work, including observing and timing activities, then uses the chart to record how it is carried out. Moving down the rows, one can trace how the left hand, the right hand and the brain are engaged in the task of soldering. Included in this description is an account of the sub–goals (e.g. hold iron, move solder to joint), the planning and sequencing of activities (e.g. the sequencing of the actions on successive rows, the instruction to await cooling) and the "brainwork" involved (memorizing current information, decision–making and visual control). Standard symbols are used for different sorts of activity. A practical variation of this approach, widely used in industrial training at the time, especially in areas such as industrial assembly tasks, was "skills analysis" developed by Seymour (1966). Careful skills analysis served to develop ways of carrying out repetitive tasks effectively and helping people acquire skills quickly.

7.2.2.2 Information processing approaches

A common approach to incorporating psychological factors in task analysis entails modelling human information processing. Information processing models in cognitive psychology are quite familiar. From the early 1950s R B. Miller, probably the most influential figure in task analysis, published a number of articles setting out principles and guidance for analysing tasks. Miller's approach, reported in numerous articles and technical reports, consisted of two main stages, *task description* and *task analysis* (e.g. Miller, 1962, 1967, 1974).

A *task description* is a statement of what an operator has to do in his or her job expressed in *systems* or *operational* terms i.e. describing what must be done by the operator to change the state of the system. One way of expressing this is in a table. Table 7.2 illustrates part of a job description concerning maintenance of a radar system. The left–hand column in Table 7.2 contains one of several component statements for the task, namely adjust radar receiver. The general heading "control" lists component tasks – power on, AC voltage adjustment, POS regulated voltage etc. The "activity" column states what to do to maintain the particular control and "indication" lists cues for carrying out the task. Finally "remarks" is used to record any other information thought to be relevant and which does not have a home elsewhere.

Implicit in this table is the common theme of dealing with tasks hierarchically – turn power on is a part of adjust radar receiver which is a part of maintain radar system. Any hierarchical system of task description, where lower descriptors are subsumed within higher descriptors, must have some method of conveying how the lower descriptors are organized to meet the requirements of the higher descriptor. For example, being able to make the various control actions in this task is hardly satisfactory if they are made in the wrong order. In Table 7.2 the "indication" column contains cues for action to prompt the execution of the different control actions in adjusting the radar receiver properly. There are more effective methods for organizing this sort of information which will be discussed in Section 7.3.

Table 7.2 A task description table (adapted from Miller, 1962), showing the analysis of a radar system adjustment task.

JOB ELEMENT FORM					
Position	Line mechanic — Radar system				
Duty	1. Adjust system				

TASK	TIME minutes		ELEMENTS			REMARKS
	In seq.	Out seq.	CONTROL	ACTIVITY	INDICATION (include when to do task and frequency of task)	Alternatives and/or precautions
1.1 Adjust radar receiver	40	40			Adjust every 25 hours of a/c time. See a/c log.	
			1.1.1 POWER ON button	Press	Inverter starts and makes audible hum, pilot light comes on, range indication lights come on, tiltmeter pointer comes on scale.	Avoid starting systm with covers removed from high voltage units: personal hazard.
			1.1.2 AC voltage adjustment (screwdriver)	Turn	AC voltmeter aligns to 117±4 volts.	
			1.1.3 POS regulated voltage adjustment (screwdriver)	Turn	POS regulated voltage meter indicates 300±5 volts.	
			1.1.4 BRIGHT control knob	Turn clockwise	Sweep trace becomes visible on CRT.	
			1.1.5 FOCUS control knob	Turn as required	Sweep trace becomes sharper (focused).	

In Miller's scheme this phase of "task description" is followed by a phase called "task analysis" where the analyst explores the *behavioural* structure of tasks. For this Miller proposes an information processing model, presented graphically in Figure 7.1 and entailing stages through which signals pass from the task environment through *reception of task information, interpretation and problem solving* to *motor response mechanisms* dealing with the manner in which the response was selected (through *interpretation and problem solving*) in order to effect a change in the environment. Supporting this performance is *retention of task information* holding current task information, such as the current status of specific parameters, as well as learned rules and principles governing decision–making. Influencing all activities is the *goal orientation and set*. The representation in Figure 7.1 is consistent with many such human–system interaction models presented in ergonomics and applied psychology.

Miller's approach is pragmatic. His purpose is not to try to defend a specific view of human information processing, but to present a practical framework for considering different influences on performance. Miller suggests that an analyst should consider execution of a task in terms of these information–processing stages in Figure 7.1 and judge where difficulties are likely to arise. Identifying a potential weakness prompts the analyst to seek a solution. For example, if it is judged that short–term retention will be affected in a task where the operator has to remember a number of system variables, then an external memory aid, such as an instrument or a note–pad, is advised. Other models of the human–task interaction, or even models of human behaviour, may serve exactly the same purpose. Whether other approaches serve this end more or less successfully is a separate issue that will not be considered here.

A major problem with distinguishing between *task description* and *task analysis* is that it is not always clear where one should end and the other begin. This distinction may apply reasonably well in tasks where people carry out a number of self–contained actions. In these cases, we may list the distinct activities according to Miller's task description phase, then explore them in turn by his task analysis approach. In many tasks, however, the component activities are integrated by substantial control structures, incorporating problem solving and decision–making. Supervisory control tasks in power stations, for example, are all concerned with doing lots of simple things like reading instruments, switching on pumps and adjusting valves, but doing them in accordance with the need to control a complex hazardous system. In such tasks systems implications are necessarily intertwined with behavioural implications. In Section 7.3 we shall consider an approach which avoids this uneasy distinction between *task description* and *task analysis* in dealing with complex tasks.

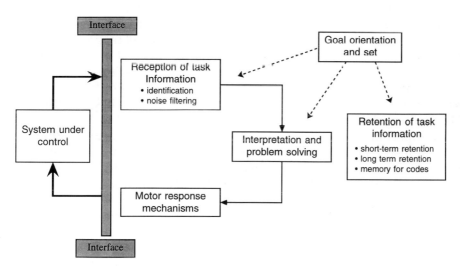

Figure 7.1 Schematic representation of Miller's scheme for task analysis.

7.2.2.3 Task classification

Categorization of task elements is evident in the early work of Gilbreth. The rationale for any such scheme is that by establishing a task element as a member of a category, it can be treated by applying to it measures that have been shown to be successful for other members of that category. If we recognise that a particular task element is concerned with monitoring a trend, for example, and we know how to present trend information, then we can use this categorization to suggest a form of information representation for the task element currently being considered.

Most approaches to categorization in task analysis are *rational*, where a researcher recognizes that a certain class of tasks have characteristics in common and suggests to other people that this is a useful way of seeking hypotheses. For example, Kragt and Landeweerd (1974) categorize process control tasks in terms of monitoring, adjusting, minimizing the effects of breakdowns and handing over process control responsibilities (to other personnel). Implicit in this scheme is that each category embodies the same sorts of behaviours and so research carried out on instances of each category will apply to other instances not hitherto encountered. There is a logical flaw in this assumption in that novel instances may bring with them unforeseen implications for example, contextual factors often limit the extent to which design conditions can be generalised. Nonetheless, classification schemes are useful in providing guidance, provided the analyst is scrupulous in evaluating any resulting designs.

An important extension of categorization is illustrated by Gagne's work in instructional psychology. Gagne has developed a scheme of task categories based on conditions for learning. For example, Gagne, Briggs and Wager (1988) distinguish between: problem solving; the application of higher order rules; the application of rules and defined concepts; the application of concrete concepts; and making discriminations. In other papers these elements are set out differently, but their underlying purpose remains the same. A task element is assigned to one of these categories. From this, it is possible to suggest the conditions for instruction appropriate to that category. The extension placed on Gagne's scheme is that these categories also relate to one another in the following hierarchical fashion:

- Problem solving

involves the formation of

  - Higher order rules

  which require as prerequisites

    - Rules and defined concepts

    which require as prerequisites

      - Concrete concepts

      which require as prerequisites

        - Discriminations

This scheme, therefore, relates task decomposition, as seen in Miller's approach, to behavioural decomposition, to serve as a framework for instructional design.

7.2.3 Collecting information

An important aspect of any task analysis is the collection of information, including, information related to managerial preferences, information needs, operator knowledge requirements, task cycle times, performance errors etc. The methods for doing these things include interviewing, verbal protocol analysis, questionnaires, observation, simulation, examining production and safety records, etc. Some people refer to these data collection methods as task analysis methods, which adds further to the plethora of methods and techniques that the reader has to contend with. Competence in appropriate techniques of information collection is essential. However, of prime importance is the appropriate identification of situations where the costs of using a specific technique are really justified. In the majority of situations, interviewing domain experts is quite sufficient. Where this proves less than satisfactory and the task element currently under scrutiny is seen as sufficiently important, then applying a more costly technique is justified.

7.3 Hierarchical task analysis

A major impetus for developing task analysis methods is change in technology and work practices affecting workload, cognitive demand, labour turnover and the means available to help people master and carry out their tasks. The methods advocated by

Seymour and Crossman became less appropriate as short–cycle manufacturing tasks became less important. Crossman (1960) charts these changes in technology and their implications for human performance with particular reference to process control tasks. Crossman's review illustrates the psychological implications of moving from manual production through to continuous processing where the operator is divorced from the actual manufacturing vessels, for safety reasons and to enable control of larger systems. The crucial factor in supervising a continuous process from a control room is that the operator cannot directly observe the phenomena under control and must operate through the medium of instruments that a human designer has chosen to represent the process. Thus process control is, largely, an interface design problem and the impetus to extend task analysis methods to cope with these changes is similar to the impetus provided by developments in HCI.

Hierarchical task analysis (HTA) was developed by John Annett and Keith Duncan (Annett and Duncan, 1967; Annett, Duncan, Stammers and Gray, 1971; Duncan. 1972, 1974) to provide an approach to analysing tasks which would cope with, among other things, the increasing number of system supervision tasks. When operating a continuous process plant, for example, the operator has to do a number of simple things, such as switching equipment on and off, opening, closing and adjusting valves. These things are often done from a control room with no significant physical effort involved. The complexities of these tasks are concerned with collecting and processing information to judge deviance from operating targets and then plan and coordinate actions to re–establish these targets. HTA is best seen as a general framework in which task analysis and human factors design decisions are made.

7.3.1 Goals and operations

In HTA tasks are analysed by considering the *operation* that has to be carried out to meet a given system *goal*. A goal is often expressed in terms of a production target along with the constraints that must be observed in meeting such targets (i.e. goals are not treated as psychological constructs). An *operation* is what people carrying out the task do to a system in order to move it towards its goal state. Definitions of these terms within HTA are discussed by Shepherd (1989). In recreational, domestic and creative situations people set their own goals for the part of the world they are trying to control, then use what skills they have to operate on their environment to achieve these goals. This also applies to many HCI tasks where a computer application is designed to meet the goals of the user rather than a manager specifying how work is carried out.

7.3.2 Examining human–task interactions

Goals are examined by two main methods – examining the *human–task interaction* or by *redescription*. To examine the human–task interaction Annett and Duncan suggest that an operation (i.e. what the operator does), should be thought of in terms of "input", "action" and "feedback". That is, competence at an operation implies an ability to collect information (*input*) pertinent to the execution of the task; an ability to carry out the *action* selected to move towards the goal state; and the ability to monitor appropriate *feedback* to determine whether the action is being executed correctly and is appropriate for dealing with the goal in question. There is no explicit *decision–making* component in this scheme, but use of feedback to regulate action to meet the goal implies the skill that the operator possesses. The I–A–F classification enables the analyst to consider, systematically, the likely sources of human error in the conduct of an operation. If an *input* or a *feedback* weakness is suspected, the analyst would be directed towards considering the display of information to the operator, or training in the discrimination, organization and interpretation of signals. If an *action* weakness is suspected, the analyst could be directed to consider equipment re–design or training. The I—A—F classification is an *information processing model of skill*, used in a similar fashion to Miller's scheme, illustrated in Figure 7.1. Some analysts will feel more comfortable with a model containing an explicit decision–making component, like Miller's. A theme of this chapter is to emphasise that task analysis is a *framework* in which different approaches may be used according to requirement and preference. In principle, the human–task interaction may be examined using any information processing model (or other cognitive model) or classification scheme felt by the analyst to be useful in the domain in question.

7.3.3 Examining goals by redescription

If exploration of the human–task interaction proves difficult, unsatisfactory in generating useful hypotheses, or the analyst feels that he or she has not yet gained a suitable grasp of the issues (e.g. the contextual constraints) then the other way of exploring a goal is by *redescription*. A goal is redescribed in terms of a set of sub ordinate goals and an organizing component known as the "plan", which specifies the conditions under which sub–ordinate goals have to be carried out to meet the system goal in question. Repeating redescription results in a hierarchy of operations and plans. This is illustrated in Figure 7.2 using an adaptation of Miller's radar adjustment task. To provide this illustration with a context, the task examined is <u>0. Maintain radar systems in flight</u> (Miller's analysis deals with ground–based maintenance – Figure 7.2 developed an in–flight variant, but the two versions are easily compared). This is redescribed in terms of nine subordinate goals and a plan which specifies the conditions when they are carried out (note sub goals 4 to 7 have been included as tasks equivalent to <u>Adjust radar receiver</u> in order to show how the hierarchy works).

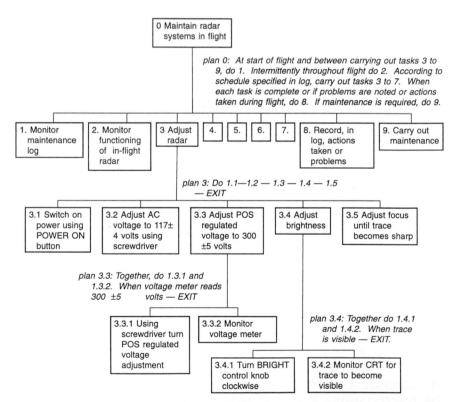

Figure 7.2 Adjust radar receiver (from Table 7.2), represented in a hierarchical task analysis format. Table 7.2 describes a ground maintenance task. To illustrate the way in which HTA can integrate on–going system monitoring with procedures, this version adapts Miller's context to present an in–flight maintenance task.

Normally each of these would be examined to determine whether further redescription is justified. For the sake of illustration, only <u>3. Adjust radar</u> has been redescribed. Whereas plan 0 shows a comparatively complex set of *conditions*, plan 3 is a straightforward *fixed procedure*. Again, for the sake of illustration, sub goals 3.3 and 3.4 are redescribed. Each of these show a form of time–sharing plan. In both cases the operator is required simultaneously to manipulate a control, whilst monitoring a target. The action is continued until the criterion is met.

By using a common example, we can immediately draw some comparison between Miller's representation, in Table 7.2 and HTA. Both analyses contain similar information, but by integrating cues and actions HTA organizes it in a way such that performance issues can be understood in context. The time–sharing examples described above may appear trivial, but in a different context these observations are critical. Williams (1992) describes the task of inspecting pressure vessels in nuclear power plant for flaws. Failure to detect flaws could prove catastrophic. This task is carried out by a technician passing an ultrasonic probe across the surface of the pressure vessel. Ultra sound reflections are monitored and displayed on a cathode ray tube as a series of peaks and troughs. Presence of a flaw creates excessive peaks. The technician's task is to monitor the cathode ray tube to identify these extreme instances. However, while monitoring, the technician must maintain correct adherence and pressure of the probe and ensure that all parts of the surface are covered systematically. Thus the technician must time–share between <u>maintaining adherence between probe and surface</u>, <u>maintaining the route</u> and <u>monitoring the display</u>. Each of these elements is comparatively straightforward on its own, but not when they are being done together. Whether or not time–shared tasks actually present problems to the operator cannot be determined from the HTA alone. The HTA merely raises a possibility that would need empirical confirmation if the consequences of the problem were deemed serious.

Time–sharing is not simply revealed through individual plans. If we trace up the hierarchy we see other possible interactions. In the radar task in Figure 7.2, plan 0 shows that some sub goals are carried out according to mutually exclusive cues (e.g. schedules for making adjustments), while others are prompted by system events. If two or more unacceptable system events coincide, the operator becomes more heavily loaded. If these unscheduled events occur while a scheduled procedure is being undertaken, then there are similar implications for loading. The HTA may need to be revised to assign priorities to the technician. In some contexts these coincidences can become a real problem. In process control an unscheduled event may trigger a number of safety responses whose execution needs sensible planning. These problems are compounded by the fact that emergencies occur rarely and there is little opportunity to practise the integration of skills necessary.

7.3.4 Types of plans

Through the use of plans HTA enables complex interaction of task elements to be recorded. The manner in which several comparatively simple plans in a hierarchy combine to describe a complex tasks is discussed and illustrated by Shepherd and Duncan (1980). Table 7.3 shows a listing and description of some main types of plan, but it must be acknowledged that actual plans encountered in task analysis can be a mixture of these. Such planning can be presented in a number of ways — text, flow diagrams, matrices, or rule–sets.

7.3.5 Stopping analysis

Tasks, goals or operations should not be examined unless performance is judged to be unacceptable — otherwise it is a waste of resources. To deal with this Annett and Duncan propose the P x C rule, where P refers to the probability of inadequate performance and C the cost of inadequate performance. If this product is acceptable then there is no need to progress with the analysis. The P x C rule is an important *rule–of–thumb*, reminding the analyst to weigh both of these factors. If an operation is likely to be carried out badly (high P), yet resultant error is of no consequence (insignificant C), then P x C will be insignificant and the operation will not be worth examining.

If an operation is likely to be carried out reasonably well (low, but finite, P), but error will result in a catastrophe with loss of life (unacceptably high C), then P x C will be unacceptable and examination and suitable treatment must follow. The analyst can apply this rule before considering a hypothesis and afterwards. If without any training and within an existing interface design P x C is judged unacceptable, the analyst can propose modifying the interface or propose training, then re–apply the P x C rule . In each of these cases, the decision rule should be extended to anticipate the costs of the innovation, such that costs do not exceed benefits. Issues associated with this stopping rules are discussed by Shepherd (1985).

Table 7.3 Different types of plan characteristic encountered in hierarchical task analysis. Instances and combinations may be identified in Figure 7.4.

Plan characteristic	Description
Fixed sequences	Sub-goals are carried out in order. The signal for carrying out a subsequent goal is feedback that the previous goal has been attained.
Cued actions	Each sub-goal is carried out when particular system event occurs, such as an alarm. This is akin to a conditioned response.
Contingent fixed sequences	Sub-goals are carrried out in order but, following successful feedback from the previous operation, the operator must wait for a system cue.
Choices	These are logically similar to cued action in that sub-goals are carried out in accordance with prevailing circumstances. However, the basis for a choice is a reasoned decision, rather than an invariant response.
Cycles	In some tasks, operators or users have to repeat a sequence of sub-goals until conditions arise when they are prompted to stop. Conditions for stopping can include an instruction from a supervisor, such as at the end of a shift or a safety condition. Alternatively, the stopping condition is monitored by the operator as an activity within the cycle — commonly encountered in process control.
Time-sharing	When 2 or more sub-goals must be carried out more or less together.
Discretionary plans	Sometimes the operator is at liberty to carry out sub-goals without constraint.

HTA continues until the analyst has reason to stop and a hypothesis has been recorded. This means that the analysis has been taken as far as is necessary to consider all constituent problems. This has always been one of the most useful yet little appreciated features of HTA. Some people use task analysis only as a first step in a design process, followed by design and evaluation. This is very inefficient.

7.3.6 Tabular representation

Hierarchical diagrams, such as Figure 7.2, are useful in showing how elements interact, but are less useful for recording potential problems or design hypotheses. Table 7.4 shows how the HTA in

Table 7.4 Illustration of a tabular format for HTA using the radar adjustment task from Figure 7.2. Only the "Task Analysis" columns are essential. The remaining columns may be adapted to the requirements of the analyst.

Task Analysis	Redescribed	I-A-F	Notes
0 Maintain radar systems in flight			
plan 0: At start of flight and between tasks do 1.Intermittently throughout flight do 2. According to schedule specified in log carry out tasks 3 to 7. When each task is complete or if problems are noted or actions taken during flight, do 8.If maintenance is required, do 9.			
1 Monitor maintenance log	no	I	Ensure a format for the log which prompts technician to carry out routine tasks and reminders to check-up on unscheduled contingencies are clear. Review ceasing redescription.
2 Monitor functioning of in-flight radar system	no	I	How are key parameters displayed for monitoring? Review ceasing redescription.
3 Adjust radar receiver	yes		This will normally be required very 25 hours.
4 *for illustration only*	no		
5 *for illustration only*	no		
6 *for illustration only*	no		
7 *for illustration only*	no		
8 Record, in log, actions taken or problems noted	no	I	Ensure layout of log is clearly designed to record action taken. Devise means of highlighting and bringing forth problems.
9 Carry out maintenance	no		Requires redescription.
3 Adjust radar receiver			
plan 3: Do 1.1—1.2 — 1.3 — 1.4 — 1.5 — EXIT			
1 Switch on power using POWER ON button	no	F	Avoid starting system with covers removed from high voltage units: personal hazard. Redescription would focus on the feedback to indicates proper functioning of the system — hum, pilot light, range indication lights, tiltmeter pointer.
2 Adjust AC voltage to 117± 4 volts using screwdriver	no	F	
3 Adjust POS regulated voltage to 300 ±5 volts	yes		
4 Adjust brightness	yes		
5 Adjust focus until trace becomes sharp	no		
3.3 Adjust POS regulated voltage to 300 ±5 volts			
plan 3.3: Together, do 1.3.1 and 1.3.2. When voltage meter reads 300 ±5 volts — EXIT			Siting of adjustment screw given need to monitor voltage may be problematic.
1 Using screwdriver turn POS regulated voltage adjustment	no	A	Review equipment design or training re comment on plan 3.3.
2 Monitor voltage meter	no	F	Review equipment design or training re comment on plan 3.3.
3.4 Adjust brightness			
plan 3.4: Together do 1.4.1 and 1.4.2. When trace is visible — EXIT.			
1 Turn BRIGHT control know clockwise	no		
2 Monitor CRT for trace to become visible	no	F	Criterion for visibility appears too subjective. Check that subjective criteria satisfy the requirements of operational staff. Modify training or job design as appropriate.

Figure 7.2 is represented in a tabular format. The task analysis columns on the left show the same information as the diagram. The column headed "redescription" informs the reader whether more detail can be found. In this version an I–A–F column is included to indicate whether the analyst judges that there might be problem in the way the operator handles information (I), carries out the action (A) or monitors and uses feedback (F). Finally the "notes" column is used to keep track of possible problems needing to be checked out or hypotheses for improving performance. Tabular formats can be modified to suit various requirements, such that information of interest can be logged against respective task elements. The only columns that must feature are the task analysis column and an indication of whether redescription has stopped at a particular point.

7.3.7 HTA – a framework for analysing tasks

A consequence of the proliferation of methods and techniques in task analysis is that would–be analysts have tended to view different task analysis methods as different tools suited to different applications. It has been an aim of this chapter to emphasize that task analysis is a problem–solving activity in which the analyst moves strategically towards the identification of problems and design suggestions, rather than follow a step–by–step procedure.

At the outset, the analyst cannot know which techniques will be needed because the nature of the task to be examined is not yet understood. Figure 7.3 sets out a framework emphasizing the *process* of carrying out task analysis, working towards a *product* in the form of an HTA diagram or table. This framework is not a formal set of procedures for completing an HTA but an account of the sorts of skills and considerations the analyst brings to bear. The underlying philosophy is entirely consistent with the principles set out by Annett and Duncan, who were mainly concerned to assemble and integrate useful principles for analysing tasks rather than specify a rigid technique. Each stage in the framework will now be described:

1 *Identify and state the goal to be examined.*
A first step in analysing a task is to focus upon the main goal. Sometimes, as an analysis progresses, it becomes apparent that it commenced at too detailed a level of description and so a broader goal must be considered. Because tasks and goals can be described at different levels of detail it is usually easy to step up a level and use the work done so far as part of its subsequent redescription. For example, an analyst might have been guided to focus on adjust radar receiver as in Table 7.2. However, it soon becomes apparent that this itself forms part of a wider task, so the analysis steps up a level to

<u>maintain radar systems in flight</u> (I am sure Miller never saw <u>adjust radar receiver</u> in isolation but the case can be used to illustrate this point). Finding the right level to start analysis develops with experience. However, there are analytical techniques which can help this focus. For example, Eason (1989) describes "Open Systems Task Analysis" as a means of understanding the boundaries of the problem being addressed; Flanagan (1954) describes the "critical incident technique" to help the analyst focus on important aspects of the task in response to examination of actual past problems or near misses.

Progressing through this framework, the analyst will continually cycle back to stage 1 to address new sub ordinate goals that have emerged through prior redescription of goals already examined (during Stage 8).

  2 *Explore its constraints*

Shepherd (1989) defines a task in terms of meeting a goal in accordance with available resources (i.e. what the operator is able to do in principle, given interfacing tools such as knobs, dials, buttons, keyboards, colleagues, screwdrivers etc.) in accordance with constraints. Two main types of constraint are considered. Firstly, there are constraints placed on the operator in *making acceptable responses*. These are often of a technical nature. For example, any practice which causes a spark in an inflammable area may cause an explosion. This is important knowledge to help indicate whether analysis should be taken further and to be borne in mind later when plans are to be developed. Secondly, there are *design* constraints – electronic devices causing sparks cannot be used in inflammable areas – so, certain forms of tools of job–aids cannot be prescribed. Similarly, if people carry out the task infrequently, training benefits may be limited and job–aids preferred.

  Exploring constraints tends to be informal and intuitive and either kept in the back of the analysts mind or recorded in the "Notes" column. Sometimes constraints are not obvious at a particular level of description and are only recognized when the goal is explored further. It is easy to see how constraints are *inherited* in tasks. In the radar example, the background noise and physical confines of the activity are general and will apply to all goals subsequently encountered. The space and orientation constraints in using the screwdriver to adjust AC voltage, however, are local to that goal.

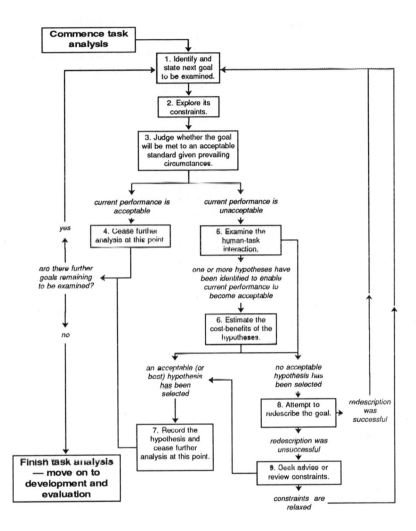

Figure 7.3 A framework for task analysis, illustrating the cycle of activities typically involved in the conduct of a hierarchical task analysis.

Their only influence on other parts of the task is in making the AC adjustment more difficult hence placing greater loading on the operator during any time–sharing. Constraints are important in task analysis and are often not formally recognized. There is scope for exploring these issues further.

3 *Judge whether the goal will be met to an acceptable standard given prevailing circumstances.*
This relates to the stopping criterion (the P x C rule), i.e. deciding whether the goal is worth examining further. Judging acceptability of current performance entails establishing what the client values, and sometimes formally examining production and incident records to ascertain probabilities and costs. It is, of course, unlikely that an analysis will stop after only the main goal has been recorded, but as the analysis progresses and goals are considered at a lower level, then sub goals become worth examining in this fashion.

4 *Cease further analysis at this point.*
Following Stage 3, analysis at a particular point may cease.

5 *Examine the human–task interaction.*
Where performance warrants attention, examination should first consider the *human–task interaction*. This may mean attempting to understand information processing, cognition, attitudes, etc. This is often done informally by the analyst relying on experience or human factors knowledge. Or it can be done using a modelling approach, e.g. Miller's framework in Figure 7.1, or a formal cognitive modelling method, such as GOMS (Card, Moran and Newell, 1983) or TAKD (Diaper, 1989).

6 *Estimate the cost–benefitsof the hypotheses.*
Cost–benefit analysis becomes increasingly important as technologies for controlling systems or dealing with human factors solutions become more expensive. Training simulation is a good illustration because the technology required to obtain high fidelity simulation in many domains is very expensive and may not appear to be justified, even in terms of the costly events it may avert. It is, however, important to recognize that as task analysis progresses and further opportunities to use the same equipment or technology present themselves, benefits may start to overhaul costs. Therefore, it is important that no potentially useful hypotheses are totally discarded on cost grounds, but kept alive to be reviewed later. Keeping track of progress is one of the many areas where computer support would be welcome.

7 *Record the hypothesis and cease further analysis at this point.*
Careful record keeping is necessary to specify any hypotheses generated.

8 *Attempt to redescribe the goal.*
Redescribing tasks is a skill which develops with practice. Benefit can be gained by considering examples in similar domains. For example, process control and maintenance tasks are illustrated in Kirwan and Ainsworth (1992); information technology tasks are illustrated in Shepherd (1989). No matter where the redescription came from, it is crucial to check that the subordinate goals and their plan

complement one another and really are *equivalent* to the goal they are collectively redescribing.

  9   *Seek advice or review constraints.*

Sometimes redescription proves impossible for the analyst. This may be because no way of redescribing can be seen by the analyst or it may mean that no way can be seen within the given set of resource constraints. The analyst may seek advice. Such advice may provide help in suggesting a method of redescription, or it may provide a more acute examination of the human–task interaction, leading to a design hypothesis.

If a constraint is challenged successfully, e.g. more funds are made available, the analyst may use the hierarchical structure to trace up the hierarchy to establish where the constraint first became effective. Then the analyst can trace those aspects of the task already examined, which were affected by the original constraint. This all gets very complicated and, fortunately, there are not many occasions when this opportunity arises. A computer tool to help back–track in this way would be very welcome.

7.4 Application of task analysis to HCI

The aim of this volume is to show how various disciplines contribute to the field of HCI. It is not possible to provide a lengthy bibliography to show how more traditional task analysis methods serve HCI, because such literature does not exist on any noticeable scale. HCI researchers have tended to develop their own techniques to examine problems. Moreover, practitioners within the main task analysis fields are often working practically in organizations where publication is not encouraged. This section will draw attention to benefits of applying task analysis methods in the HCI domain.

7.4.1 Relevance of task analysis to HCI tasks

A first important point to make is that HCI tasks are usually components of non–HCI tasks. When people interact with computers, they do so for a purpose and this purpose and the manner of their interaction is influenced by the other events that have caused them to turn to the computer. A travel agent or an electricity board clerk has interacted with a customer before and while interacting with the computer. This will shape the manner in which computer interaction takes place. This issue is dealt with in chapter 9 of this volume. Moreover, seen in the context of a real occupational task, the intricacies of HCI may be trivial, bearing in mind the P x C rule. If they are not trivial, then they can often be understood using the general methods of conventional task analysis. Alternatively, the analyst may feel justified in using a formal cognitive modelling approach within the broader HTA framework. An important feature of the task analysis framework is justifying where effort should be expended in task analysis.

Shepherd (1989) discusses an intervention demonstrating how an even–handed approach to task analysis is preferred to focusing too readily on prominent HCI issues. This case was concerned with an accountancy–related clerical task in a large service organization. The task was seen as an HCI task by management in view of the emphasis on data entry and retrieval via computer terminals. Indeed, the computer screen design was uninspiring and often inconsistent, so there was a temptation to dive straight in and focus on these aspects. However, a broader analysis placed the HCI issues into perspective. Despite the presence of computers, the broader task analysis showed that the real problem resided in the manner in which clerks were required to investigate problems with customers over the telephone, rarely involving use of the computer. They used the computers to store and retrieve relevant information, but it was clear that operators could learn the computer tasks effectively and errors were easily recoverable.

Another example (Shepherd, 1986) showed the converse. Management of a process plant assumed that a new computer–based plant display would present their experienced operating staff with no problems. They saw task analysis as a method of analysing and designing familiarization training. In carrying out the task analysis it was revealed that mastering the HCI task was far from being a simple familiarization exercise. It was shown that the configuration of information on the screens was inconsistent with what the operators were required to do. Thus detailed analysis of the human–computer interaction was justified to facilitate screen redesign.

Even where an HCI task does warrant examination, it is often quite satisfactory to proceed with HTA. Form filling tasks, such as entering customer records in a telephone service industry (e.g. mail-order, gas and electricity) are easy to deal with as they are largely procedural. An illustration is given in Figure 7.4. Plan 0 shows a typical cycle of answering the telephone and dealing with various enquiries. Plan 2 is a list of condition–action statements. Such plans can often prompt menu design in computer systems. Plan 2.2 shows a procedure to prompt form filling. Plan 2.2.1 is again procedural and captures the sequence of communicating intermittently with the customer and the computer. It is dangerous to use the task hierarchy to map directly on to a proposed screen hierarchy because it does not address issues such as task frequency, but the purpose to be served by the screen hierarchy in supporting user performance is far clearer having completed the HTA.

One of the most common forms of HCI is using an applications package such as a wordprocessor or spreadsheet. An illustration of applying HTA to a wordprocessing task is shown in Figure 7.5. Such packages entail a vast range of functions. The problem for the user is knowing which ones to use and how to use them to attain their goals. The danger in trying to encompass all functions in one task analysis is that the analysis becomes a categorization of everything in the package with no feel for how functions are used.

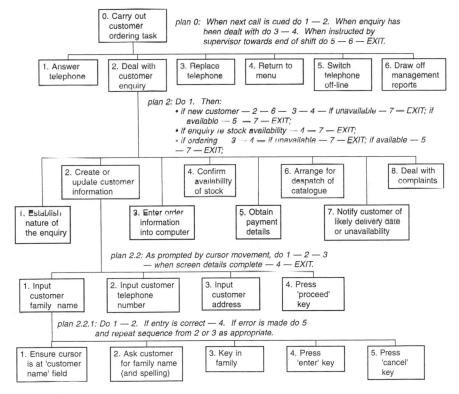

Figure 7.4 A telephone customer service task, entailing human–computer interaction, represented as a hierarchical task analysis. This sort of task analysis can be easily extended and provides an opportunity for readers to try out HTA for themselves and explore different approaches to organizing the task.

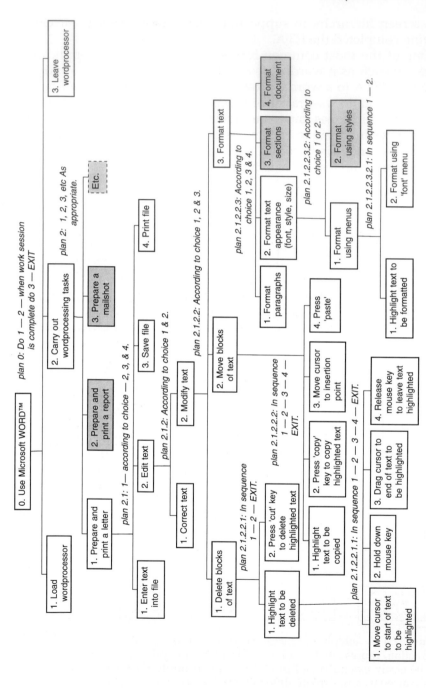

Figure 7.5 Examining the functions of a word processing package using hierarchical task analysis, focusing on "prepare and print a letter". Shaded boxes represent sub-goals to be explored as more demanding word processing skills are developed.

A useful strategy is to consider typical tasks for which the package might be used, starting with something quite simple. A simple application is using the wordprocessor to prepare and print a letter, which is developed as goal 2.1. To do this, the user must 1. Enter text into file, 2. Edit text, 3. Save file and 4. Print file. This is a task complete in itself – a completed letter will result. These goals are redescribed as necessary. The example shows Edit text redescribed as Correct text and Modify text. Modify text is redescribed in terms of deleting, moving and formatting. The first step in deleting is highlighting, which is a common interfacing skill, seen again in Moving text (goal 2.1.2.2.2.1) and formatting text using menus (goal 2.1.2.2.3.2.1). This enables economy in analysis, opportunities for consistency checking in the package and a rationale for identifying portable sub–skills that can be taught in an early demonstration. Figure 7.4 has only redescribed a few goals to illustrate the approach.

Moving on to Prepare and print a report the analyst will find much in common with what was done with Prepare and print letter. The idea is to try to use the structure developed to date and see how it can be extended to accommodate the new task being considered. The shaded boxes in Figure 7.5 show some of the new goals that might be considered when Preparing and printing a report. These include formatting sections and documents and using style–sheets to ensure consistency of presentation Further additions would be to add creating page numbering, creating contents pages, etc.

There are several practical advantages of this step–by–step approach of focusing on explicit tasks such as prepare and print a letter to prepare and print a report. Firstly, it helps the analyst focus on the practical tasks and practical cues that are necessary to master the package. Secondly, if the analysis is being conducted to develop content and structure for a manual or training programme, this approach will focus on what is necessary and sufficient for the training in question – there is no need to teach mail–merge to people who are simply going to type letters and reports. Thirdly, it is helpful to use these intermediate tasks during training, because it provides a series of meaningful *functional contexts* in which the trainee can gradually learn to cope with more and more of the package and is given encouraging feedback in the form of concrete achievement.

Plans, in the analysis of using applications packages, tend to fall into two main categories– choices and procedures. *Choices* invariably relate to the things the user wants to do, while *procedures* describe the sequence constraints in doing these things.

7.4.2 Cognitive task analysis

The developments in technology, discussed earlier, have placed greater emphasis on cognitive rather than manual aspects of skill. As a consequence, some people have called for the development of "cognitive task analysis", arguing that existing forms of task analysis are inadequate. By "cognitive task analysis" people tend to mean "cognitive modelling". Approaches to cognitive modelling are discussed in chapter 5.

In this chapter task analysis has focused on a systems perspective to identify the demands placed upon human beings in systems. This is important, because any form of task analysis should consider these demands in an even–handed manner. It makes no sense to assume a task has certain important characteristics at the outset, since the actual nature of the task in terms of system demands and criticality cannot be known. There is a danger, when looking at practical problems, in focusing on interesting behaviours which are not justified by any assessment of their criticality, since resources may be wasted. Carrying out "cognitive task analysis" makes more sense if it is done in the context of a broad task analytic framework.

The benefits of a broader task analysis framework to the application of cognitive modelling go beyond helping identify where such effort is justified. HTA also sets a clearer context for the problem to be solved. Examining a human–task interaction is served by seeing how the task element in question fits into the hierarchical structure. Thus, the conditions that the operator experiences prior to the task in question, how other task elements must compete for cognitive resources, what options or consequences will follow the task element in question, are all made clearer. For example, in analysis of process control tasks, we are constantly faced with operators having to carry out diagnosis. It is important to know whether the operator has been monitoring the task prior to the disturbance, since this will certainly affect the working knowledge available to carry out the task. It is important to know whether diagnosis has to compete for mental resources with other tasks, such as planning safety contingencies or monitoring other safety systems, or whether there is excessive time pressure. It is important to know the range of options available – deciding whether to continue production or shut down is a simpler choice than having to select from a range of remedial actions as a consequence of diagnosis. It is also important to be aware of the stresses on the operator in terms of the consequences of making a mistake. Unless these contextual factors are understood, cognitive analysis will be of little value because the behaviours investigated may have no bearing on what actually happens and the contextual constraints affecting behaviour cannot be known.

7.4.3 Using hierarchical task analysis in human factors design

Human factors design entails providing specification for a range of system elements that will influence the manner in which people carry out tasks. The environment in which people work in any task can be described in terms of:– the goals to be attained; the information available to provide evidence of the current system state and feedback concerning action taken; the resources available in terms of controls and other response facilities; system constraints that must be taken account of in making decisions (e.g. the dynamics of the system under control); motivating factors that affect the urgency and care of performance; and environmental constraints that will affect the manner in which information is processed to make decisions. In traditional applications of task analysis the task is set by constraints of the environment; the aim of task analysis is to identify what these "natural" components are. For example, a problem might be to identify the cues used by an aircraft pilot carrying out manoeuvres in order to develop simulation. There is no changing many of these cues because they are, in part, determined by gravity. In HCI we often have the opportunity, through the medium of software, to modify how the task is represented to the user. For example, the interface designer can automate routines and develop metaphors for representing functions to the user which will prompt the use of various tools at the interface.

Human factors design is concerned with optimizing task components such that, together, they meet system requirements within resource constraints. This is usually done through attention to common stages in the human factors life cycle. The first recognized stage is *allocation of function*, to decide whether human beings or machines (often automation) are best suited to carry out a particular system's function. Similarly, *job–design* addresses how functions are best distributed between members of a team to ensure that the overall goal is met. *Information specification* indicates the information that must be available to an operator or user to carry out a task properly, while *interface design* prescribes how this information is displayed. The design of *job–aids* or *help facilities* together with *training design* provides the means by which skills are supported to complement other features of task design. A common weakness in human factors design and system management is to treat each of these elements separately. This is generally quite wrong. It is uneconomical and promotes inconsistencies between solutions. Much of computer system design, expressed in terms of more traditional ergonomics, is concerned with *allocation of function* and *functional representation*, through interface design.

HTA provides a useful input to human factors design because it is concerned with:– what people do (through goals); how they do it (through plans); the information they need (through cues within plans and implicit in the feedback necessary for completing sub goals); and the response facilities they need (by the sub goals expressed). It is helpful in making *allocation of function* decisions through the hierarchy of functional goals. In principle, any intermediate goal could be allocated to the computer, with the means of triggering the goal expressed as an interface tool. For example, process plant monitoring of early generations of plant entailed making direct measures of process parameters (e.g. using dip–sticks to judge level). The operator then compared these direct measures with what they thought they should see. A task analysis of this would entail expressing the intermediate goal of <u>maintain product flow–rate</u> then redescribe this to a level of <u>collecting plant information</u>, <u>making a comparison with the desired state</u> then <u>remedying any deviation</u>. With developments in technology, sensed information is translated into an electronic signal. This is then compared with a set point by a local micro–processor, to produce an output signal. The output signal then works a solenoid in an automatic valve to alter the product flow. Thus, <u>maintain product flow–rate</u> becomes a task allocated to a machine. The operator's job now is simply to indicate when this control should be implemented. This can be done by providing a button, hard–wired or part of a computer interface, to switch on the controller. In principle, any hierarchy of functions, such as provided by HTA, can be treated in this manner. This principle can be extended to many HCI applications if the execution of sub–goals can be allocated to a computer.

A *specification of information* to carry out a task can be developed by examining, systematically, all of the information flows implicit in the task. Shepherd (1993) has outlined a scheme where an HTA is subjected to a translation process such that all goals and plans are identified in terms of specific types, each warranting specific forms of information to support performance. Many activities, for example, are simple actions, each requiring a cue to invoke it, an identifiable control to carry it out and feedback to indicate when it is complete or whether the control needs adjustment. The full scheme considers activity elements including *actions, communications, monitoring* and *decision making*, with several instances of each type. A final broad category is that of *sequencing* which results from examining plans. This shows how sub goals relate to each other – a specific goal might *follow* another; might be carried out *at the same time* as another; or might be carried out as an *alternative* to another. These sequencing elements do not specify information as such, but they specify which information should be displayed with other information. In a fixed procedure, for example, information to support a subsequent operation does not need to occupy the same screen as the information to support the current operation. In time–sharing, the information sets for the respective operations need to be accessible from one another.

Job–aids also follow from the task analysis. Job–aids, manuals and help facilities tell the operator or user what to do next when certain conditions arise. *What* has to be done is stated explicitly in HTA in the goal statement. *When* it has to be done is stated in the plans. Translating this form of task analysis into a clear job–aid is quite straightforward (see Shepherd, 1989). *Training* is also facilitated by the structure of the task analysis to schedule training to enable skills to be developed in a systematic fashion.

This section has been necessarily brief. Its aim has not been to suggest that task analysis methods themselves solve all of these design problems, but simply to point out that the task analysis is both important and helpful in a coherent approach to design. It sets out what people have to do in a task and, therefore, the purpose that any design must serve. It helps the designer focus on critical aspects of the task warranting attention. Also, through the medium of the hierarchical task structure, it offers a representation of the task which the designer may use to organize various design solutions.

7.5 Concluding remarks

Reviewing earlier approaches to task analysis highlights some useful lessons. An important observation is that task analysis is only ever done for a purpose. It is not an end in its own right. It is not an attempt to model behaviour or cognition and should not be judged as such. Principal lessons learned from the task analysis literature that apply equally to tasks involving HCI are as follows:

1 Tasks carried out by human beings within systems have to be defined with reference to system demands and constraints.
2 Analysis is justified only in terms of its contribution to the broader human factors intervention.
3 Effort in analysis should be directed only to those aspects where effort is justified.
4 Tasks can be examined by studying the *interaction* between the human operator (commonly referred to in HCI literature as the "user") and the task, often by using some psychological model of the operator or user.

5 The grain of analysis can be adjusted by *redescribing* a goal into its component goals and an organizing or planning component to provide some structural relationship between elements.
6 Task analysis is a hypothesis–generating activity and not a method of modelling cognition.
7 Analysis continues until hypotheses have been generated for dealing with the entire task.

Of particular importance is the emphasis upon a framework for task analysis to embody these principles. This framework may entail the analyst undertaking a wide range of different task analysis methods and techniques, including cognitive modelling approaches. Applying methods of task analysis within a rational framework provides a thorough and economical basis for identifying performance problems and a foundation for specifying options.

Further reading

Duncan, K. D. (1974). Analytical Techniques in Training Design. In E. Edwards and F. P. Leeds (eds), *The Human Operator and Process Control*. London: Taylor and Francis.
Task analysis is discussed widely in most texts of industrial psychology, systems psychology and ergonomics. Discusses basic principles of task analysis in the area of systems psychology

Patrick, J. (1992). *Training – Research and Practice*. London: Academic Press.
A general discussion of task analysis especially with reference to personnel psychology and its applications.

Drury, C., Paramore, B., Cott, H. V., Grey, S. and Corlett, E. (1987). Chapter 3.4 – Task Analysis. In G. Salvendy (eds), *Handbook of Human Factors,* pp. 370 – 401. New York: John Wiley and Sons.
Reviews different methods of task analysis.

Kirwan, B. and. Ainsworth, L. K. (1992). *The Task Analysis Guide.* London: Taylor and Francis.
In addition to providing an extensive catalogue of different approaches, this provides a number of detailed case studies and show how task analysis is applied in various ways.

Shepherd, A. (1989). Analysis and training in information technology tasks. In D. Diaper (eds.), *Task Analysis for Human–Computer Interaction*, pp. 15 – 55. Chichester: Ellis Horwood.
This offers a comprehensive account of hierarchical task analysis, providing advice on how it is carried out and illustrates its application to HCI tasks.

Chapter 8

Ethnography: aligning field studies of work and system design

Jeanette L. Blomberg

8.1 Ethnography

The term ethnography refers both to the process of conducting field research and to the written text produced as a result. Ethnographic textual accounts reflect specific interpretive modes and analytical conventions which provide particular views of the social world. As employed in the HCI and system design communities, ethnography most often refers to an approach used to develop understandings of everyday work practices and technologies in use. While there is a great deal of variability subsumed within the practice of ethnography, most practitioners share a few basic presuppositions.[1] These include: a commitment to studying activities in the "natural" settings in which they occur; an interest in developing detailed descriptions of the lived experience; a focus on what people actually do, not simply on their accounts of behaviour; and a concern with understanding the relation of particular activities to the constellation of activities that characterize a setting.

Ethnography developed within anthropology as a way of gaining insights into the life experiences of people whose everyday reality was vastly different from that of those living in Western developed societies. Anthropology's early focus was on studying small scale, non–Western societies where little could be assumed about the

---

[1] Those interested in learning more about the foundations upon which ethnography is based should consult Agar, 1980, 1986; Clifford, 1988; Clifford and Marcus, 1986; Geertz, 1973, 1983; Pelto, 1970; Van Maanen, 1988 among others.

descriptive and interpretive categories relevant to members of those groups or useful in "explaining" their behaviour. Anthropologists rely on firsthand experience to shape their inquiry, viewing early formulations as partial, tentative, and open to revision as new experiences challenge existing ideas. Increasingly anthropologists have become aware of the ways their own life experiences necessarily inform the descriptions and interpretations they make of the behaviour of others. While not abandoning the basic view that knowledge of others can best be gained by direct experience, there is a growing recognition that such experiences are inevitably colored by one's position in relation to these others.[2]

The ethnographic approach also is employed in sociology, where it developed, in part, in opposition to survey research. The focus of study in sociology primarily has been on "sub–groups" within industrial societies (e.g. youth, addict, ethnic groups). It is within sociology that the sub–field of ethnomethodology developed (see Chapter 9). In the HCI and CSCW literature the terms ethnography and ethnomethodology are sometimes used interchangeably. However, ethnomethodology refers to a particular analytical perspective with respect to the object of study, while ethnography is practised by individuals with varying theoretical and analytical perspectives (ethnomethodology among them).[3] This terminological confusion may have resulted from the fact that many ethnographers working in HCI and CSCW are trained as ethnomethodologists or are sympathetic to ethnomethodological views.

Central to the practice of ethnography in both anthropology and sociology is the view that it is difficult for individuals to articulate the tacit knowledge and understandings they have of familiar activities. Because of this, it is critical that the things people say about their own activities and about the activities of others be supplemented with firsthand observations of behaviour. It is equally important that these observations be made in the actual settings in

---

[2] There is a vast and growing literature, particularly in feminist and postmodern anthropology, which provides a critique of the adequacy of traditional anthropological interpretations (cf. Clifford, 1988; Haraway, 1988; Kondo, 1986; Rosaldo, 1989; Wolf, 1992).

[3] Heritage (1984:4) provides this definition of ethnomethodology, "The term 'ethnomethodology' thus refers to the study of a particular subject matter: the body of common-sense knowledge and the range of procedures and considerations by means of which the ordinary members of society make sense of, find their way about in, and act on the circumstances in which they find themselves."

which the activities of interest typically occur since to remove an activity from its everyday setting is to alter it in fundamental ways (Lave, 1988). It follows, therefore, that there is a strong conviction that field studies form the basis of an ethnographic investigation. Ethnography at its best provides more than detailed description of everyday activities. It focuses an interpretive light on those activities, making visible the lived experience of distant and not–so–distant others.

8.2 Ethnography and HCI

Attempts to adapt ethnography to the goals of HCI began in the 1980s and were motivated by three emerging realizations. First there was a developing awareness that the narrow focus on isolated individuals using computational artifacts was inadequate; to understand human–machine interactions one had to look at the socially situated nature of those interactions (e.g. Blomberg, 1988b; Suchman 1983a, 1983b; and more recently Heath and Luff, 1991; Luff and Heath, 1993; Jordan, in press; Whalen, in press). Second there was an emerging consensus that human intelligence was socially constituted and achieved, and as such could not simply be recreated in a computational device (Dreyfus, 1979; Suchman, 1987). At the same time it was proving extremely difficult to bring the social world into some relation with computational artifacts that attempted to embody human intelligence. Third there was a growing interest in developing computer technologies that acknowledged and supported the cooperative[4] nature of human activity (Bowers and Benford, 1991; Greif 1988; Grudin, 1990c). It was thought by some that ethnography could provide the intellectual and analytical power needed to develop broader, sociologically informed views on the relation between humans and computers.

Prior to this time most studies of human–machine interaction consisted of experimental or laboratory assessments of individual performance on isolated tasks, analysis of the adequacy of selected user interface features, and comparisons between different user interface strategies. While these studies generated valuable information (e.g. the limits of individual performance capabilities, differences between novice and skilled users, trade–offs among specific user interface choices), they were ill–equipped to provide

---

[4] Cooperative here does not necessary imply non–problematic or without conflict.

insights on the everyday experience of using (interacting with) new technologies. Experimental or laboratory studies attempt to control for environmental differences and to eliminate "extraneous" variables in favor of better assessing quantitatively a small number of specific variables. However, the laboratory isn't the real world; few if any of the social resources typically available to users are present in the laboratory setting (Blomberg, 1988b; Lave, 1988). For example, Blomberg (1988b) found that users experiencing difficulties with an unfamiliar photocopier often consulted co–workers known to be more knowledgeable about the operation of the machine before they referred to available documentation. In laboratory studies the tasks given to users are highly constrained and must be accomplished within artificially short time frames so that quantitative measurements can be obtained. Because of these inherent limitations, laboratory studies by themselves were unable to extend our understanding of how the larger social environment of machine use shapes the experiences individuals have with new technologies (Chapter 4 makes some related points).

Dissatisfied with the existing research paradigms, HCI researchers and professionals began to look for other approaches that could provide a broader view on the human–machine experience. Wixon, Holtzblatt and Knox, (1990, p. 330) comment, "The questions faced are not adequately addressed by quantitative models predicting how fast subjects can perform benchmark tasks or the decrease in error rates from method A to method B. The HCI professionals often need to develop new, non–traditional techniques that yield an *understanding* of real customers solving real problems in the real world." The argument being made was that deeper understandings of existing work practices would result in the design of systems better suited to the needs of their users. Likewise, "It has been suggested that user acceptance would be increased if problem formulation, design, and system–building were informed by reliable information about the needs and desires of potential users, as well as the setting in which systems are intended to be used" (Forsythe, 1992, p. 505). Ethnography was viewed as a way of gaining insights into the nature of human activity that could provide the grounds for the design of new technologies.

Explorations of the relation between ethnography and system design have developed in three general directions: (1) studies of *work*, (2) studies of particular *technologies* in use and (3) participatory/work–oriented *design*. Although researchers, as well as specific projects may address concerns relevant to each of these general areas of research, projects often can be differentiated by their emphasis on organization of work site activities, *particular* technologies in use, or the design of new technologies.

8.2.1 Studies of work

A number of projects initiated in the 1980s and continuing today have the goal of providing a deeper understanding of work in settings where new technologies might one day be used (Anderson, Hughes and Sharrock, 1989; Brun–Cottan et al., 1991; Forsythe, 1992; Forsythe and Buchanan, 1991; Filippi and Theureau, 1993; Goodwin and Goodwin, in press; Harper, Hughes and Shapiro, 1991; Heath, Jirotka, Luff and Hindmarsh, 1993; Hughes, Randall and Shapiro, 1992; Orr, 1990; Orr and Crowfoot, 1992; Suchman, 1993; Whalen, 1993, Rouncefield, Hughes, Rodden and Viller, 1994). Their focus is on explicating how work is accomplished in varied and complex settings. While these studies differ with respect to how closely coupled they are with specific design agendas, they initially proceed relatively unencumbered with the problems of design. Consider, for example, a study of air traffic controllers (Harper, Hughes and Shapiro, 1991). This study was initiated without a specific design agenda but later laid the groundwork for a series of design oriented projects (Hughes, Randall and Shapiro, 1992; Bentley, 1992). These subsequent projects, while taking up the problem of design, viewed the design component as somewhat separate from the challenges of representing and interpreting the work of air traffic controllers. Hughes, Randall and Shapiro, (1993, p. 130) describe the relationship that obtained between system designers and ethnographers in their study of air traffic controllers; "While both sides (ethnographers and system designers) agreed that an effective strip display[5] system would have to resonate effectively with existing work practices, it was the task of the ethnographic study to specify what these were *without any presumptions about how they could or could not be supported by any subsequent computer support system*" (italics added). In this case the ethnographers' task was to "elaborate and explicate" relevant practices, setting aside for the moment how such revelations might contribute to system design.

The Workplace Project (Brun–Cottan et al., 1991; Suchman, 1993) also focused primarily on developing understanding of work in

---

[5] A strip display is an electronic representation of a flight strip which "is used to represent the passage of an aircraft through controlled airspace" (Hughes, Randall and Shapiro, 1993:128).

context. This ethnographic study of ground operations at an airport had as its primary objective explicating the relations between work and technology in a multi–activity, technology–intensive work setting. While this three–year study had no explicit design agenda (i.e. no technologies were being designed specifically in relation to its findings) the study has provided important insights about the spatio–temporal coordination of activities, the prevalence of indigenous innovation, and the ways heterogeneous technologies are assembled into working systems that have influenced technology design efforts (Weiser, 1993). In another case, an ethnographic study of the practices of doctors and patients in clinical settings that offer migraine diagnosis and treatment is helping to inform the design of "expert systems" that provide patients with information about their condition and its possible treatments (Forsythe, 1992). At the same time this study is identifying contradictions in some of the underlying assumptions upon which "expert system" development often is grounded.

8.2.2 Studies of technology in use

Ethnography has also been applied to develop understandings of the situated use of *particular* technologies or classes of technologies (Blomberg, 1987, 1988a; Heath and Luff, 1993; Nardi and Miller, 1990, 1991; Nardi and Zarner, 1991; Gantt and Nardi, 1992; Nardi, 1993; Whalen, in press). Some of these studies are directed at evaluating existing technologies to improve upon their design. For example, Nardi and colleagues (cited above) have studied the use of spreadsheet software and CAD systems as a means of designing more successful end user programming systems. End users of both spreadsheets and CAD systems are able to customize and extend system capabilities. Their view is that a better understanding of the everyday practices of people using these customizable systems contributes to the design of innovative end user programming languages and environments that allow individuals with detailed task–specific knowledge to design and build their own applications. Their work also highlights the importance of collaborative work practices in supporting end users who attempt to design new or extend existing applications.

In another example, Blomberg (cited above) studied the introduction of a computer–based design tool, Trillium, into the user interface design community of a technology development company. This study showed that a reciprocal relationship obtained between the technology and the settings of its use; not only were the working relations adjusting to the introduction of this new technology, but the technology was being shaped by the requirements of its use (see Mackay, 1990 for a similar observation). For example, pressures to modify Trillium developed in different directions within two design groups that adopted Trillium. These differences were the result of the levels of computer expertise represented within the design teams as well as the relation of the Trillium–generated code to the code that was to control the user interface on the final product. In a related way the organization of the work differed markedly in the two design groups as a result of the distribution of design and computer skills within the groups and the demands of the larger product development teams. The overall findings of this study, that "design" continues after a system is introduced and that working systems include not only the hardware and software but also the organization of social resources, have implications for the design of computer tools to support the varied and dynamic practices of user interface designers. The study also raises design issues related to questions about the ease with which end users should be able to modify a technology and about the emergence of specialists to moderate between work practitioners and computer systems.

8.2.3 Participatory/work–oriented design

Participatory/work–oriented design approaches hold that design should proceed with the active involvement of those who will use and be affected by a new technology. Participatory approaches developed in Scandinavia where there was a concurrent emphasis on workplace democracy, quality of working life, and skill preservation (Ehn, 1988; Floyd et al., 1989; Greenbaum and Kyng, 1991; Muller and Kuhn, 1993; Schuler and Namioka, 1993). For many working in this area, the focus is on *designing* systems wherein an understanding of the working practices of end users may emerge as a result of extended interactions between designers and work practitioners, but is not a goal of the project. While ethnography is not explicitly employed in many participatory design projects, designers often observe and participate in the working lives of the intended users much as they would if they were involved in an ethnographic study. If, however, as some rightly argue (Anderson, 1994), ethnography is more than the application of a set of field methods in that it assumes an explicit analytical and interpretive relation to its subject matter, then perhaps it is misleading to characterize these design projects as ethnographically informed.

Recently, however, some practitioners of participatory design have explicitly incorporated "work analysis" based on field investigations into their design projects (Mogenson, 1994; Bodker et al., 1993; Simonsen and Kensing, 1994). The AT project was initiated to explore how organizational change in the Danish national labour service might be supported through technology and to investigate the possibilities for tailoring software systems to meet local conditions within the labor service. The project adopted ethnographic methods (e.g. interviews and participant observation) to help in "understand(ing) the work at a theoretical level" (Bodker et al., 1993, p. 9). The field study and work analysis aspects of the project also proved useful in developing the real life working "situations", including a description of the work organization, the professional roles represented at the work site, and realistic problem situations. These characterizations of the work site provided the basis for the Organizational Game (Ehn, Molleryd and Sjogren, 1990) activity where work site participants participated in discussions about realistic problem situations they might encounter at work. The Organizational Game activity was used to stimulate discussions about current work circumstances and possible future work scenarios.

Others, not as closely tied to participatory design approaches as they developed in Scandinavia but sympathetic to many of their underlying concerns, view the iterative development of an understanding of the work to be an integral part of their overall project (Blomberg, Suchman and Trigg, 1994). This interest in and commitment to abstracting insights about the work and its relation to the designed artifacts from particular sites of work activity may be related to the type of technologies under development. For example, when designing generic products or the underlying technologies that make up the components of working systems (as opposed to custom systems crafted for particular work settings), the ability to translate and transfer the lessons of particular site–specific designs to a wider range of products and work settings becomes important. In such contexts the design effort continues after a site–specific system has been developed. For example, the Work–Oriented Design project (Blomberg, Suchman and Trigg, 1994) focused on designing user applications, while at the same time developing ethnographically–informed representations of the work that could be used in subsequent product–focused design deliberations. This project will be discussed at greater length later in this chapter.

8.2.4 Aligning ethnography and design

One of the major challenges confronting those who believe ethnography has something to offer system design is how to bring descriptions and analysis of work practices to bear on the design of new technologies. The movement from ethnographic study to design is complex, presenting no simple relation between the findings of an ethnographic study and design specifications. The studies cited here have approached this challenge in a variety of ways. Brun–Cottan et al. (1987), Suchman (1993) and Blomberg (1987, 1988a) rely on designers to take from the studies those lessons they believe useful to their design concerns. Bentley et al. (1992) see the ethnographer as a bridge between the work domain and the system design domain, wherein the ethnographer acts as a stand in for the work practitioner in design deliberations. As justification for this view, they cite the difficulty of finding opportunities for users to participate in all phases of the design. Hughes, Randall and Shapiro, (1993, p. 134) describes the process as a dialogic one wherein the fieldworker is "interrogated" by the designers on the team. Nardi (1993, p. 6) and her colleagues argue that empirical studies "create an atmosphere in which the actual experiences of users become a part of the discourse of design."

Recently, Shapiro (1994) has asserted that ethnographers of work only reluctantly include a discussion of design implications because of the view that design implications are outside the realm of what can justifiably be said based on the observations made in the study. He argues for "hybrid forms" of inter–disciplinary work for design that would allow social scientists to step outside the restrictive boundaries of particular academic disciplines (including various forms of ethnography) and embrace more fully the problems of design.

For others, in particular those working in the participatory design tradition, the problem is not formulated as one of abstracting from studies of work those insights that might inform design. Ethnographic methods join other techniques such as future workshops,[6] organizational games and cooperative prototyping to create a context for design. The field investigations are not viewed as separate from other design activities; designers, social scientists,

---

[6] The future workshops method was developed to support groups in influencing decision making in planning processes (Jungk and Mullert, 1981). It has been employed by researchers working in the participatory design tradition to support the process of organizational and technological change.

and even the workers themselves, may take part in "work analysis". However, for all, "... design requires sites (times, places and artifacts) through which shared understandings of work can be constructed across multiple perspectives" (Suchman, 1994a, p. 2).

8.2.5 Representations of work

Creating the context in which design can proceed in relation to specific work settings requires having available ways of representing emerging understanding of the work and their relation to the designed artifacts.[7] Textual accounts, typical of ethnographic research, by themselves often are inadequate for communicating the dynamics of the work setting to system designers. Some find it useful to supplement textual accounts with collected segments of videotape showing work site participants talking about their work, engaged in a work activity, or using mock–ups or prototypes (Brun–Cottan et al., 1991, Blomberg, Suchman and Trigg, 1994; Suchman and Trigg, 1991). Others are experimenting with enhancing traditional storyboarding techniques to incorporate photographs depicting people engaged in the represented work. In this way the storyboards connect back to the actual people who do the work and settings in which it is done (Swenton–Wall and Mosher, 1994). Still others take the position that understanding of the work is embedded in the designed artifacts (e.g. mock–ups, prototypes) and that these artifacts can aid in the construction of shared understanding of the work (Kyng, 1994).

8.3 The Work–Oriented Design project

A recent example of how ethnographic methods have contributed to system design is the Work–Oriented Design project (conducted by the author, Lucy Suchman and Randy Trigg) initiated to explore the possibility of bringing site–specific studies of work into a productive relation with technology design. The project originated within a research organization of a large American corporation where new technologies to bridge between paper and electronic domains were under development. The effort began as a collaboration between researchers, product developers, and work site participants. One of

---

[7] For an extended discussion of techniques for representing work see Suchman (1994).

the goals of the project was to design applications for a set of emerging image processing technologies (e.g. electronic forms processing, handprint recognition, extraction of circled text, and OCR). While focusing on specific technology objectives is not necessarily characteristic of projects where design and studies of work are interleaved, the desire to connect the project to product development efforts elsewhere in the corporation and the necessity of enlisting the participation of system designers inside the research organization encouraged pursuit of particular technology directions.[8] The general approach employed in the Work–Oriented Design project to link field studies of work and design involved cycling between field studies, design, and user experience with mock–ups and prototypes of new technologies (Blomberg, Giacomi, Mosher and Swenton–Wall, 1993; Blomberg et al., 1994).

The work site for this project was a large law firm in the Silicon Valley of California employing over 200 attorneys and 300 support staff, specializing in both corporate law and litigation. This site was selected because of the mix of technologies (copiers, printers, fax machines, PCs, etc.) currently in use, the firm's continuing orientation to paper albeit in an increasingly computerized environment, and the variety of documents and document–related practices at the firm. The firm's interest in participating in this project, as well as its proximity to the research centre, also influenced the selection. While one of the goals of the project was to design and prototype end user applications, no commitment was made to the firm to deliver a fully functioning system for use; work site participants simply were offered an opportunity to reflect with us on their current work practices, to preview innovative technology directions, and to help shape future products.

Fieldwork began with interviews and guided tours of the firm's operations in which we acquired a general overview of the organization of work and an outline of document–related activities. During this initial period of fieldwork we became aware of a collection of activities around which much of the work in litigation was organized.[9] These activities of "document production" centre

---

[8] It would have been difficult, for example, to get research participation in a project to extend the functionality of commercially available software even if work site participants viewed this as a significant advance.

[9] While the Work-Oriented Design project pursued design activities on both the corporate and litigation sides of the practice, only our efforts in litigation are described here. Blomberg, Suchman and Trigg, (1994) and Rao et al. (1994) describe the work undertaken on the corporate side of the practice.

around processing documents (often numbering in the thousands) that are taken from a client's files and used to support arguments in the case. Document production proceeds, in part, because of the legal requirement that relevant documents (e.g. those "responsive" to the case) be made available to the opposing side. Document production requires that junior attorneys review the entire corpus of documents to determine which documents must be turned over. Document production workers assign to each page of every document a unique identification number (Bates number) which is later used in locating specific documents. To facilitate identification and retrieval of relevant documents from among the thousands typical of large cases, an on–line index to the paper documents is created. The index consists of information about each document that is entered into a database. The work of creating the on–line index is carried out by litigation support workers.

Based on early conversations with attorneys at the firm we thought the image processing technologies we were developing might be able to support certain aspects of the document production activity, in particular the creation of the electronic index. However, to this point we had not directly encountered the work of creating the on–line index. From the perspective of the attorneys, the work of creating the on–line index involves "subjective" and "objective" coding of documents; junior attorneys would quickly go through the document corpus to ascertain to which issues of the case each document pertained (subjective coding), and litigation support workers would code each document for such information as the date, author, recipient and document type (objective coding). Early in our fieldwork one attorney described the work this way:

> "You have, you know, 300 cartons of documents and you tear through them and say, I'm going to put Post–its on the ones we have to turn over. And then, ideally, you hire chimpanzees to type in *From, To, Date*. And then, ideally, you then have lawyers go through it again and read each document, with their brains turned on."

During a later meeting in which we introduced attorneys to the capabilities of the image processing technologies we had another opportunity to discover how the attorneys viewed the document coding operation.[10]   This time, however, the remarks were in relation to how our technologies might be able to automate the coding process. An attorney remarked:

> "If this works, it could save us just a fortune. I'm now negotiating for offshore data entry in the Philippines, because it's cheaper. In which we send things DHL. They do the objective coding, 40 cents to 80 cents a page. No thought, just author, recipient. And if you could have, not even paralegals, sort of, you could hire 9 year–olds to sit there, or just train the program, after *To* that was the recipient, *From* was the author, and *Re* was the subject, and *Date* was date. Feed that just stuff the thing in the scanner and shoot it through, and then to make sure it worked, do it again, and then compare the two. You could save me millions."

From the point of view of this attorney the work of objective coding was routine work that required little thought and, as such, was a perfect candidate for automation, possibly by means of our technology. This proposal that we participate in designing a technology that automated the work of objective coding was not only ethically troubling to us (Blomberg, 1994; Blomberg et al., 1994), but was based on the attorneys' very limited and distant view of the work.[11] It was clear that if we were to develop an application to support the work of objective coding, we would need to involve the document coders directly and learn a great deal more about their work. At that point we began to focus our fieldwork on the document coding practices, first by interviewing the supervisor of litigation support (where the coding was actually done), and later by observing the work of document coders and data entry workers.

In an interview, the supervisor of litigation support told us that the attorneys had a limited and inaccurate view of the work of document coding due in large measure to their lack of familiarity with the demands of the work. As she put it:

---

[10] Because the Work-Oriented Design project was committed to involving members of the law firm directly in application design, we held a series of review meetings where the technologies under development were described.

[11] As evidence for attorneys' lack of familiarity with the coding operation, attorneys gave us conflicting responses when we asked where the coding was actually done.

"The attorneys need to understand what the process of getting a document from hardcopy to abstract is because on the one hand they think it's a very streamlined, easy process and when I tell them that no I can't create a two hundred page database in 30 days they don't understand why. They get very frustrated. They have no idea why that can't happen."

She went on to express a variety of reasons why the attorneys' automation "fantasy" wouldn't work. For example, she mentioned that coding even such mundane information as the date of the document was not always straightforward. A document might have multiple dates; the date it was written, the date it was signed, and the date it was faxed. Deciding which date to code required knowledge of the case and interpretation of a document's content and relevance. Not only would 9 year–olds be unable to perform this work, but it would be highly unlikely that knowledge of the case and of a document's content could be embedded in a technology to allow coding to proceed without human intervention.

Later when we observed document coders at work, we saw them reading the documents to arrive at judgments about how best to code them. Because documents, not individual pages, are coded, the first challenge facing the coders is determining a document's boundaries. Coders are simply presented with boxes of "paper". The paper clips that sometimes joined pages together can not be assumed to hold a single document. Deciding to code the pages joined together as single documents, multiple documents, or a single document with multiple attachments might require reading the text. Once having determined a document's boundaries, coders could begin to code for the date, author, document description, document type and so on.

It became apparent from our discussions with the supervisor and our observations of the work that the attorneys' suggestion of a simple mapping between the work of document coding and our image processing technologies (i.e. "train the program" to do the work of the document coders) was unrealistic. However, we went on to explore possible ways that the technologies we were developing might help to reduce tedious aspects of the work of document coding, while at the same time supporting coders as they made informed judgments. We continued to inform our understanding of the work of document coding through discussions and observation and began working with the supervisor and her staff to develop prototype applications to support their work.

Specifically, we initiated discussions about the relation of our technologies to their work, sketched out possible application designs, and demonstrated early mock–ups and prototypes of the application.

During this period, the supervisor and her staff were experimenting with their own alternative strategies for creating the on–line index. When we first encountered the work, the coding was done using paper forms. Document coders transcribed relevant information from the document onto the form. The form was then given to data entry workers who keyed the information into an on–line database. Quality control workers later checked the database entries against the form, occasionally consulting the original document to resolve problems. Later there was an experiment to code directly on the documents, eliminating the paper forms altogether. In this case coders used highlight marking pens to specify relevant text found on the document (e.g. dates, names, Bates numbers). Information not directly available as text on the document (e.g. document type, document source) was written on the document along with instructions to data entry workers. The data entry workers then worked from the marked–up document instead of the form, and quality control workers checked the database entries against the marked up document. For a variety of reasons (e.g. the cost of producing photocopies that could be marked on, difficulty locating information on the marked–up document), they later returned to using forms. At the time of this writing experiments are underway to code directly on–line, merging the document coding and data entry operations.

It was in this context of *in situ* experimentation that we undertook our application design effort. Recognizing both the need of litigation support workers to adapt to changing local conditions and their inclination to extend current practices, the prototype application we developed provides flexible support for the coding and data entry. Using our application, information can be coded on machine readable paper forms, the document pages, or directly on–line. Once the paper form and/or the document are marked–up they are scanned into the system where our image processing software interprets the marks. Information on the form that can be automatically abstracted shows up as filled–in fields on an electronic form. Information that was circled on the document is collected together and presented to the user as a composite image on the screen. Users then paste the OCRd text into appropriate fields on the electronic form. Images of the form and document pages can also be viewed on–line allowing litigation support workers to check the accuracy of the handprint recognition and OCR. Because the document image is viewable and editable, coding may be done completely on–line.

The prototype provides flexibility by allowing users to code information either on the machine readable paper form or on the document itself. Our observations indicate that characteristics of the task and document type influence where information is most efficiently coded. For example, the designation of document type (e.g. agreement, letter, financial statement, etc.) may be more easily indicated on a form that provides a somewhat fixed range of document types to choose from. On the other hand, in–text coding of proper names (where the set of names appearing in the documents grows as the documents are coded) may be more easily indicated by circling the names as they appear on the document. Additionally, document types that are similar in format and length (e.g. memos) may be more efficiently coded by marking on the document directly since the location of specific information (date, author, subject) does not vary significantly from one document to the next. Conversely document types that vary greatly in format and length may be more efficiently coded using a paper form where information located throughout a document can be gathered onto a single page facilitating data entry and quality control. The prototype also allows coding to be done prior to scanning (on the paper form and/or document) or after scanning (on the on–line electronic image of the document).

Because of our recognition that a great deal of judgment is exercised by document coders, the design did not attempt to automate the coding process. Instead, the idea was to minimize the need to directly transcribe (copy by hand) information from the document to the paper form and to maximize the ease with which the database could be checked for accuracy. While the prototype did not include a facility for allowing litigation support workers to design and modify the machine readable forms, we recognized the need for such a capability given how variable individual cases were.

This example shows how ethnography can help shape a design by making visible aspects of the work that might otherwise go unrecognized. Had we relied on the attorneys' characterizations of the work of document coding we would have failed to appreciate the informed judgment required to accomplish this work. At the same time if we had not observed the evolution of the work over some weeks, we might have believed that the document coding practices were more uniform and fixed than was the case. Importantly, we were able to appreciate that any system we developed would need to flexibly respond to the evolving demands of the work and the interest of the litigation support workers to experiment with their work processes in an effort to increase efficiency and improve their product.

8.4 Main features of the Work–Oriented Design project

The Work–Oriented Design project is one example of how ethnography can be linked to the design of new technologies. This project began with the presupposition that the insights gained from field studies of work can have their greatest impact on technology design if the design occurs concurrently and in relation to the field studies, and the work site participants cooperate directly in design deliberations and have an opportunity use the emergent technology. Not all attempts to link ethnography and design have required that the field studies be so directly tied to design or that work site participants be included in design considerations, but they all share the perspective that a detailed understanding of peoples' everyday experiences can provide useful insights for the design of new technologies.

8.4.1 Interleaving field studies and design

Interleaving field studies and design requires that early accounts of work activities and early design concepts be viewed as tentative. While early designs will be based on partial understandings of the work, opportunities to revise these early characterizations arise as the project moves between field studies and design. Design interventions can contribute to the fieldwork by helping reveal aspects of the work previously not well understood. New insights into the work may come to light as workers use, or imagine using, mock–ups or prototypes based on early understanding of the work.[12] Likewise early design concepts, when viewed as open to revision, are more easily shaped by the everyday realities of the workplace. Early designs are measured by their ability to stimulate discussion

---

12 Ehn and Kyng (1991) present a detailed discussion of the value of mock-ups and prototypes in cooperative design. See also Kyng (1991), Mogensen and Trigg (1992), Mogenson (1994).

about the work and its relation to the technologies under
development.

8.4.2 Gaining access to the details of specific work practices

A starting premise of ethnographically–informed design projects is
that looking in detail at how people work can provide a basis for
innovative, well–integrated design. To acquire a detailed view of
the everyday requirements of specific work activities requires going
beyond traditional methods of organizational research (e.g. surveys
and focus groups) to engage the people who actually do the work in
the setting in which it is done. This means observing work as it
unfolds, talking with workers as they go about their work, and
enlisting workers in design deliberations.

As demonstrated in the above example, people who have only a
distant relation to the work are unqualified to provide accurate
descriptions of it. The attorneys' view of the work of document
coding failed to acknowledge the nature and extent of the judgment
being exercised by the coders. Only after talking with the coders and
observing them at work did we begin to understand what was
involved in creating the on–line index. Because aspects of the work
that are most central to its accomplishment often are so routine as to
be unremarkable even by the people who actually do the work, talk
about the work must be coupled with direct observations of the
work.

8.4.3 Video analysis

Video records of people working, talking about their work, and using
prototype technologies are viewed as a valuable resource in later
analysis and reflection (Suchman and Trigg 1991; Jordan and
Henderson, in press), and in communicating with project members
unable to participate in fieldwork or those working on related design
and product development efforts.

8.4.4 Case–based prototyping

The Work–Oriented Design Project recognized the value of actual
case examples of everyday practice as an aid to design. Prototypes
developed in relation to actual cases make it possible for users to
assess the design with respect to their everyday work. Case–based
prototypes also can "trigger" discussions that might not occur in the

absence of an artifact that partially embodies the imagined new work practice.[13] More generally, the level of commitment to and investment in using a prototype seems to depend on a strong relation between the prototype and the participants' everyday work activities, manifest, in part, by the incorporation of materials from the work site. The ability to assess the value of an application design and of the underlying technologies depends on creating a situation where the prototype can be used to accomplish tasks that originate from participants' own work requirements. In the case of the document coding application, the machine readable forms retained many of the characteristics of forms already in use at the law firm, while at the same time adding new capabilities, and the documents used to demonstrate the prototype came from an actual case being litigated at the time of our project.

8.4.5 Continuing design

Indigenous innovation[14] and continuing design in use characterize most workplaces. After design professionals have left the scene, the ongoing process of adapting technologies to the changing requirements and day–to–day contingencies of the work persists. Technology integration is an integral and sustaining aspect of successful technology utilization and must be supported by the way technologies are designed and in the provisions made for their continuing development (Bjerknes, Bratteteig and Epeseth, 1991).

8.4.6 Comparative generalizations

Extracting from specific design projects those lessons and insights about the work and its relation to the designed technology that might be relevant to other related design efforts increases the potential impact of a specific project. In this sense there is a recognition that design, grounded in the realities of a specific work setting, can be useful for design deliberations that are removed in time and space from the original site. However, having opportunities and representational vehicles through which the

---

[13]The notion of case-based prototypes as triggers for discussion and mutual learning is developed in the writings of Trigg, Bodker and Gronbacek, (1991), Mogensen and Trigg (1992) and Mogensen (1992).

[14] Indigenous innovation is change that is initiated from within the work group and not dictated from the top of the organization or brought in from the outside.

original work practices and design context can have a continuing presence in future deliberations is as challenging as it is critical.

8.5 Ethnography and conversation analysis: complementary approaches

Chapter 9 discusses the application of conversation analysis to understanding the relation between talk, visual conduct and the use of computer systems. The insights that are gained from such analyses have direct bearing on how computer use is conceptualized and on the computer systems that are designed. Conversation analysis and ethnography can be viewed as complementary approaches. Conversation analysis sometimes occurs as part of an ethnography wherein activities identified as central to the concerns of the ethnographic study are analysed using the techniques of conversation analysis. The fine–grained analysis of audio and video recordings characteristic of conversation analysis are indispensable for revealing aspects of human action and interaction not discernible using the observational techniques of ethnography alone.

The results of an ethnographic study also may assist in interpreting the isolated interactions which are the focus of a conversation analysis. While there are those who assert that a conversational analysis should and need only make reference to what is actually hearable or observable on an audio or video recording, others underscore the importance of knowledge of the larger social context in which the interaction being analysed occurs. Some argue that lacking context it is impossible to fully appreciate and give meaning to the isolated interactions of a conversation analysis.

In considering the relation of ethnography and conversation analysis to system design it is important to note that particular design issues may be more productively addressed using one or the other of these approaches. For example, the design of the behaviour of a user interface (e.g. sequencing of messages in response to user actions, menu design) might be aided by a conversational analysis of the actual use of related or prototype systems (see Chapter 9 for an extended example of such a study). On the other hand an ethnographic study of the organization of work at a particular site might be useful in informing how system capabilities (OCR, forms processing, full text retrieval, etc.) could be combined and integrated into a system that supported the described work practices (the

Work–Oriented Design project discussed above is an example). In addition, the prototype designed for the litigation support workers described above could benefit from a detailed conversation analysis of its use in the context of the everyday activities of document coding.

8.6 Future directions

The promise of integrating and aligning technology design and field studies of work is yet to be fully realized. Ethnographically–based design projects, still few in number and primarily exploratory in nature, are just beginning to provide concrete examples of the value of bringing knowledge about specific work practices into a close relation to the designed artifacts, and of the requirements for creating an environment wherein the worlds of design and work analysis can come together.

A future challenge will be developing ways of moving from specific sites of ethnographically–based design to the design and development of generic products. The difficulty is not only that the requirements placed on a technology vary across the settings of its use, but that multiple voices, many not typically represented in work–oriented design projects, will shape the final product (e.g. product strategy, marketing, sales, service, product integration). What emerges from a cooperative design project may in the end bear little resemblance to the product that reaches the marketplace (Anderson and Crocca 1992). It will be necessary to find ways of including a wider range of perspectives (and participants) in these design projects if we expect the resulting products to reflect design concerns that originate from sites of intended use.

The issue of how ethnographically–informed design projects scale to larger projects that take place over years and that involve many, geographically distributed, people also needs to be addressed. For example, are there times in the overall development effort when a close relation to end–user sites would be most productive? Are there specific aspects of the development effort where such a relation is more critical (e.g. product concept, user interface development, sales approach)? Are there ways of sustaining a close relation to a work site so that work site participants can be involved in design deliberation at different times in the development process?

Finally, the claim that technologies designed with a closer relation to the potential sites of their use will better meet the needs of their users must be read against the everyday political realities of the workplace. The power work site participants actually have in shaping their work situation (including the technologies they use) is usually limited (Blomberg, 1994; Schuler, 1994; Suchman, 1994b). Work–oriented designers may find themselves implicated in power struggles over (re)specification of the work and participating in an agenda of job elimination in the name of increased productivity. Achieving the goals of ethnographically–informed design often requires confronting unequal distributions of power within the workplace and multiple, conflicting visions of the future.

Acknowledgments

I would like to thank Lucy Suchman and Randy Trigg for their many contributions to the development of ideas presented in this chapter and the work upon which it is based. They, along with Richard Hughes, read and commented on an earlier version which helped to clarify and refine some of the arguments herein.

Further reading

Blomberg, J. et al. (1993). Ethnographic field methods and their relation to design. In D. Schuler and A. Namioka (eds), *Participatory design: Principles and Practices*, pp. 123-155. Hillsdale, NJ: Lawrence Erlabaum Associates

Jordan, B. (in press). Ethnographic workplace studies and computer supported cooperative work. In D. Shapiro, M. Tauber and R. Traunmueller (eds), *The design of computer–supported cooperative work and groupware systems*. North Holland, The Netherlands: Elsevier Science.

These articles describe field methods and analytical strategies used in ethnographic studies of work and organizations. They also discuss how ethnographic techniques can be productively applied to problems in system design.

Bentley, R. et al. (1992). Ethnographically–informed system design for air traffic control. In J. Turner and R. Kraut (eds), *Proceedings of CSCW '92*, pp. 123-129. NY: ACM.

Hughes, J. et al. (1992). Faltering from ethnography to design. In *Proceedings of CSCW '92*, pp. 115-122. NY: ACM.

These articles provide further examples of the potential of ethnographic studies to inform system design. Included is a discussion of the problems and challenges faced by those attempting to bridge between ethnography and design.

Nardi, B. (1993). *A small matter of programming: Perspectives on end user computing.* Cambridge,MA: MIT Press.

This book documents how field studies of the use of end user applications (e.g. spreadsheets, CAD systems) have provided important insights into the requirements on systems that hope to support the ability of their users to customize and extend them. The argument for moving beyond a narrow focus on individual cognition to consider the collaborative work practices of end users is convincingly made.

Shapiro, D. (1994). The limits of ethnography: Combining social sciences for CSCW. In *Proceedings of CSCW '94.* NY: ACM.

This article argues for the value of "hybrid forms" of social science research which the author believes have the greatest chance of contributing to the design and development of computer systems. At the same time he argues that efforts to develop these hybrid forms will result in advances in the core disciplines (e.g. ethnography, cognitive science, activity theory).

Chapter 9

Conversation Analysis: human–computer interaction and the general practice consultation

David Greatbatch, Christian Heath, Paul Luff and Peter Campion

9.1 Introduction

In recent years, we have witnessed a growing diversity of research concerned with the 'interaction' between individuals and computers. In part, this interest has been driven by rapid technological change and a growing concern with the cooperative and organizational implications of complex systems. It has also however, been informed by the burgeoning critique of more traditional approaches to human–computer interaction. A number of the critiques of these approaches to HCI have focused on the inappropriateness of using metaphors drawn from computer systems to conceptualise thought and action (see, for example, Button, 1990). More generally they have delineated the shortcomings of goal–oriented and plan based models of human conduct which underlie a number of conventional psychologistic and cognitive approaches to system use (cf. Dreyfus, 1992; Coulter, 1979, 1989; Winograd and Flores, 1986; Lave, 1988; Still and Costall, 1991). As Suchman (1987) and others have cogently demonstrated, such debates have profound implications for our conception of the cognitive and the ways in which we can fruitfully investigate the 'interaction' between individuals and computers.

In this chapter, we will illustrate one way in which Conversation Analysis might be used to explore human–computer interaction. The illustration is drawn from our current study of the introduction of computerized information systems into primary health care and, in particular, into the general practice consultation. The study is primarily concerned with the impact of the technology on professional practice and interpersonal communication. The aim of the chapter is to show how Conversation Analysis may contribute to our understanding of the "interaction" between individuals and computer systems.

Link. → | Conversation Analysis emerged about thirty years ago as part of a broader research initiative known as Ethnomethodology. Ethnomethodology developed from studies undertaken by Harold Garfinkel (1967) from the 1950s onwards. He developed a radically distinct approach to the study of social action; an approach which places the situated and interpretative character of human conduct at the forefront of the methodological agenda and which is concerned with discovering the social organization underlying the production and intelligibility of ordinary, everyday social actions and activities.

The pioneering research of Harvey Sacks and his colleagues, Emanuel Schegloff and Gail Jefferson, has directed some ethnomethodological studies towards a concern with language use and social interaction. It was recognized that the analysis of social interaction, in particular talk–in–interaction, provided the possibility of developing a "naturalistic observation discipline which could deal with the details of social action(s) rigorously, empirically, and formally" (Schegloff and Sacks, 1974, p. 233). These early beginnings have inspired a substantial body of empirical studies which have explicated the systematics underlying a wide variety of social activities not only within conversation but also within a range of organizational settings (see, for example, Atkinson and Heritage, 1984; Button and Lee, 1986; Conein, de Fornel and Quere, 1989; Boden and Zimmerman, 1991; Drew and Heritage, 1992). In a recent bibliography Coulter (1990) includes more than 1400 citations to Conversation Analytic and Ethnomethodological studies .

In the following we will begin by briefly discussing some ways in which Conversation Analysis has been used to explore HCI and then proceed to introduce one or two methodological considerations. Following this introduction, we will draw on our current study of the medical consultation to illustrate the ways in which Conversation Analysis might be used to examine human–computer interaction. The paper will conclude by discussing some of the more general implications of Conversation Analysis for design and HCI.

9.2 Conversation Analysis and HCI

A substantial body of research has drawn on the findings and conceptual distinctions developed within Conversation Analysis to characterize human–computer interaction, and in some cases this research has been incorporated into the design of complex systems. For example, research in Conversation Analysis on the production and coordination of turns of talk in conversation (Sacks, Schegloff and Jefferson, 1974) has been used to characterise human–computer interaction (cf. Norman and Thomas, 1990; Thomas, 1990). Similarly others such as Frohlich, Monk and Drew (forthcoming) and Raudaskoski (1990) have drawn from work in Conversation Analysis concerned with the ways in which speakers locate and repair problems in "hearing, speaking and understanding", to examine the errors and difficulties which emerge in human–computer interaction. The studies have led these researchers to conclude that conversational practices may provide an important resource for the design of complex systems and in particular the forms of interaction between the user and the computer.

Such research has made an important contribution to our understanding of human–computer interaction and, in common with a number important critiques of HCI and Artificial Intelligence, such as Dreyfus (1992), Suchman (1987) and Winograd and Flores (1986), have played a significant part in developing alternatives to more traditional approaches to human–computer interaction. However, these attempts to apply Conversation Analysis to the study, and design of human–computer interaction (see for example Gilbert, Woofitt and Fraser, 1990), have been subject to sustained criticism. It has been argued that such research conflates two distinct concepts of rules. In particular, whereas the "interaction" between computers and humans is governed by rules which stipulate a range of options open to the user and the system, in Conversation Analysis rules are treated as resources which speakers may orientate to, utilize or disregard subject only to the fact that they may be held morally accountable for their actions (cf. Button, 1990; Button and Sharrock, forthcoming). As such, it is suggested that the approach and findings of Conversation Analysis cannot be simply transposed to human–computer interaction.

Perhaps the most fruitful, yet methodologically and empirically demanding, use of Conversation Analysis to examine human–computer interaction is found within a body of research characterized as "Work Place Studies". Whilst no means all Work Place Studies are informed by Conversation Analysis or Ethnomethodology (for example, Hughes et al, 1992; Hutchins, 1990; Joseph, forthcoming; Filippi and Theureau, 1993), a growing number of researchers have drawn from Conversation Analysis in order to explicate work, interaction and the use of new technology in complex organizational environments including: Suchman, (1987, forthcoming); Goodwin and Goodwin, (1992); forthcoming); Whalen (1992); Zimmerman (1992); Heath and Luff, (1992, forthcoming, Heath, Jirotka, Juff and Hindmarsh (1993); Greatbatch, Luff, Heath and Campion (1993). These studies cover a broad range of settings, including offices, airport operation rooms, emergency dispatch centres, rapid urban transit control rooms, City trading rooms and primary health care. These researchers have found, that although Conversation Analysis cannot be simply "applied" to the activities in such settings, since those activities are neither conversational nor necessarily accomplished through talk, it provides an important resource with which to explicate the interactional organization of work and technology.

9.3 Methodological considerations

The primary sources of data for these studies are audio and audio–visual recordings of "naturally occurring" interactions. On occasions these recordings are augmented by field observation, though there remains some debate as to whether more traditional ethnographic methods can be incorporated into Conversation Analysis (cf. Hopper 1991). Audio and video recordings have considerable advantages over more conventional forms of data used in the social sciences, such as field notes or the responses to questionnaires. They provide the researcher with access to the richness and complexity of social action, allowing particular events to be repeatedly scrutinized and subjected to detailed inspection. In contrast for example to field notes, they provide raw data to which a range of analytic interests can be applied, unconstrained by the concerns of a particular research study. Moreover, audio and video recordings enable other researchers within the scientific community to evaluate the strength of particular analyses with respect to the original data and thereby provide an important constraint on the quality and rigour of findings. Audio and video recordings give researchers a cheap and reliable technology which provides repeatable access to specific details of real world actions, activities and events; a microscope with which to study human life. As Atkinson and Heritage suggest:

> In sum, the use of recorded data serves as a control on the limitations and fallibilities of intuition and recollection; it exposes the observer to a wide range of interactional materials and circumstances and also provides some guarantee that analytic considerations will not arise as artifacts of intuitive idiosyncrasy, selective attention or recollection, or experimental design (Atkinson and Heritage, 1984, p. 4).

Conversation Analysis, unlike certain forms of linguistics, is not concerned with language *per se*. Rather, its interest in language derives from a recognition that talk is a primary vehicle for the accomplishment of social actions in human society. Its concern is with the social organization of ordinary, naturally occurring, human conduct, and the resources that members of society rely upon for the production and recognition of social activity. It focuses on the socio–interactional organization which underlies the production of talk, and the ways in which turns at talk accomplish specific actions by virtue of their sequential character and design. In contrast to some theories of language use and linguistic analysis (e.g. speech act theory), it is assumed that a turn at talk and the action it accomplishes is inseparable from the context in which it occurs. Thus, Conversation Analysis focuses on the situated organization of talk and involves the detailed inspection of the organization of utterances from within the situation in which they are produced and rendered intelligible. Through these analyses it is able to derive generalisable descriptions of the resources through which specific actions and activities are systematically accomplished.

Although it has a general concern with the situated character of human conduct, Conversation Analysis places rigorous constraints on the way in which talk–in–interaction can be explicated with respect to the "context–at–hand". All too often "context" in the social sciences is treated as a realm of local variables which can be invoked to account for the character of a particular activity. Indeed, even in certain forms of qualitative research, we find concepts such as "frame" being used to characterize (and perhaps determine) patterns of conduct. Context is treated as external to, rather than part and parcel of, social action. By contrast, in Conversation Analysis, the detailed inspection of *in situ* human conduct is concerned with the identification of features of context which are relevant to the participants themselves. Context consists of and is reflexively constituted in and through the participants' actions and activities. Conversation Analysis not only seeks to identify features of the context which are relevant to the participants, but more importantly to explicate the practices and procedures utilized by the participants in the production and intelligibility of social actions and activities in real world situations (see, for example, Sacks, 1964, and Schegloff, 1988, 1991).

In general, talk and aspects of bodily comportment in interaction are organized locally, with each action orientated to the immediately preceding action(s) and activity(ies). While each utterance or action is produced with respect to the immediately preceding action(s), it simultaneously contributes to the framework to which subsequent actions will be addressed. As Heritage (1984) suggests, the conduct of participants in interaction is doubly contextual, both "context shaped and context renewing". In consequence, the character of an action or activity and its organization can only be determined with reference to its location within the local configuration of conduct. Schegloff and Sacks suggest:

> a pervasively relevant issue (for participants) about utterances in conversation is "why
> that now," a question whose [...] analysis may also be relevant to find what "that" is.
> That is to say, some utterances may derive their character as actions entirely from
> placement considerations. (Schegloff and Sacks, 1974, p. 241)

Audio and video recordings provide researchers with a medium through which they can repeatedly inspect social activities in the context of their occurrence. Thus, researchers can begin to chart the character and social organization of these activities, with respect to the orientations of the participants themselves. We can consider an utterance or bodily movement with respect to the circumstances of its production and its significance for subsequent action. By repeated inspection of the data, we can begin to assess how the participants themselves display an understanding of, and act upon, each other's actions and activities. Through this analysis we can slowly begin to develop insights into the socio–interactional organization through which participants produce their own conduct and recognize the actions of co–participants. In other words, the researcher utilizes the sequential character of the participants' conduct as a resource for developing an understanding of the organization of the various actions and activities. By inspecting the ways in which the participants respond to and display an understanding of each other's conduct, the researcher can begin to develop observations which are sensitive to the orientations of the participants themselves. Sacks, Schegloff and Jefferson suggest:

> [It] is a systematic consequence of the turn taking organization of conversation that it
> obliges its participants to display to each other, in a turn's talk, their understanding of
> the other turn's talk. More generally, a turn's talk will be heard as directed to a prior
> turn's talk, unless special techniques are used to locate some other talk to which it is
> directed .... But while understandings of other turns' talk are displayed to co–
> participants, they are available as well to professional analysts, who are thereby
> provided a proof criterion (and a search procedure) for the analysis of what a turn's
> talk is occupied with. Since it is the parties' understandings of prior turns' talk that is
> relevant to their construction of next turns, it is their understandings that are wanted
> for analysis. The display of those understandings in the talk in subsequent turns
> affords a resource for the analysis of prior turns, and a proof procedure for
> professional analyses of prior turns, resources intrinsic to the data themselves (Sacks,
> Schegloff and Jefferson, 1974, p. 728–9).

9.4 An example

Our study of human–computer interaction in the medical consultation has two broad dimensions. On the one hand, it is assessing the impact of computerization on communication between patient and doctor. On the other hand, it is explicating the ways in which human–computer interaction and social interaction may be co–ordinated and shaped by reference to each other.

The data used in the study consist of video recordings of medical consultations, augmented by field observation and discussions with the doctors concerned. Approximately one hundred consultations were recorded before the introduction of the computer system and one hundred and fifty after its introduction. The recordings have been collected at regular intervals so that we can detect changes in the use and effects of the computer system as the doctors become more familiar with its operation, constraints and potential. Seven GP's are represented in the recordings, four of whom have been involved in each phase of recording.

The data were gathered in an inner city practice in North West England. The system used in the practice is known as VAMP, which is the most common system in the United Kingdom, being currently installed in approximately 2,200 general practices (Nazareth, King, Haines, Ragel and Myers 1993; Jick, Jick and Derby, 1991). VAMP is accessed through standard keyboards and monitors, located in the reception area and in each consulting room. It provides two linked features that are used in the consultation: a computerised record system for the documentation and retrieval of medical biographical information and a facility for issuing prescriptions. Since the introduction of the system in 1990, the practice has made use of both of these functions. However, within the consultation, computer use is concentrated largely in the prescription phase of the consultation (see Greatbatch, Luff, Heath and Campion, 1993).

Our data show that it is common for doctors and patients to discuss various matters while prescriptions are being produced. These often concern the type, strength, form, dosage, quantity and possible side-effects of the items being prescribed. Alternatively, however, the discussions may be about topics that do not concern the prescription itself, but rather the general state of a patient's health, other medical complaints, psychosocial issues, problems in the family, and "small talk" about such matters as holiday plans and the weather.

Whilst reviewing the recordings of consultations involving the use of a computer, we were struck by the extent to which the use of the system appeared to be inter–related with communication between doctor and patient. Firstly, it quickly became apparent that when patients produce unsolicited talk whilst the computer is in use, they often begin to speak immediately after keystrokes which complete a discrete activity, such as entering the name of a drug. Secondly, we found that the doctors also regularly coordinate their social interactional conduct with the use and operation of the system: for example, delaying responses, or pausing in the midst of their utterances, until they have completed a sequence of keystrokes or until a change on the screen takes effect. Finally, it was noticeable that social interactional considerations can, in turn, affect how the system is used. This ranges from brief cessations of system use as a doctor glances at a patient through to collaborative readings of screen–based text, some of which are initiated by the patients.

In order to illustrate the conversation analytic approach, we will focus on the first of these three areas: the coordination of patients unsolicited talk with the doctor's use of the system.

9.4.1 The coordination of patients' talk with system use and operation

The fact that patients often produce unsolicited talk immediately after keystroke sequences or individual keystrokes which complete a discrete activity suggested that they may be attempting to synchronize their talk with the doctor's use of the keyboard so as to avoid interrupting an activity in progress. In order to explore this possibility, we searched our database in order to locate and transcribe every instance in which patients began to speak on their own initiative while a doctor was using the computer. The transcripts we produced captured not only what was said, but also overlapping talk, pauses within and between the doctors, and patients' utterances, the direction of the parties' gaze, bodily movements such as nods of the head, the positioning of keystrokes in relation to both verbal and non–verbal actions, and the occurrence of changes on the screen. This involved customizing and adding to the transcription systems used within conversation analytic research.[1]

We began by examining in detail the cases in which patients begin to speak immediately after keystrokes which involve the completion or execution of a keyboard task, such as specifying the form, dosage or quantity of a prescribed drug. Having formulated a candidate analysis, we then turned to consider a range of 'complex', 'marginal' and 'incongruous' cases in which the pattern is either less clear cut or

---

[1] A simplified version of the transcription system for talk is:

[	A left bracket indicates the point at which overlapping talk begins.
=	Equal signs are used to indicate that the utterances of different speakers are "latched". They are also used to link continuous talk by a single speaker that has been distributed across non-adjacent lines due to another speaker's overlapping utterance.
(0.5)	Numbers in parentheses indicate the length of silences in tenths of a second.
(.)	A dot in parentheses indicates a gap of less than two tenths of a second.
Wo::rd	Colons indicate prolongation of the immediately preceding sound.
. , ?	Periods, commas and question marks are used to indicate falling, non-terminal and rising intonation respectively.
( )	Empty parentheses indicate that the transcriber was unable to hear what was said.
°hhh	h's preceded by a circle represent inhalations.

not in evidence. As we shall see, our examination of the latter confirmed our candidate analysis.

9.4.2 The initiation of talk (without delay) after the completion of discrete keyboard–based activities

The fact that patients are often able to synchronize their talk with the completion of discrete keyboard activities suggests that they are able to anticipate potential boundaries in the use of the keyboard. Repeated viewing and careful transcription of the data revealed several aspects of system use that appear to be implicated in this process. In particular, patients appear to be synchronizing the initiation of their unsolicited talk with visible aspects of the doctors' use of the computer system. This involves them monitoring the doctors' conduct for evidence of upcoming boundaries in the use of the keyboard. Thus in the majority of the cases in which patients begin to speak immediately after the completion of a keyboard–based activity, we found that the doctors, conduct was consistent with at least temporary disengagement from the task of typing, and that this was available to the patients early enough for them to be able to gear up to speak without delay.

A summary of those aspects of the doctors conduct which are implicated in these displays of potential disengagement from keyboard use follows:

1 As the doctors strike the key which completes or executes a task, the positioning of their other hand does not suggest that it will be used to strike another key immediately after the present keystroke. So, for example, it may be held motionless, the fingers outstretched and relaxed, or away from the keypad altogether.

2 The doctors strike the "final" key with greater force than normal, possibly thereby marking out activity completion. So, for example, in keystroke sequences which involve a series of alphanumeric keystrokes followed by a carriage return keystroke, the carriage return keystroke often is harder than the preceding alphanumeric keystrokes.

3 The doctor's preparation and enactment of the keystroke which completes or executes the activity may provide further evidence that a boundary is imminent. Note that in order to strike a key with additional force, the doctors necessarily (i) lift their fingers more than is normally the case, and (ii) bring them down with a more pronounced thrust. Thus, even before the sound of the keystroke is heard, a patient may have evidence that it constitutes a potential boundary in system use.

4 As the doctors release the final key, they position their hands in ways which are consistent with at least a temporary disengagement from use of the keyboard.

5 In a number of the cases, as the "final" keystroke is made the doctors begin to move their gaze from the keypad to the monitor.

Taken together, these features mark out potential boundaries in keyboard use. They also provide patients with resources for anticipating those boundaries and gearing up to speak simultaneously with their onset – that is, without delay. The features can be illustrated by reference to Extract 1. Here a patient produces an unsolicited utterance ("You see if I could...") immediately after the completion of an alphanumeric–carriage return sequence of keystrokes.

(1a) [C:2:3: Transcript One]

```
   1   Dr:   is all connected (0.2) with u:hm (0.7)
   2         with all this this:=
                 [
   3   P:        (            )
   4   Dr:   =this worry (and) stress. °hhhhhhh U:hm
   5         (3.1)
<  6   P:    You see if I could- I'd be all right if
   7         I could just- you know slee:p,
```

Doctor presses carriage return

Patient begins to speak after doctor lifts his finger away from key while continuing to look at monitor

(1b) [C:2:3: Transcript Two: Detail of Lines 4-6]²

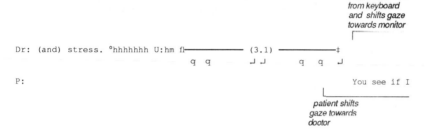

Doctor lifts *hand* from *keyboard* and shifts *gaze* towards *monitor*

```
Dr: (and) stress. °hhhhhhh U:hm fl───────── (3.1) ─────‡
                                  q  q      ⅃ ⅃      q   q   ⅃

P:                                              You see if I
```

patient shifts gaze towards doctor

As the doctor makes the carriage return keystroke which precedes the patient's utterance, several aspects of his conduct combine to project a possible lull in his use of the keyboard. As he presses the carriage return key with his right hand he gazes at the monitor. His left hand is placed on his lap, and as such there is no indication that this hand may be about to be used to make a subsequent keystroke. As the carriage return key is released, and the second click of the keystroke is heard, the doctor lifts his right hand quite sharply away from the key. The inactivity of the left hand, the inception of the gaze shift away from the keyboard, the comportment of the right hand project a potential boundary in the use of the keyboard by the doctor.

A further example can be found in Extract 2. Here the patient begins to speak after the second of two consecutive carriage return keystrokes, each of which complete a discrete keyboard task.

---

2   q   Indicates a keystroke.

   q   Indicates that a key is pressed with greater force than normal.

   ⅃   Indicates a carriage return keystroke.

    Although each keystroke is denoted by a single symbol (q or ⅃) it is important to note that the sound emitted by a keystroke actually involves the merging of two sounds: a 'click' as the key is pressed, a "click" as it is released. While this is not represented in the current transcripts, it will be mentioned in discussing the data extracts.

(2a) [HY:2:1 Transcript One]

```
    1   Dr:    with Parkinson's (.) °hhh er: treatment.
    2          (2.2)
<   3   P:     I do find it very (.) difficult to get
    4          comfortable in bed
```

Doctor makes second carriage return keystroke as he looks at monitor

Patient begins to speak as doctor lifts hand away from keys while continuing to look at monitor

(2b) [HY:2:1 Transcript Two: Detail of lines 1–3]

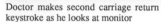

Detailed analysis of this case lends support to the contention that patients orient to displays of disengagement. As the doctor makes the first of the two carriage return keystrokes, he not only shifts his gaze from the keyboard to the monitor, but also holds his left hand motionless above the character keys. However, upon releasing the carriage return key he immediately thrusts his finger back down towards the key to make the next carriage return keystroke. Thus before the second beat of the sound of the initial carriage return keystroke is complete, it is already apparent that he intends to strike the carriage return key again.

In contrast, upon releasing the second carriage return keystroke, he starts to lift the hand up and across (slightly) to the left, opening out the fingers from their previously "cocked" position. As such, given that his left hand remains still, his actions may now suggest activity completion; a boundary in the use of the keyboard. And it is here, immediately after the second carriage return keystroke, that the patient starts to speak. As in Extract 1, then, the patient's speech is coordinated with bodily movements that are consistent with disengagement from the use of the keyboard.

The import of these and related features as resources for the projection and recognition of boundaries was confirmed by our subsequent analysis of incongruous cases. We found that even where utterance initiation does not occur immediately after a keystroke which completes a discrete task, the patients continued to display an orientation to the principles we had explicated in our candidate analysis.

9.4.3 Incongruent cases

Delayed initiation: Support for our candidate analysis was forthcoming when we turned to consider cases in which patients begin to speak in the context of a "boundary", but not immediately after a "final" keystroke. Thus in many of these cases the doctors hand and/or bodily movements do not project possible disengagement from the use of the keyboard. Moreover, the initiation of the patient's utterances often occurs after the doctors' conduct has retrospectively indicated or underlined that a boundary has been reached.

The way in which patients may withhold utterance initiation until evidence of potential disengagement is available can be illustrated by reference to Extract 3.

(3a) [[OB:2:1 Transcript One]

```
    1  P:    You can just use your loaf can't you.
    2  Dr:   Yeah.
    3        (.)
    4  Dr:   °hh
  < 5  P:    And those paracetamol are very good.
```

(3b) [OB:2:1 Transcript Two]

Doctor looks at keyboard as completes sequence of keystrokes

Patient speaks as doctor takes inbreath and looks at monitor

Doctor looks at patient

```
                    Patient dressing
       ------------------------------------------------------
P:    can't you.              And those paracetamol
                    q q   ⌐
Dr:                      Yea:h. - °hh
           ------------------------------┘
            Doctor gazing at keyboard
                             └_____┘
                             Doctor shifts gaze
                             toward monitor
```

Here the doctor conduct upon pressing and releasing the carriage
return key is not consistent with potential disengagement from
keyboard use. As the carriage return key is released he continues to
gaze at the keyboard. However, subsequently, as he takes a brief
inbreath, the doctor shifts his head slightly in the direction of the
monitor. It is immediately following this move that the patient
initiates his utterance.

Thus while the striking on the carriage return key with greater
intensity than preceding keystrokes may have served to alert the
patient to the occurrence of a potential boundary, he does not begin
to speak until conduct (the gaze shift) consistent with disengagement
from keyboard use is forthcoming from the doctor.

In cases involving delayed initiation of talk, patients also attend to
aspects of the operation of the system which can be taken as
indicating a boundary in computer use: e.g. changes on the screen,
sounds emitted by the system, the operation of the printer. For
example, in Extract 4, a patient's talk occurs a full second after the
completion of a keystroke sequence. The positioning of the talk does
not appear to be responsive to the conduct of the doctor. Rather, the
patient appears to coordinate his talk by reference to changes taking
place on the screen.

(4a) [OB:3:7: Transcript One]

```
    1   P:     he's- he's he's going down the dumps °hhh
    2   Dr:    Yeah
    3          (1.5)
<   4   P:     Because I have some of the homemade stuff you
    5          know.
    6   Dr:    Yeah.
```

(4b) [OB:3:7: Transcript Two; Details of lines 1–4]

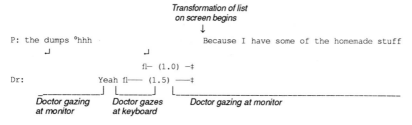

Here the doctor completes an alphanumeric–carriage return
sequence and then gazes at the screen, his hands poised just above
the keyboard, suggesting that further keystrokes are imminent. After
several tenths of a second, however, it becomes evident that the
system is in the process of wiping away all but the top two items of a
long screen–based list. It is at this point that the patient begins to

speak. Cases such as this illustrate how patients may take aspects of system operation as indicating that, although displays of disengagement are absent, further use of the keyboard is not imminent,

Utterance initiation in the midst of keystroke sequences: In a number of cases, patients, utterances are produced in the midst of sequences of keystrokes, rather than at boundaries: e.g. following alphanumeric rather than carriage return keystrokes in alphanumeric-carriage return sequences. Here, then, the patients start to speak at points which do not appear to constitute the completion of a discrete keyboard activity. In these cases, however, it is not unusual to find that the doctors have comported themselves in ways similar to those found in the cases considered above.

(5a) [HY:2:1 Transcript One]

```
1  Dr:    Okay? That's great.
2         (2.0)
< 3  P:   The only thing other problem I do have u::hm I  4
   sleep quite fitfully.
```

(5b) [HY:2:1 Transcript Two]

Doctor initiates sequence of keystrokes   Doctor lifts hand after third alphanumeric keystroke   Patient begins to speak

```
                    Patient gaze on doctor
------------------------------------------------------------┐
P:                                  The only other problem I do have u::hm I
                        ɋ   ɋ   ɋ      ɋ                          ɋ ɋ ˩
Dr:  That's great. fl├──────(2.0)──────┤
     └_____┘
                    Doctor gazing at monitor/keyboard
                                                      ↑   ↑
                                              glances at medical records
```

Having completed his utterance, the doctor initiates an alphanumeric–carriage return sequence of keystrokes. He strikes three character keys, the first two with the left hand, the third, centrally positioned key, with the right. Immediately following the latter, the patient initiates a turn at talk. While this keystroke does not represent the completion of a discrete keyboard task, the doctor's conduct does suggest the possibility of activity completion. Thus, he strikes the third key slightly harder than the preceding two, his left hand held still above the keyboard. Upon releasing the key, his left hand remains motionless, as he raises his right hand with a pronounced movement (in preparation, it turns out, for a subsequent shift back across to the right of the keyboard). By the end of the sound(s) emitted by the keystroke, the fingers of the doctor's right hand are out of range of the keys; his left hand is motionless. His activities are thus consistent with the completion of a sequence of keystrokes and at least momentary disengagement from use of the keypad.

Counter examples: In other cases utterance initiation follows a keystroke that is produced in conjunction with conduct which, given our candidate analysis, one might expect to be associated with the withholding of turn initiation (Extract 6).

(6a) [P:2:3 Transcript One]

```
1  Dr:    It may not help at all we'll have to see. (.)    2
I'll just give you twenty for now.
3  (0.6)
< 4  P:    So they won't clash with one another.
```

Doctor makes third carriage return   Doctor stills finger above
keystroke   carriage return and patient
                                              speaks

(6b) [P:2:3 Transcript Two: Detail of lines 2–4]

```
P:                            So they won't clash

       ⌐ ⌐ ⌐        ⌐ ⌐ ⌐
Dr:    twenty for now. ------
```

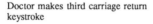

Doctor gazing at keyboard
                    ↑
            Doctor holds hand
            held still above key

After a series of alphanumeric keystrokes, the doctor makes three rapid and pronounced carriage return key strokes. Following the third of these the patient initiates an utterance. What is interesting about this case is that on first inspection the doctor's conduct might appear to be counter to that associated with the initiations considered above. Thus there is no discernible movement of his head or eyes towards the monitor as he makes the third carriage return keystroke. Moreover, as he releases the key, he leaves the finger poised just above, an action clearly the possibility of an imminent keystroke. However, on closer inspection, the doctor's hand movements do appear to be consistent with possible activity completion.

The important point is the rapidity with which the carriage return keystrokes are made, one after the other. In order to achieve this rapidity, the doctor thrusts his finger back down towards the key immediately following both the first and second carriage return keystrokes. On the third carriage return keystroke, by contrast, he lifts the finger and holds it just above the key. Given the character of the preceding two keystrokes, then, this aspect of the doctor's conduct, combined with the left hand being held still, gives a clear sense of a boundary; a brief lapse in the use of the keyboard: the sudden stilling of the finger above the key, as opposed to the immediate thrust downward, serving to mark out a potential boundary.

This case demonstrates the danger of assuming that given bodily movements, or lack of them, will automatically be taken as signifying (or not) a boundary in keyboard use. Quite clearly, the interpretation of such movements is shaped by the context in which they occur, and this must be borne in mind in interpreting the findings reported in this paper.

9.4.4 Discussion

Through detailed analysis of video recordings of computer use in medical consultations we have been able to reveal how patients attempt to synchronize their talk with the use and operation of the system. Specifically, they monitor the doctor's conduct, as well as the operation of the computer, for evidence of the completion of screen based activities. They appear to be attempting to avoid interrupting the activity in progress in circumstances in which they have limited access to the "actual details" of the activity itself.

The grosser examples of this phenomenon are available from relatively casual inspections of the recordings, and could possibly have been noted by a participant observer using standard ethnographic research techniques, or by the doctors or patients themselves in the context of *post hoc* interviews and/or questionnaires. However, in order to explicate the processes involved in even these relatively simple cases, it was necessary to replay our recordings many times, carefully transcribing and re-transcribing the events, and reassessing our analysis in the light of new findings and observations. Moreover, it would have been impossible to provide a systematic and detailed analysis of those cases without the use of video, and the possibility of repeated scrutiny of raw data which it presents. This clearly demonstrates that the use of video recording technologies enables researchers to reveal and analyse fine–grained, "seen but unnoticed" aspects of human conduct which are otherwise unavailable for systematic study. If we had relied solely on data generated through field observation, practices and reasoning utilised by the participants in coordinating their conduct with the use of the computer would have remained largely, if not wholly, unexplicated.

Our analysis also underlines that, in contrast to many of those methodologies which involve quantification and/or experimental techniques, conversation analytic research does not begin with *a priori* hypotheses which are then subjected to empirical testing. Rather, it uses inductive search procedures in order to locate recurring patterns of action and interaction; the patterns in this case concerning the relationship between the initiation of talk by patients and the use and operation of a computer system.

In analysing these patterns, the aim has been to explicate the participants' orientations; the practices that they use and rely upon as they converse while a computer is in use. The central resource out of which our analysis has emerged has been the moment–to–moment understandings of their circumstances that the parties unavoidably display as they interact with each other. In cases such as those considered above, for example, the patients display an understanding of the current state of the GP's use of the computer. Specifically, by initiating a turn at talk, they can be seen to propose that the doctor has completed a keyboard activity: that a boundary in keyboard use has been arrived at. In fact, we are currently developing our analysis to consider the subsequent conduct of the doctors and patients. As such, we are extending and developing a sequential analysis which incorporates both social interaction and human–computer interaction.[3]

Whilst in this chapter we have primarily addressed the ways in which Conversation Analysis might be used to explore the use of information systems in general practice, the approach is currently being used to examine work, interaction and technology throughout a range of "organizational" environments. An example drawn from our own research is Heath and Luff's study of London Underground

---

[3] Our concern is with explicating how interlocking human–computer interaction and social interaction unfolds, moment-by-moment, with parties displaying understanding of each others' conduct *vis-à-vis* each other and the computer.

Line Control Rooms (cf. Heath and Luff, 1992a). The study has begun to explicate the ways in which personnel within the Control Room coordinate a range of actions and activities when dealing with the day–to–day problems which inevitably arise within the running of a major urban transport system. In particular, the study has begun to identify interactional practices and procedures through which personnel distribute information to each other and "peripherally" monitor each others' activities. The study has also begun to identify how personnel systematically produce particular (technologically informed) activities, whilst simultaneously participating in the activities of colleagues, so that for example an utterance may be designed for various participants who stand in different relations both to the speaker's activity and the actions which they themselves are "producing". These observations have been used to develop various implications for the design of Control Room systems.

A second example drawn from our work involves more advanced technologies. At the Rank Xerox Research Centre in Cambridge we have been involved in the evaluation and design of a Media Space: an audio–visual and computing infrastructure which provides mutual access to scientists and administrative staff working in different 'physical' locations within the laboratory (cf. Gaver et al., 1992; Heath and Luff, 1992b). We analysed video recordings of the use of the system (and use of related systems elsewhere in Xerox). It was found that video–mediated communication reveals asymmetries which, as far as we are aware, do not arise within other forms of human interaction. In particular, we find that the technology provides visual access but undermines the interactional significance of non–verbal behaviour. In the light of these findings and more general observations concerning the inability of Media Space to support collaborative work (as opposed to interpersonal 'communication'), we have been undertaking a series of experiments, through which we are developing and evaluating more suitable forms of audio–visual interconnectivity (cf. Gaver, Sellen, Heath and Luff, 1993; Heath, Luff and Sellen, 1994). In both these examples, Conversation Analysis not only provides a body of observations concerning the socio–interactional organization of technology use in a particular environment, but generates findings which are of practical relevance to the design of the complex systems.

9.5 Considerations and design

Conversation Analysis and Ethnomethodology may not only enrich our understanding of the *in situ* accomplishment of certain forms of human–computer interaction, but may also provide findings which are relevant to the design and the deployment of new technologies. Taking general medical practice, we can begin to consider the ways in which the system might be reconfigured to avoid some of the problems currently faced by "users", both doctor and patient, and to enlarge and enrich the forms of "interaction" which the system will support. So, for example, we might explore redesigning the 'computer dialogue' so that discrete activities were routinely completed by particular keystrokes, or add selected displays, which, if available to the patient, could provide support for document–focused collaboration between the participants. More generally, we can begin to see the ways in which a detailed understanding of an individual's use of an information system within an interactional environment such as a medical consultation raises some interesting issues concerning the limitations of screen–based documents and some of the advantages of the original paper–based system. For example, despite the limitations of paper–based records, they are not only ecologically flexible, allowing the doctor to carry and reposition the document, but they "tailorable", allowing the doctor to shape and interpret contributions with respect to fine distinctions in the ways in which text is written and positioned (cf. Heath, 1982).

Elsewhere, we have discussed the ways in which Conversation Analysis augmented by field work may be relevant to requirements analysis and different stages of the design process (Heath and Luff, 1992a, b; Luff, Heath and Greatbatch, 1994). Indeed, it is increasingly argued that developments in social science may provide a distinctive approach to 'user–centred design'; an approach which brings to the forefront the social and interactional character of technologically supported work in complex organizations. However, we should not ignore the training implications of Conversation Analytic work. For example, as indicated above the study discussed here has generated a collection of observations which are relevant to helping doctors (and perhaps even patients) manage screen–based systems within the consultation and to avoid some of the pitfalls which inevitably arise when a "new technology" is deployed within a working environment.

Perhaps as important, however, Conversation Analysis and Ethnomethodology may provide a vehicle with which to re–address a number of the key issues and concepts within human–computer interaction and within disciplines such as computer science. Consider, for example, the concept of 'task' or the concept of 'the user' which inform a broad range of empirical research and which are of profound relevance to the design of new technologies. More conventional treatments of task, their emphasis on individual cognitive abilities and the goal–oriented models of human conduct they embody, appear inappropriate when considering the doctor's actual use of the computer in the consultation. *In situ*, we find that the doctor has to coordinate use of the system with the contingencies at hand, the unanticipated contributions of the patient and the practical circumstances of use he or she faces. The task, say entering information into the system, is interactionally coordinated with the patient, and inseparable from the moment–by–moment demands which progressively emerge. The doctor's use of the system, his skills and abilities in accomplishing various tasks within the consultation, are dependent on and inseparable from, his or her abilities to coordinate actions with those of the patient. Similarly, whilst the doctor may in principle be considered "the user", his or her use of the system is not independent of the patient's contributions, but embedded in the ongoing collaborative accomplishment of various activities in concert with the patient. However specialised, and however asymmetrical the subsequent interaction, tasks are accomplished in collaboration with others; they are dependent upon a socio–interactional organization which provides for the proper and relevant accomplishment in actual situations. To lose sight of this social organization is to ignore the foundations upon which the skilled use of technology rests.

9.6 Developments

It is possible that we will witness a growing interest amongst scholars from various disciplines in drawing on Conversation Analysis and cognate approaches to explore aspects of the "interaction" between human beings and computers over the next decade. Part of the drive towards such approaches inevitably derives from the growing concern with more conventional forms of Requirements Analysis and more generally with their apparent inability to avoid difficulties, and occasionally disasters, when technologies are deployed into real world, organizational settings. Indeed, whether it is an official investigation into the introduction of Computer Aided Dispatch into London Ambulance Service, or the Taurus system into the London Stock Exchange, it is interesting to note our attention is drawn to the fact that the original design of the new technology in various ways failed to take into account the work and communicative practices of the people who were expected to use the new systems. There is, therefore, a growing recognition that in the design and deployment of new technologies we need a more thorough and wide ranging understanding of the *in situ* organization of tasks and communication that the particular system is seen as either supporting or even replacing, otherwise we will inevitably be faced with unanticipated and in many cases unwanted consequences.

Conversation Analysis provides one amongst various approaches through which we can begin to explicate the social organization of work and interaction in organizational settings. It has both advantages and disadvantages. It can provide a relatively rigorous and detailed analysis of the socio–interactional organization of complex tasks and activities, and delineate the ways in which tools and technologies feature in accomplishment of particular actions. Its source of data, audio and audio–visual recordings, not only allow the researcher to subject conduct to repeated scrutiny, using slow motion facilities and the like, but the actual analysis and if necessary its implications for design can be evaluated (by co–researchers, the academic community, designers, etc.) against the raw data (the video recordings of the work situation). For design, video could also support "traceability"; providing a resource throughout the process of design that can allow critical decisions to be made with reference to actual materials collected in a relevant setting.

In the light of the need for new and distinctive approaches to Requirements Analysis and design, it is likely that there will be growing emphasis on exploring ways in which Conversation Analysis and other naturalistic approaches to human conduct, can be transformed from an intellectual and "scientific" methodological orientation to an applied and procedural method to support design. Some ways in which this might be done for Ethnography is discussed by Blomberg (chapter 8) and in a recent paper by Hughes, King, Rodden and Andersen, (1994). It is not clear whether it will be possible, or even advantageous, to attempt to develop a "quick and dirty" method for Conversation Analysis. Nonetheless, it is apparent that such an approach could contribute to design through small scale empirical studies of work and interaction in particular settings, (cf. Suchman, forthcoming; Heath and Luff, 1992a). The growing body of findings in Conversation Analysis however, coupled with recent studies of work and interaction in complex technological environments, do provide an important resource for the analysis and comprehension of system use and human conduct in day to day, organizational settings.

One suspects that in the long term, the more important contribution which will be made by Conversation Analysis will be through the ways in which its empirical studies not only generate a distinctive body of knowledge concerning the use of tools and technologies in real world environments, but lead to a reconsideration of a number of the key conceptual distinctions found in HCI and related disciplines. However, research into the organization of work and interaction in complex organizational environments also raises serious empirical and methodological challenges for Conversation Analysis itself. Unlike conversation, and talk in the various institutional settings so successfully charted by Conversation Analysis, technologically informed conduct not only demands serious consideration of visual as well as vocal actions and activities, an area already extensively addressed in Conversation Analysis (for example Goodwin, 1981; Heath, 1986), but also directs our attention towards the inter–relationship of various concurrent activities which are being accomplished by the participants alongside and within their talk and interaction. Even in a relatively conventional interactional environment such as the medical consultation, we can see how the actions of doctor (and patient) are not only geared to each others' contributions, but also to the text and textual changes manifest through the computer system. The implications of such activities for Conversation Analysis become even more severe when one considers the complexity found in multi–party technological settings such as Control or Operation Rooms (cf. Suchman, forthcoming; Goodwin and Goodwin, 1992; Whalen, 1992; Heath and Luff, 1992b). Here we find personnel participating in and systematically coordinating multiple activities simultaneously with each other, few of which are accomplished through "mutually focused interaction". Whilst we believe that Conversation Analysis can make an important contribution to HCI, it has to be recognized that "tool saturated environments" and the complex activities they embody, provide an unprecedented methodological and empirical challenge to Ethnomethodology and Conversation Analysis.

Further reading

Heritage, J. C. (1984). *Garfinkel and Ethnomethodology.* Cambridge: Polity Press.
This provides a clear introduction to Ethnomethodology and Conversation Analysis.

Atkinson, J. M. and Heritage, J. (eds). (1984). *Structures of Social Action: Studies in Conversation Analysis.* Cambridge: Cambridge University Press.
This is a key collection of empirical studies in Conversation Analysis, including papers on ordinary conversation, institutional interaction and visual conduct.

Drew, P. and Heritage, J. (eds.) (1992). *Talk at Work: Interaction in Institutional Settings.* Cambridge: Cambridge University Press.
A recent collection of studies which use the approach and findings of conversation analysis to examine institutional interaction.

Heath, C. (1986). *Body Movement and Speech in Medical Interaction.* Cambridge: Cambridge University Press.

The book involves the analysis of visual as well as vocal conduct within a Conversation Analytic framework.

Suchman, L. A. (1987). *Plans and Situated Actions*. Cambridge: Cambridge University Press.

This study of computer use provides a seminal critique of conventional approaches to HCI.

Chapter 10

Activity theory, CSCW and organizations

Frank Blackler

Information and communication technologies are presenting a new set of challenges to the theory and practice of organization. The way in which they interlace with tacit skills has exposed processes that previously were ignored, taken for granted, or misunderstood in established behavioural approaches to work system design. At the same time the new technologies are precipitating new approaches to management, supporting organizations which are "communication intensive" with little hierarchy and strong links to other organizations. Such considerations indicate the need for new approaches to understanding the role of technologies within organizations. Activity theory offers one such approach, reconceptualising as it does the relationships between individuals, communities, technologies and actions.

Activity theory has its origins in the work of Lev Vygotsky, a Russian psychologist who worked in the 1920s and 1930s. Current versions of the approach he pioneered have much in common with contemporary anthropology, ethnomethodology and actor network theory in the way they explore the relationships between everyday practices, material artifacts, language, social systems and cultures. The approach is distinctive in the way it models expertise as an active, collective phenomenon, and in the importance it ascribes to collective learning.

Activity theorists analyse activity as a socially stabilized and transformational endeavour, and analyse thinking as internalized cooperation. Technologies in general and language in particular are treated as integral features of the systems through which, by collective endeavour, the world is changed. A number of contemporary approaches in Western social science have explored similar orientations to activity theory (an early example is Bateson, 1972 a contemporary which demonstrates similarities is actor network theory, e.g. Law, 1992). Yet not all Western observers have found activity theory easy to grasp. This is almost certainly because of the way the approach seeks to avoid dichotomies that have a long history in Western styles of thinking. Thus, it endeavours to avoid segregating thought from action, the individual from the collectivity, and the social from the technical. Instead, activity theory focuses on the relationships between such factors, indicating that technology development is a social intervention, best undertaken from an appreciation of the ways in which communities of practitioners distribute and coordinate their efforts.

In the account of the approach which follows a contemporary version of activity theory is used to analyse a medical records system. First an historical overview of the development of activity theory is presented, followed by a discussion of the ways in which new technologies are transforming work and organizations. Engestrom's contemporary version of activity theory is next introduced, and used to analyse a case of computerized medical records and the activities of staff in a health care centre. The chapter concludes by drawing attention to the similarities between activity theory and contemporary social theory, and by underlining the relevance of the approach to key social and organizational problems associated with advanced technologies.

10.1 A brief history of activity theory

At least since Descartes sharply differentiated mind from body dualisms have been a feature of the Western intellectual tradition. This is very evident in Western psychology where, in their efforts to develop psychology as an experimental science, psychologists endeavoured to study individuals as if they can be separated from their contexts, treating technological and cultural factors as contextual variables that may be sharply distinguished from the individuals who are affected by them. In sociology similar processes can be seen. For example, Parsonian social theory (Parsons, 1951) treated social rules and norms as if they could be studied at a general level far removed from those supposedly enacting them while, in contrast, symbolic interactionists have tended to treat rules and norms as if they provide merely the general context within which individuals act.

However, as Knorr–Cetina (1981) pointed out in the early 1980s, social theory has been shifting away from approaches which seek to consider the context in isolation from the individual, or the individual in isolation from his or her context. Explanations are being developed which focus explicitly on the relationships between actions and context. Attempts are being made to avoid separating doing, thinking, feeling or evaluating, from social, economic, political and cultural processes. Thus, contemporary constructionism assumes that just as culture is a part of self so, too, do people play a role in the creation of culture; peoples' active involvement is an integral feature of everyday practices. Detailed empirical work in this tradition include Callon, Law and Rip's (1986) study of the sociology of science and Suchman's (1987) ethnomethodological study of human–machine interaction. So widespread and influential are such approaches nowadays that Starr (1992) suggests they have come to represent an "invisible college", "an intellectual movement that as yet has no name".

In psychology, however, this intellectual movement has had far less of an impact than it has in sociology. Some psychologists have made concerted efforts to stimulate interest in such approaches (e.g. Gergen, 1985) but traditional approaches, which sharply distinguish between "self" and "society", have proved especially entrenched in Western psychology (see Kvale, 1992). It is of particular interest to find, therefore, that a psychological approach whose origins reach back to the early decades of this century anticipated contemporary approaches to social theory and is currently offering a significant contribution to their development.

Russian activity theory managed to avoid the dichotomies of mind/body, individual/community, technological/social, and language and action that remain at the foundation of much Western psychology because of the way that Vygotsky deliberately set out to develop an alternative. Vygotsky's writings spanned a remarkable range, including art, literature and semiotics. His working life was short yet, as Kozulin (1990) points out, by the time of his death at the age of 37 he had, almost singlehandedly, sketched the outlines of a psychology of culture and consciousness. Vygotsky himself was an enthusiastic supporter of the Bolshevik revolution, but under Stalin his work was to be banned. His followers in Russia (including Leont'ev, Luria and Davydov) continued to develop aspects of his orientation, but it has been only comparatively recently that the approach has been debated and extended outside the Soviet orthodoxy.

While it was to take half a century for American psychologists to move away from simple behaviourism and to acknowledge the significance of language to both thought and action, language assumed a central role in Vygotsky's approach. Rather than being controlled by external stimuli he assumed that behaviour is controlled by semiotic mediation and the enactment of meanings. Human development, Vygotsky suggested, can be understood as a transition from "natural" forms of behaviour to higher mental functions. Because of the relationship between higher mental processes and signs, symbols and language, higher mental functioning is, Vygotsky believed, intimately linked to social and cultural processes.

Vygotsky rejected the idea that Marxist ideology could provide a blueprint for scientific research, but his efforts to link the individual and the cultural were profoundly influenced by some of Marx's ideas, in particular by Marx's conception of human nature. Marx believed that it makes no sense to say that human nature is fixed. He attributed a key role to productive activity: mankind has to interact with nature to survive, converting raw materials into goods for human use. Accordingly, for Marx, productive activity conditions everything else. People continually make themselves through their productive activity, "as individuals express their life, so they are". Moreover productive activity is fundamentally social, Marx maintained. The relations of production constitute the economic structure of a society, and give shape to particular legal and political infrastructures.

Marx's notion of productive activity was wide, including both material products and mental ideas. His suggestion was that different societies in different times provide varying resources and opportunities for the activities of their members. Thus, for Marx productive activity and the human nature it expresses is an historically developing process; it is not the consciousness of humans that determines their being but social experiences which shape their consciousness. Impressed as he was by the notion that higher mental processes have their origin in social and material ones Vygotsky developed the view that psychological processes can only be understood through an understanding of the (culturally provided) factors which mediate them. Marx's notion of productive activity indicates that through the use of tools people alter their environments; similarly, Vygotsky thought, through the employment of signs (language) people alter themselves.

Two comparisons between this approach and familiar approaches within Western psychology emphasize the significance of this point. First, Vygotsky's culturalist approach to language and learning contrasts markedly with Piaget's individualistic orientation. Piaget maintained that children necessarily pass through a stage of egocentric speech before they use language socially; his view was that they have to learn to externalize previously internal thought. Vygotsky's view was the opposite: children learn to internalize their speech which is, from the start, oriented to their external social environment. Second, in their studies of intelligence and learning Western psychologists have placed a heavy emphasis on measures of individual achievement and intelligence. For Vygotsky, however, what should be measured is not a child's existing performance but his or her ability to interact with teachers and thus to extend his or her knowledge and abilities. The "zone of proximal development" is the term Vygotsky used to describe the difference between what a child can presently do on his or her own and what he or she would be able to achieve in collaboration with an adult. Developing his view of the social nature of learning Vygotsky suggested that it is in coordination with more proficient members of their community that competencies develop.

According to Vygotsky, therefore, a person's actions, language and learning can only be understood as part of a broader social endeavour. As others developed this approach the concept of "activity" was to become central to the Vygotsky tradition. "Activity" is a more general concept than either "operation" or "action" (examples of activities would be "work", "play", "study" and "war") and more specific than either "society" or "culture". Yet it implies all these. As Leont'ev (1978) explained, just as the concept of "action" gives coherence to related operations, so the notion of "activity" gives coherency to related actions. For Russian theorists, interested as they were in the relationships between mind and culture, activity provided the smallest unit of analysis which would preserve the link between mind and society and the coherence of different actions and movements. The conceptions people have of their activities are best understood as socio–cultural interpretations that are imposed on particular circumstances by participants themselves.

The American psychologist Wertsch (1985) has illustrated this with an example from education. When given the same task to work on with a child, teachers and parents may approach the situation somewhat differently; teachers may interpret the activity in terms of providing learning opportunities for the child (thus prompting the child to experiment in order to solve the problem for itself); parents, on the other hand, may interpret the task in terms of goal achievement (thus prompting the child towards a rapid production of the correct solution). The teacher and the parent in this example have quite different conceptions of appropriate activity in the same situation; neither may necessarily articulate their approaches, which will probably remain tacit, but both will show skill and creativity in enacting their understandings of appropriate behaviour.

What is immediately noticeable about this formulation is the resemblance of the notion of activity to a number of mid–range concepts that Western anthropologists and sociologists began developing in the 1970s. The concept closely resembles Goffman's "frames", Schank and Abelson's "scripts", Strauss's "social worlds" and Bordieu's "habitus" (Goffman, 1974; Schank and Abelson, 1977; Strauss, 1978; Bordieu, 1977). Like them the notion of activity identifies classes of actions in terms of the contexts that people consider appropriate for them. Behaviour is not determined by physical contexts rather, understandings of what is appropriate to do in a particular circumstances are enacted by the participants themselves. How such understandings are acquired, and how they may be developed, are central concerns of activity theory.

While Vygotsky's colleagues and followers in Russia were to continue developing the notion of activity (see Lektorsky, 1990) it is only comparatively recently that the significance of the approach has become appreciated in the West. German theorists of "critical psychology" (see Tolman and Maiers, 1991) drew from Russian ideas. In Finland, Engestrom (1987, 1990) presented a contemporary version of activity theory. Meanwhile, activity theory had been introduced to the English–speaking world by the Americans Cole, John–Steiner, Scribner and Souberman, (1978) and Wertsch (1979) and, as a result of their efforts, Vygotsky's approach has, in recent years, become influential in American educational theory (see especially Scribner, 1986; Brown, Collins and Duguid, 1989; Lave and Wenger, 1991). Links between Americans and Scandinavians interested in developing the approach have been established over this period and connections have been made with others such as Suchman, whose ethnomethodological approach to situated action is well–known, and Hutchins, who has analysed distributed cognition (see the collection edited by Chaiklin and Lave, 1993).

Activity theory now has a well developed presence in Western social science. The concerns of activity theorists to understand the links between actions, language and communities resonates with the interests of social theorists in how everyday practices interlace with social institutions. As is illustrated below, the distinctive contribution that the approach offers lies in:

(a) the analysis it offers of how human activity is inevitably mediated by human creations such as technologies, language, and institutional arrangements. (These, and the relations between them, are depicted as "activity systems".)

(b) the emphasis it places on the point that ways of acting are grounded in tradition and shared by a community. (These are depicted as "communal narratives".)

(c) the analysis it provides of how individuals perpetuate   practices but also change them, and in the suggestion that   developments in practices are made possible by the   incoherencies and conflicts which are inherent within activity systems. (These are depicted as the "zone of proximal development".)

10.2 Activity theory, information systems and HCI

Within the HCI community in recent years some dissatisfaction has been expressed about predominant orientations to the subject. Contributing to a a discussion on this point Bannon (1991) traced the history of HCI. The subject area, he pointed out, developed out of European "ergonomics" and American "human factors engineering", approaches that had their origin in attempts to ensure that complex machine systems would not be built that were incompatible with peoples' physical or cognitive abilities. The advent of widely available computer systems in the 1980s led to a revized emphasis, of course, where first "ease of learning" and later the "user friendliness" of advanced machines were to become central concerns. Yet, Bannon argues, such developments departed only marginally from earlier tendencies to treat humans as if they are simply another component within a technological equation. To the extent that HCI practitioners overlook the role of computer systems within the broad complexity of work values and motivations, and treat work as if it is merely the solitary interaction of worker and machine, their insights into work behaviour will obviously remain constrained.

Quite how HCI theory can be expanded to embrace a broader perspective is not, of course, an easy matter. The further attention shifts away from anthropometric or individual cognitive issues to social and cultural ones the more difficult it is to produce guidelines for designers. Clearly, user practices must become the centre of the design process; but for this to be possible applicable approaches for analysing the complexity of factors surrounding them and how they can change and develop need to be created.

It is in exactly this respect that activity theory offers a distinctive contribution, providing as it does a framework which analyses the place of technology in work, and work itself as a collaborative endeavour. As already indicated, the approach has developed over a number of decades, but its application to work behaviour is relatively new. Applications of the approach to work systems began appearing in the 1980s (including cleaning work, Engestrom and Engestrom 1986; flexible manufacturing, Toikka, Hyotylaines and Norros, 1986; social work, Arnkil 1988; and teaching, Engestrom, 1990). Activity theory has only very recently been applied to information systems and human computer interaction issues however. One of the earliest reports was Bodker's (1989, 1991) exploration of the relevance of Leont'ev's ideas to interface design. Bodker emphasizes how the user interface should not be conceptualized by designers as independent from the activities it is intended to support. The operations–focused, end–user orientation she develops analyses computers as extensions of the body, integrated into broader systems of coordination and communication. Bodker's analysis of HCI issues in terms of activity theory is typical of much of the commentary on the relevance of activity theory to advanced technologies to date: problems are analysed at a broad level and issues are interpreted retrospectively (Bodker, for example, presents a reinterpretation of the well publicized UTOPIA project).

Perhaps the strongest general reflection of the relevance of activity theory to advanced information and communication systems has been provided by Raeithal (1992). Raeithal distinguishes between the various influences inspiring key orientations in the general area, recording how the key influences on mainstream computer scientists (e.g. Turing, Quine), contrast with the postmodern influences on Winograd and Flores' alternative (Heidegger, Wittgenstein, Searle, etc.) and with the origins of contemporary activity theory (Vygotsky, Leont'ev).

Raeithal compares his own interpretation of activity theory with the general interpretation of the approach suggested some years earlier by Engestrom (1987). This approach has been especially influential in Finland and Scandinavia in recent years and, as already noted, in the USA. Engestrom's version of activity theory has been used to analyse information systems design (Kuuttii, 1991) and, as discussed below, to help in the development of a computer supported cooperative work (CSCW) system in a medical centre (Engestrom, Engestrom and Saarelma, 1988; Engestrom, 1990, 1991, 1993; Kuutti and Arvonen, 1992).

10.3 The problem: extending HCI into the design of CSCW systems

10.3.1 CSCW and the need for a theory of working

A contemporary issue in the developing field of HCI that activity theory is especially well placed to address is computer supported cooperative work (CSCW). It is appropriate to note that ever since the early days of socio–technical systems thinking (that is, nearly thirty years before work systems based on micro–electronics began to appear, see Trist and Bamforth, 1951) practitioners and theorists interested in developing human–centred systems have sought to avoid technological issues becoming the driving force in work systems development. In recent years, however, this has become a burning issue within the IT community as early preoccupations to make computer hardware work efficiently or to program it in an orderly way have given way, first, to efforts to satisfy the needs of individual users (Friedman, 1989) and, most recently, to efforts to develop systems that will support collaborative working (Galegher, et al, 1990). As Greenbaum and Kyng's (1991) report of discussions amongst systems designers illustrates, such a shift in orientation has precipitated major dissatisfactions with established approaches to HCI. Interest in "computer supported cooperative work" especially is directing attention away from information flows, expert rules, individual workers and isolated problems, to the ways in which computing systems relate to collaborative activities. This requires a sophisticated understanding of social processes, including the relationships between technologies and social interactions, the nature of mutually supporting competencies, group dynamics and the organizational problems that complex systems present.

The technology of computer supported cooperative work includes message systems, computer conferencing, shared data systems, co-authoring systems, group decision support technologies and team development tools including multi–media communication technologies. There is no ready–made approach that will help designers overcome the complex social and behavioural issues that such technologies raise. Given their relative novelty (such technologies only began appearing in the mid–1980s) this is, perhaps, hardly suprising. Moreover, as McCarthy (1994) points out, much discussion in the early years of these technologies was dominated by interest in the "CS" of CSCW, concentrating as it did on issues associated with the technical performance of such systems (e.g. Gibbs and Verrijn–Stuart, 1991).

The "CW" aspect of CSCW has been less successfully considered, perhaps because it is so much more intractable. The earliest writers about such technologies were relatively cautious in the comments that they made about the possible interpersonal and organizational impacts they might have (see Greif's 1988 collection of early papers). But many subsequent commentators were to throw caution to the winds. The introduction to a special edition on CSCW in the *Communications of the ACM* in 1991 urged that "collaboration is a sign of maturation ... computing is coming of age ... the potential for supporting collaboration is limitless ... there is excitement and opportunity in seeing what is coming: there is risk in ignoring it". Many such commentaries seem as much designed to impress or to startle as to inform; indeed, the rhetoric to be found even in the serious literature on CSCW seems designed to persuade, e.g. the terms "computer supported cooperative work", and "intellectual teamwork" (see especially Kling's 1991 observations on this). The worst of this literature demonstrates a naïvety about the complex nature of collaborative processes and an almost heroic disregard for the differences between face–to–face interactions and computer mediated exchanges assuming, as it does, that CSCW mediated communications will effortlessly support cooperative activities between individuals who are separated in both time and space (for an example see Wilson, 1991).

Recent attempts to explore the "CW" in CSCW include, of course, a growing number of well–worked empirical studies which, in general, steer clear of hyperbole. Yet as McCarthy (1994) points out in a review of such work, the focus of much of the research in this area has been on office work only and, within this milieu, on the adequacy of particular channels of communications. Interest in the "CW" of CSCW has, in other words, tended to focus on certain rather specific issues relevant to communication, rather than on the nature (and variety) of work expertise and of the complexities of collaboration.

The conclusion suggested by these points is clear. A theory of working and, in particular, a theory of cooperative working is the necessary prerequisite for a theory of computer supported cooperative working.

10.3.2 New technologies, and changing experiences of work and organization

The significance of the need for a theory of cooperative working to underpin CSCW development is underlined by the issues touched on in the opening paragraph of this chapter. Conventional theories of organization (and the approaches to design that were built upon them) are being undermined by the impacts the technologies are having on work skills and organizational practices.

First, because of the intimate way in which computer technologies interlace with everyday practices they are disrupting social processes which, hitherto, have been ignored, taken–for–granted, or misunderstood by technology designers and behavioural analysts alike. Tacit skills, communication patterns and procedures of sense–making are being displaced in unexpected ways by such "advanced" information and communication technologies.

The organizational psychologist Karl Weick (1985) was among the first to comment on this development. Weick's general approach to organizations emphasizes the importance of sense–making in collective endeavour (Daft and Weick, 1984). Despite their many advantages in manipulating, transmitting and displaying data, the new information and communication technologies are "information deficient", he pointed out, in the constrained and restricted representations of reality that they present. Data transmitted by computers lacks the richness of other informational processes. Deficient in sounds and smells, they cannot be looked at from different angles, are less likely to be talked through, are often presented in ways that make it difficult to see the wood for the trees and, in the manner of their presentation, computer generated information can feel final and non–negotiable.

Weick's suggestions anticipated many of the points so clearly presented in Zuboff's (1988) case studies of the effects of computers on the experience of work. The skills of effective collaboration are being disrupted by I.T.–based work systems. Conventional "action skills", she suggests, depend on peoples' physical involvement in a task, are based on immediate responses to physical cues and face–to–face exchanges, are developed by doing (so are often tacit) and are situated (i.e. are rooted in specific contexts). But, in both the factory and the office, these skills are being displaced by technologies which, rather than depending on immediate inferences and spontaneous responses, require operators to rely on the cerebral skills of induction and deduction and a detailed knowledge of procedures.

However, it is not only through what Zuboff calls their "informating" effects that the new technologies are transforming organizations. The technologies are associated also with the widespread social, political and economic changes that are occurring in contemporary capitalism. A variety of interpretations of what is happening in these fields can be identified in the literature. Piore and Sable (1984), for example, pointed to the disintegration of the conditions necessary for a mass–market production system, as domestic markets have been penetrated by externally produced products and as the advantages of large, dedicated mass production systems have been undermined by computer based production systems producing low–cost, high–quality goods for niche markets In their more extensive interpretation of such trends Lash and Urry (1987) pointed to the changes currently taking place in capitalism, comparing the significance of contemporary changes with the transformations of earlier epochs. Just as early "liberal capitalism" gave way to "colonial capitalism" so, they suggest, colonial capitalism is now being replaced by an era of "disorganized capitalism". Such an era is characterized by an international division of labour, international capital flows, cultural fragmentation and, importantly, a dependency on electronically transmitted information.

It would be incorrect, of course, to assume that the new information and communication technologies are determining the changes that are taking place in contemporary capitalism. Castells' (1989) analysis of the situation points to a more complex relationship. Governments across the developed world have, he notes, enacted post–Keynesian policies by weakening trade unions, developing fiscally austere policies, retreating from policies of wealth distribution, and reducing the size of the public sector. The new technologies have supported and enhanced such developments, as they have facilitated the internationalization of financial markets, the transformation of production processes, and the creation of information networks. Conventional distinctions between mass– and customized–markets are rapidly being eroded in this situation, as organizations are developing flexible modes of production, dispersing their operations, and developing competitive strategies in alliance with others.

Despite their differences in orientation these various commentators suggest that organizational changes associated with contemporary developments are considerable. Communication and control operations supported by new technologies are, it is being suggested, facilitating the demise of bureaucratic approaches to organization, promising vigorous internal networks, collaborative work relationships, and significantly reduced hierarchical structures of control in organizations (see, for example, Sproull and Kiesler, 1991). Moreover, rather than taking on all–comers, using "in–house" skills and resources, firms are tending to compete in alliances with other organizations, be these suppliers, customers, or firms possessing complementary skills and competencies (Kanter, 1989; Malone and Rochart, 1991). Networking technologies in general and CSCW technologies in particular are an essential component of such developments.

While many proponents of CSCW write enthusiastically about the benefits of such changes it is as well to note that they are not beneficial for everyone. Reich (1991) discusses how in the globalized, informated, economy, wealth creation is becoming dependent on esoteric "knowledge workers" (they are, the way Reich uses this term, entrepreneurs by another name) who command large salaries, and who are increasingly isolating themselves from the rest of the community. Castells' (1989) perspective on such an issue again places the difficulties in a broader perspective: organizations' traditional dependency on geographically located communities is being replaced by a dependency on electronic information flows.

The "cooperative work" aspect of "computer supported cooperative work" is not, therefore, as straightforward as it might first appear to be. It is misleading to assume that computer technologies may merely be grafted onto existing patterns of work and cooperation. On the contrary, advanced technologies disrupt existing patterns of expertise and are associated with the development of wholly new systems of collaboration, competition and social differentiation.

Compare these insights, not only with the over–optimistic claims within some of the present day literature on CSCW, but also with the comments of social scientists in the early 1980s. Then (e.g. Buchanan and Boddy, 1983) it was fashionable to emphasize how the new technologies of computing were not deterministic in their effects but open a range of choices for managers, from centralization to decentralization and from automation to job enrichment. It makes sense to say that such choices do, certainly, exist. Yet the impacts of computing technologies reviewed here indicate how misleading it would be to conceive of these technologies merely as flexible tools for organizations, to be used in ways that managers deem appropriate. The developments summarized in this section suggest that organizations which are becoming heavily dependent on new information and communication technologies are, simultaneously, being imploded into electronic representations on machines and exploded into (global) information networks.

Rather than providing systems that effortlessly enhance existing practices the new technologies are, therefore, raising fundamental questions both about the nature of work, the nature of collaboration, and about the nature of organization itself. How can the changes in expertise demanded by technologies, which require people to rely less on their immediate responses to the environment and more on their abilities to interpret decontextualized symbols, best be understood and planned for? And how can the changes in patterns of collaboration demanded by technologies, which create organizations which are independent of geographical locations, devoid of hierarchies, and with unclear boundaries between themselves and their parter organizations, be conceptualized and managed?

10.3.3 Using activity theory to analyse CSCW: the case of a health care centre

While it cannot provide answers to all the issues raized in such questions, activity theory does offer a number of significant contributions to them. Engestrom's reports of a medical health centre in Finland provide the best documented example of an attempt to apply the approach in an analysis of a CSCW system.

Engestrom, Engestrom and Saarelma (1988) describe how a distinguishing feature of excessive users of the services of a medical health centre in Finland was their presentation of multiple problems, possibly linked by psychosomatic factors (which, of course, can be difficult to diagnose). Yet a characteristic of the health care system provided in Finland at that time was the discontinuity of treatment that patients received. Following general procedures in the Finnish health care system, patients visiting the health centre Engestrom studied were randomly allocated to whatever doctors were available. Thus, patients would routinely be allocated to doctors who had never seen them before, and the chances of the doctors recognising the possible psychosomatic origins of whatever symptoms were being reported were significantly reduced.

The computerized medical records in use in the Centre might have been expected to compensate for the fact that doctors in this system would often find themselves treating patients they had not seen before, by providing easily accessed records to inform doctors about the complexity of the patients' history of complaints, and thus alerting them to the possibility that the any current symptoms might need to be interpreted within this broader context. The records system in use in the centre (FINSTAR) was adapted from an American system COSTAR however, a highly inflexible records system. COSTAR was modelled on the conventional view of medical note taking, which privileges the relationship between the individual doctor and his or her individual patient. The developers of these systems had, in other words, assumed that computerized records are little more than personal notes by a particular doctor for him or herself. The system had not been designed to facilitate cross–referencing or data analysis, nor as a vehicle of communication and cooperation between different medical staff collaborating in their treatment of a given patient.

Engestrom's research confirmed that although some doctors might carefully extract patient data from the computerized records available to them, others found that, in the time pressured situation in which they operated, they had little opportunity or incentive either to reflect on such data, or to use up surgery time by entering more than very brief additional comments themselves into the record system. The predictable result was a tendency for doctors to compartmentalize problems currently being presented to them from the more general and complex case histories of their patients.

Engestrom asks, should this situation best be analysed as either a technical problem, to be solved by the better design of a records system, or as a motivational problem, to be solved by encouraging doctors to change their attitudes towards the use and maintenance of the record system? The answer he offers draws from his interpretation of the Vygotsky tradition.

Engestrom builds his general account of human activity by contrasting it with the activity of animals. Human activity systems are radically different from animal systems because of the range of mediating factors which occur within them. Tools and concepts, created by humans themselves, mediate the interactions between actors and the object of their activities. Traditions, rituals and rules mediate the relationship between the individuals and their communities. The division of labour mediates relationships between the community and the actions of its various members. This complex of mediating relationships is given coherency by the goals or objectives which unify overall collaborative endeavour; activity systems are distinguished by the objects towards which they are directed.

Note that the notion of mediation (by tools and concepts, rules and roles) is central to Engestrom's presentation of activity theory, adopting as he does Marx's emphasis on how "man the tool–maker" creates tools (which he interposes between himself and his labour) and Vygotsky's extension into the notion that man creates a sign–system (which in the first place he uses to coordinate his actions with those of others, and which he later uses to regulate himself). "Mediation" should not be understood to mean that the development of tools or language (or rules and roles) make it easier to do things that somehow or other were going to get done anyway. Crucial to Engestrom's model of activity systems is the insight that the processes of mediation transform the nature of the contexts within which people act. Thus, the notion of mediation points to the occurence of wholly new events, events that would be impossible in the absence of the relevant mediating processes (e.g. "communication intensive" organizations).

The idea of mediation is not peculiar to activity theory - it appears elsewhere, particularly in theories of language and semiotics. Where activity theory is unusual, however, is in the emphasis it places on the suggestion that symbol–mediated activity should not be studied as if it is "for the mind alone". People do not only, nor do they primarily just, think. Above all they act practically, and in collaboration with others.

Two final points should be noted about the notion of activity systems. As the notion of "system" implies, elements within activity systems are mutually interactive. Thus, for example, the rules a community adopts interact with division of labour it develops, both these factors are related to the ways different technologies are developed, all interact with the conceptions communities evolve of the activities they are engaged in, and so on. Moreover it should not be assumed that the relations between the elements of an activity system will all be straightforward and non–problematical. One of the major insights developed by the approach is the notion that incoherencies, inconsistencies, tensions and dilemmas are likely to feature in all activity systems. For example, conceptions of activities may change but elements of an older activity system may remain; the demands of new technologies may jar with established social norms; more flexible organization cultures may be needed to cope with changing structures but may be difficult to develop, and so on. It is because of the determination and skill that people demonstrate in the enactment of their activities that everyday difficulties like these are overcome, and work systems appear to operate smoothly and in a machine–like way. Inspired by Marxist notions of the internal contradictions of capitalism Engestrom suggests that such tensions offer a major opportunity for change and development within an activity system. Borrowing and adapting Vygotsky's notion of "the zone of proximal development" he suggests that the immediate capacity of a social system for learning reflects the internal contradictions within it that participants are prepared to address.

In a series of papers Engestrom (1990, 1991, 1993; see also Kuutti and Arvonen, 1992) has applied his model of the dynamics of activity systems in further analysis of the health care centre. Partly through discourse analysis, partly from observation, and partly from accounts of the history of medical practice he was able to distinguish a variety of conceptions that doctors may have of their activity. Doctors may conceive of their work in biomedical terms (the treatment of somatic disease), in administrative–economic terms (the apportionment of scarce medical resources), in psychiatric terms (regarding the patients as a psychosomatic whole), in socio–medical terms (as in community medicine), or in system–interactive terms (the patient as collaborator in the solution of health care problems).

Engestrom's research suggested that, perhaps unrecognized and certainly not debated by them, different doctors in the same medical practice were enacting different conceptions of health care, in particular biomedical/administrative–economic approaches and psychiatric/socio–medical ones. The subsequent decision to refocus priorities around the latter orientation did not, however, prove straightforward. As he reports, attempts to reorient priorities in this direction were hampered by the resource system that the doctors worked within. As well as tensions between the computerized medical system and the new object of activity, that have already been described, tensions emerged between the new object of activity and: (i) the established division of labour between doctors and other health professions (the new approach required broader, overlapping work roles); (ii) the way patients were randomly allocated to doctors; and (iii) the (traditional) biomedical concepts and techniques that the doctors were accustomed to using. Note that Engestrom would suggest that such incoherencies and tension mark the scope for self–generated learning within the medical centre (its "zone of proximal development"). By recognising and confronting these difficulties staff in the centre could begin to reconstruct their activities and rebuild their activity system.

Not only, however, did the desire to enact new priorities in the health care centre require internal adjustments, such as the need to modify the patient records system. A psychosomatic and socio–medical orientation required also that new relationships should be developed between the centre and other centres, hospitals and social workers who might endeavour to help the same patients. As Kuutti and Arvonen (1992) analyse the situation, an expanded conception of health care across different, geographically separated, professional groups had to be developed.

For this to be achieved two priorities presented themselves: the need to build a shared concept of patient care across different health care professionals, and the related need to support their shared endeavour by appropriate technologies, rules and a division of labour.

Kuutti notes how the geographically separated and functionally segregated health care professionals at the medical centre, in hospitals and in the community had, in the past, each dealt with only a fragment of the total situation affecting their clients. He reports that a technical system, improvized by personnel involved in the centre, made it possible to support efforts to develop a new, expanded, conception of joint endeavour. Via an e–mail network, supported also by telephone and ordinary mail, a new community of practice was fostered around a shared concern for integrated health care provision with relevant information about patients being shared between the general practitioners, hospital doctors, nurses, community nurses and social workers. The fragmented focus that each of them had previously enacted was, Kuutti reports, overtaken by an emerging sense of shared priorities. Following discussions about an appropriate division of labour and procedural rules, the e–mail system in particular facilitated synchronized action around a developing patient–centred "master help plan".

In introducing this case the question was posed, were the problems of the patient records system that Engestrom studied best considered as technical problems or motivational ones? Following the activity theoretical analysis introduced here it will be clear why the reply is: it is both these and more. The solution to problems of the health care centre was not to be found in the redesign of its computer records system alone. A key insight from activity theory for HCI practitioners is that it is a mistake to seek to separate particular episodes from the contexts in which they are situated, to separate technological questions from behavioural ones, or to separate the attitudes of individuals from the orientation of their communities. Analysis of the inter–relationships in this case suggest its technological and motivational aspects must be located within the broader purposive, socially distributed activity system of which they are but a part. In other words, the technical system was an integral feature of the broader system of activity, and developments in working practices depended upon a complex interaction of changes. Such changes could only effectively be initiated by the participants themselves through their creativity in addressing the incoherencies of their activity system.

10.4 Main features of activity theory as illustrated by the CSCW example

Key points from the general theory of activity are summarized in Table 10.1. Earlier it was suggested that CSCW needs to be located in an analysis of working and of cooperation. Three key contributions to such an analysis emerge from the points summarized in the table.

First, activity theory conceptualizes working as an active, purposive endeavour. Expertise is distributed within a community of practitioners but activity systems achieve their coherency by virtue of the shared object of activity that unites participants. Neither social cooperation nor workplace technologies can sensibly be understood in isolation from the purposive nature of the activity system of which they are a part.

Second, expertise is "situated". Knowledge acquired from text books or classroom tuition, for example, is no more (and no less) than a resource for action in any particular situation. The process of "knowing" is related to the process of "interpretation": always provisional, inevitably developing. Understanding of an activity, participation in improvizations towards its enactment, and access to relevant debates and dialogue within a community of practitioners are essential components of this process. Thus, an activity theory orientation merges the notion of cooperative activity with the notion of collective learning.

Third, rather than studying technologies, communities or individuals in isolation from each other, activity theory emphasizes how activities are intimately inter–related with the systems through which they are enacted. Collective learning occurs with engagement, and new mediating devices may precipitate new learning. Unrecognized inconsistencies that develop within and between the elements of an activity system can provide major opportunities for engagement and dialogue.

Such points indicate that CSCW technologies in particular and computer systems in general cannot be studied in isolation from the core activities they are intended to support and that technologies themselves help sustain particular conceptions of activities. It would a mistake therefore (see for example, Kraut, Galegher and Egido, 1988) to focus on group process in the absence of a focus on group task, or to seek to maintain the supposed distinctions between social systems and technological systems. Within the perspective that activity theory encourages, technology design is social design and social design is technology design.

Table 10.1 Key aspects of activity theory

(i) Activities are enacted through purposive actions. Activities are intended to transform the world and different activities are distinguishable by their objects (e.g. for doctors in Engestrom's example objects of activity were somatic diseases, patients as a psycho–somatic wholes, etc).

(ii) They are enacted by agents who understand the object of the activity. Appropriate behaviour for certain situations are not determined by the situations themselves as stimulus–response psychology would assume; rather, agents (doctors, in Engestrom's case) make assumptions about how it is appropriate to behave in different situations.

(iii) The conceptions people hold of their activities are actively generated by them in their participation within communities of practitioners. People do not passively internalize conceptions of their activities.

(iv) Activity is enacted through a community's activity system. Activity systems are comprized of tools, concepts, social structures, and social processes. These mediate relations between individuals, communities, and the object of their activities. Activity systems are typically characterized by internal incoherencies and contradictions (in Engestrom's example these included variations in the doctors' conceptions of their activities, and in the tensions between an emerging psycho–social conception of medical activity and established concepts, procedures, and division of labour).

(v) Activity systems are rooted in their histories. (The various conceptions of medical activity noted in Engestrom's case, for example, emerged at different historical periods).

(vi) Different activities and activity systems overlap and interrelate. The output of one activity system (e.g. the qualified doctor produced by the educational system) may be an essential feature of another activity system (i.e. the doctor as a key input to a health care system). Moreover, activities may themselves become the object of further activity, e.g. when attempts are made to transform particular practices. (This is, according to activity theory, how social coordination occurs and how people (re)produce their society's cultural order).

(vii) Collective learning occurs when significant shifts occur in a community's practices and in the conceptions participants develop of their activities. This may be provoked by strains and incoherencies within an activity system which, hitherto, have become taken–for–granted. (In the health centre example health care professionals developed a wider concept of their collective activities that was supported by CSCW technologies).

Similarly, an activity theory perspective indicates that technologies should not be studied in isolation from the communities where they are to be used. It would be naïve to assume, for example, that because new channels for communication are created people will necessarily use them to communicate with individuals or sub groups that they do not already identify with; certain communications within communities of practitioners will, naturally enough, be exclusive to members of the group itself. Moreover, as was discussed earlier, computer–mediated communications provide abstract and decontextualized representations of reality which, despite all their speed and convenience, have been stripped of the richness and spontaneity of face–to–face exchanges. Decontextualized messages often have the appearance of messages coming from no–one in particular, going to no–one in particular. In terms of both the richness of information they may convey and the emotional impact such messages may have, activity theory suggests that computer mediated information systems may augment, but not replace, face– to–face interactions. Putting this another way, a sense of communal activity is a necessary prerequisite of cooperative working, the best way in which trust may be developed is by shared endeavour and face–to–face dialogue.

Nonetheless, in the context of other developments, activity theory suggests that CSCW technologies do offer significant opportunities to support collective change and development. As the case discussed in the last section illustrated, computer mediated communications can become associated with significant changes in a community's practices as expanded information and communication networks may support expanded conceptions of activity. The FINSTAR computer records system the doctors were using had been designed with a particular model of medical activity in mind. In the evolving situation changes were required to the records system certainly, but in themselves these were not enough, nor could they be designed without the ongoing involvement of the health care professionals themselves. As tensions within the activity system of health centre were exposed, however, participants became aware both of the inadequacies of their conventional approaches and of the need to develop the system through which they were enacted. The broader networked system that was improvized then helped stimulate the developing conception and methods of providing medical care that were being fashioned by the participants themselves.

10.5 Activity theory compared with other approaches

Activity theory contrasts with a number of established approaches to behavioural and social analysis and systems design. Although it can be presented as a "psychological" approach it challenges distinctions between psychology and sociology. Thus, in its emphasis on collective activities it is unlike conventional individual psychological approaches to HCI (e.g. P. Johnson, 1992). Similarly, it marks a departure from functional orthodoxies in information systems design (as, for example, identified by Hirschheim and Klein, 1989) which show strong similarities with Tayloristic approaches in the way they seek to break tasks into their smallest elements. Moreover, it departs from the two best publicized alternatives to this tradition, namely socio–technical approaches (e.g. Mumford, 1983) and approaches which examine computer systems design from a theory of power and democracy within organizations (e.g. Bjerknes, Ehn and Kyng, 1987). Unlike socio–technical theory, activity theory avoids distinctions between technological systems and social systems. Unlike power–based theories it places less emphasis on an interest group model of organizations, more on the interrelationships between activities, imaginations and social and technological resource systems.

Within the IT and HCI communities activity theory has been compared with a number of contemporary attempts to develop new approaches to design. For example, Raeithal (1992) suggests that, helpful though Winograd and Flores' (1986) attempt to introduce the theory of speech acts into the analysis of computers and cognition was (they present a model of man "as a speaking animal that loves to bargain") it falls some way short of providing a new foundation for design; critical elements are absent from Winograd's account and it reduces the concept of communication to verbal and written language only. Activity theory promises a more general framework, highlighting the incoherencies of activity systems, emphasising the relationship between verbal communication and material action, and providing a basis for cross–disciplinary, action–oriented interventions. Kuutti (forthcoming) declares a similar hope, suggesting that activity theory offers more promise for the development of a coherent alternative to conventional approaches to systems design than has been offered by a range of alternatives inspired by, for example, phenomenology (he cites Boland, 1985), transaction cost theory (Ciborra, 1987) and semiotics (Anderson, 1991).

In the present writer's view, however, it is a mistake to champion any approach as the basis for a united theoretical future. Given the complexity of behaviour a multi–perspective orientation has much to commend it. Indeed, the alternative, suggested by Starr's comments about an "invisible college" that was touched on earlier and illustrated so well by Chaiklin and Lave's (1993) collection of papers, is to seek to align activity theory with approaches which are developing similar or complementary orientations. Chaiklin and Lave bring together a range of contributions from activity theorists, critical psychologists, cognitive anthropologists and ethnomethodologists. Certainly, important differences in orientation can be identified in these various contributions; for example, while ethnomethodologists (such as Suchman) emphasize how the world is constructed in social interaction, activity theorists (such as Engestrom) emphasize the significance of the cultural and material systems employed within such processes. Lave explains this difference by suggesting that while phenomenological approaches emphasize the here and now rather than its historical origins, activity theorists concentrate on the origins rather than just the here and now. But what is most striking is not the differences between activity theory, ethnomethodology anthropology, phenomenology, and the rest, but their similarities. All provide theories of everyday practices, reversing the conventional assumption that social structures explain social cohesion to suggest that it is the recurring pattern of everyday interactions which explains social structures.

Bloch (1977) anticipated the focus of contemporary social theory on the practice of everyday life some twenty years ago when he argued that anthropologists who concentrate on exotic social rituals fail to notice the structure and development of the everyday competencies upon which community survival depends. In the early 1980s Ortner (1984), in similar vein, suggested that the theory of everyday practice was becoming the central theme of both contemporary anthropology and social theory. In the late 1980s actor network theory (e.g. Latour, 1987; Law, 1992) contributed further to this development, demonstrating that scientific practices are not, as is often assumed, in some way above contemporary culture but are integral to it. Activity theory is perhaps best understood as the latest addition to this developing orientation. Its distinctive contribution lies in the explanations it offers of social construction, social cohesion and social change.

10.6 The future

Earlier it was suggested that the new technologies are, simultaneously, imploding organizations into electronic representations in computers and exploding them into communications networks. As the subsequent discussion and the case of the Medical Centre suggested, many of the problems the technologies create can be traced to the former of these effects, many of their opportunities to the latter. Be that as it may, such developments can be expected to continue apace in the coming years. In these circumstances the new technologies are best regarded not as flexible tools (to be used, for example, to support cooperative work); rather, the new information and communication technologies are emerging as the medium for organizing itself.

Activity theory suggests that two key problems are likely to be associated with this development. First, because of the new technologies, activity systems which were previously relatively independent one from the other are becoming ever more interdependent. As in the health care example, such networks both encourage and require an expanded conception of (collective) activity. Second, as activity systems become ever more inter–related and complex they are becoming larger and, correspondingly, more difficult to manage in an hierarchical, top–down way. Widespread employee involvement in communication–intensive activity systems is essential for their effective operation.

However, although activity theory highlights such issues there is very little empirical data on them at the present time. Studies are needed as follows:

(a) Activity theory suggests that an apprenticeship–like role is essential for the transition from novice to expert; the process of becoming an expert requires more than merely the application of classroom knowledge, experts must learn how to operate as competent members of a community of practitioners. Note, however, that the experiences of socialization into work systems built around an extensive use of computers and computer–mediated communications will be very different from those of past epochs. Studies of the acquisition of expertise in these circumstances will be required.

(b) A common problem in bureaucratic organizations was the existence of work systems which systematically routinized work, effectively excluding participants from an understanding of, and meaningful participation within, the activities they were serving. Future work organizations may have a different problem; as systems become ever larger and more interlinked it will be essential, but perhaps very difficult, to cultivate and foster the necessary shared sense of priorities amongst "community" members. Studies are needed to illuminate further how a shared sense of priorities can be developed within dispersed communities united by computer mediated technologies.

(c) At the same time, where more people do become directly involved in the activities with which they are involved, anxiety is likely to become more of an issue than ever it was in bureaucratic organizations. Bureaucratic organizations offer a number of defences against anxiety (see Menzies–Lythe's 1960 study of how rules and regulations can be used to detach people from the stress of personal involvement in their tasks). As Hirshhorn and Gilmore (1992) noted, a different and more mature set of psychological skills are essential for the "organization without boundaries" where participants must become personally involved with the consequences of their actions and decisions. Studies will be needed of the emotional strains associated with the non–hierarchical systems of organization that are becoming associated with advanced technologies.

In conclusion, note that these various issues all demand an expansion of HCI activities away from attempts to understand "human factors" only, towards the broader study of "human actors". The range of behavioural issues being raized by advanced technologies demand new approaches to their analysis. Activity theorists insist that conventional dichotomies, between the social and the technical or between thought and action, are unhelpful. They point to the way in which collaboration is achieved through language and through actions, and to the complex ways in which activities, concepts, technologies, structures and processes constitute each other. As the process of organizational implosion/explosion continues, and as advanced technologies become (ever more obviously) the medium of organization, the theme of this chapter has been that the need for new systems of communal self–regulation will become urgent. Attention will shift away from conventional theories of formal organization (which consider "change" and "learning" as optional extras) towards accounts of how people organize, in which the processes of "collective learning" and "knowledge generation" are central. Activity theory promises a major contribution to such developments. It focuses on the detail of everyday practices and dialogue, and indicates how activities are systemic, self–organizing, rooted in history, and reaching out to the future. In this way activity theory pictures the creative and improvizational nature of everyday practices. It points to the ongoing opportunities that exist for social (re)construction and identifies the constraints, as well as the opportunities, that information technologies present for communal self–regulation.

Further reading

The history and development of activity theory

For readers interested in tracing the development of activity theory see the introduction by Wertsch, and the articles by Vygotsky and Leont'ev in:

Wertsch, J. (1979, 1981). *The Concept of Activity in Soviet Psychology*. Armonk, NY: M. E. Sharpe.

A contemporary collection of debates between Russian activity theorists is:

Lektorsky, V. (ed.) (1990). *Activity: Theories, Methodology and Problems*. Orlando: Deutsch Press.

Lektorsky's collection is very philosophical. Articles printed here demonstrate the links between the approach of Russian activity theorists and Marxism, the way they have sought to avoid the dichotomies that are a feature of Western psychology, and their efforts to develop the concept of "activity" into something beyond a synonym for "frame" or "script".

The landmark treatise on activity theory, which does much to resolve some of the ambiguities otherwise associated with the approach is:

Engestrom, Y. (1987). *Learning by Expanding: an Activity Theoretical Approach to Developmental Research*. Helsinki: Orienta–Konsultit.

This is not always easy to get hold of, however. Other material by Engestrom which provides an overview of his theoretical approach includes

Engestrom, Y. (1991). Developmental work research: reconstructing expertise through expansive learning. In M. Nurminen and G. Weir (eds), *Human Jobs and Computer Interfaces*. Amsterdam: Elsevier.

Engestrom, Y. (1993). Developmental studies of work as a testbench of activity theory: the case of primary care medical practice. In S. Chaiklin and J. Lave (eds), *Understanding Practice: Perspectives on Activity and Context*. Cambridge: Cambridge University Press.

Recent American (and non–Marxian) approaches to activity theory have been influenced by Engestrom's approach, but while he draws strongly from Leont'ev as well as Vygotsky, Vygotsky has been the major inspiration in discussions about activity in the American literature. See especially:

Brown, J., Collins, A. and Duguid, P. (1989). Situated cognition and the culture of learning. *Educational Researcher*, January– February, 32–42 (a number of "peer review" articles discussing this paper appeared in the May–June 1989 edition of this Journal).

Lave, J, and Wenger, E. (1991). *Situated Learning: Legitimate Peripheral Participation*. Cambridge: CUP.

Brown and Duguid relate their and Lave's ideas to organization theory in:

Brown, J. and Duguid, P. (1991). Organization learning and communities of practice: toward a unified view of working, learning, and innovation. *Organization Science* 2, 40–57.

See also:

Blackler, F. (1993). Knowledge and the theory of organizations: organizations as activity systems and the reframing of management. *Journal of Management Studies* 30, 863–884.

Activity theory and CSCW

Problems with established approaches to systems design that CSCW technologies have highlighted are discussed in:

Greenbaum J. and Kyng, M. (1991). *Design at Work. Cooperative Design of Computer Systems*. Hillsdale NJ: Erlbaum (see especially the introduction and the chapter by Bannon).

Activity theory ideas, based on the Russian tradition of activity theory, as they may relate to CSCW are discussed at a theoretical level by:

Raeithal, A. (1992). Activity theory as a foundation for design. In C. Floyd, H. Zullighoven, R. Budde and R. Keil–Slawik, (eds), *Software Development and Reality Construction*. Berlin: Springer–Verlag.

The case of the medical health centre is introduced in

Engestrom, Y., Engestrom, R. and Saarelma, O. (1988). Computerized medical records, production pressure and compartmentalization in the work activity of health centre physicians. *Proceedings of the 2nd Conference on Computer–Supported Cooperative Work*. New York: ACM. Reprinted in Engestrom, Y. (1990). *Learning, Working and Imagining: Twelve Studies in Activity Theory*. Helsinki: Orienta Consultit.

See also

Kuutti, K. and Arvonen, T. (1992). Identifying CSCW applications by means of activity theory concepts: a case example. In *Sharing Perspectives –Proceedings of the CSCW '92 Conference*. New York: ACM Press.

Activity theory and related approaches

A paper which overviews the emerging, shared orientation between activity theories and contemporary social theory is:
Starr, S. (1992). The Trojan door: organizations, work and the "open black box", *Systems Practice* 5, 395–410.

Papers presenting such "theories of practice", and a review of the similarities and differences of such orientations, are provided in the excellent collection:
Chaiklin, S. and Lave, J. (eds) (1993). *Understanding Practice: Perspectives on Activity and Context*. Cambridge: Cambridge University Press.

Chapter 11

Organizational Analysis and HCI

Matthew Jones

11.1 Introduction

Organizational Analysis in relation to HCI is concerned with understanding the influence of organizational context on the way in which computer–based information systems (IS) are used. There are many different views, however, about what organizational context is, let alone how it influences HCI, and it is therefore not possible to talk about Organizational Analysis as a single, unified approach. Instead, it must be recognized that there are several alternative approaches that draw on different disciplinary bases which themselves include a number of distinct theoretical perspectives. There is not the space in this chapter to discuss all the approaches in detail, and our aim will therefore be to sketch out some of the more important and to describe some of the major theoretical differences between them. We will also give a fuller description of one particular form of Organizational Analysis to illustrate some of the issues involved.

Organizational Analysis has only recently begun to receive wider recognition in the HCI field. Traditionally, HCI has tended to treat the organizational context within which IS are used as outside the boundary of the system which it seeks to address. While this may have been necessary as an initial approximation to enable the underlying cognitive principles to be investigated, it has become increasingly unsustainable as IS have spread from being specialized systems used by technical experts to being ubiquitous tools of general work. This is partly reflected in the growth of interest in Computer Supported Cooperative Work, where the social nature of computer use is a fundamental principle. It may be argued, however, that even without the technological developments of groupware, the continuing problems of implementation and use of single–user systems has highlighted the need to consider a wider range of factors in understanding the interaction of humans with computers, many of which may be seen to be organizational in character.

Similarly, despite the immense impact of IS on organizations, most organizational theorists have tended not to focus on the interaction of humans with computers, and even the organizational sub field of Information Systems has tended to treat HCI as insignificant detail. Consequently, awareness of HCI in the organizational literature is probably even less than that of organizational issues in HCI, as Clegg (1991) notes. This may be seen as reflecting the predominantly non–technical background of most organizational theorists and the domination of the research agenda by more evidently managerial or sociological concerns. Our discussion of the organizational literature in this chapter will therefore be primarily as a source of theoretical insight rather than of exemplary analyses.

11.2 Disciplinary backgrounds

Vaske and Grantham (1988) provide an overview of socially–oriented approaches in HCI which they identify as being based on three main disciplines. The first of these, and the one to which Vaske and Grantham give greatest attention as it is their own preferred approach, is social psychology. Its main focus is on how individual psychology is affected by other individuals in a social context. For example, how do attitudes towards computers change when individuals are required to use them in their work? Social psychology also addresses how groups can affect their individual members, how individuals can affect groups and how groups affect each other. For example, how does the use of a computer system by others affect individual attitudes? Social psychology is probably closest to traditional HCI in terms of its theoretical assumptions and underlying cognitive focus.

A second contribution, discussed in more detail in Chapter 8, comes from social anthropology. This is the study of human behaviour in terms of social customs and practices. The shared beliefs, values and behaviour of a group are described as its culture. Traditionally, anthropologists studied the culture of whole societies, often in "exotic" locations. Modern organizations, however, often have distinctive cultures, and subcultures, and these have been an increasing focus of anthropological research. An important aspect of a culture is symbolism and ritual. While these may be easier to detect in "exotic" societies, they are also present in modern organizations. For example, the installation of powerful computers for senior business executives may be related more to their status in the organization than their computing needs. Similarly, in many British organizations the "tea break" may be an important occasion for informal communication and source of social cohesion, the contribution of which may need to be considered in the design of computer–based systems.

The third field, Organization Studies, is more applied. Organization Studies is a branch of sociology which focuses on organizations, often, though not exclusively, of a commercial nature. It therefore seeks to apply sociological concepts to business organizations rather than to society as a whole. There are also some important theoretical concepts in mainstream sociology which apply specifically to organizations, such as Weber's theory of bureaucracy, which describes an "ideal form" of rational organizational control, and Marx's socio–political analysis of capitalism, which emphasises the inherent conflict of interests between different groups in an organization (for a useful introduction to sociology see Giddens, 1993). For example, the design of a computer–based system may need to conform to established bureaucratic procedures or may be affected by conflicts between different interest groups.

Other relevant theories from Organization Studies include: Scientific Management, which suggests that productivity can be maximized by task simplification and the separation of the execution of work from its control; the Human Relations school, which argues that organizations prosper when they meet the needs and aspirations of those who work in them; and socio–technical design, which argues that effective work organization requires a balancing of social and technical elements and that this is best achieved through participative design. Pugh and Hickson (1989) provide a concise introduction to these theories. Much early work in HCI may be seen as having been strongly influenced by the tradition of Scientific Management, in the sense of adopting a reductionist model of human behaviour and a distant attitude towards users, although more recently Human Relations and socio–technical ideas have become more influential.

11.3 Alternative perspectives on Organizational Analysis

Even from this brief review of the contributing disciplines, it should be clear that there are some significant differences between and within them. In terms of the typology of the social sciences developed by Burrell and Morgan (1979), these may be considered as reflecting the influence of one or other of two major intellectual traditions, each of which involves distinctive assumptions about social reality (ontology), about what constitutes legitimate knowledge of that reality (epistemology) and about how we may obtain that knowledge (methodology). Although there is considerable disagreement in the literature about what to call these traditions we will adopt the terminology of Orlikowski and Baroudi (1992) in referring to them as "positivism" and "interpretivism".

Perhaps the most fundamental assumption on which the approaches differ is that relating to the nature of social reality; in this case, the nature of organizations. The "positivist" position assumes that organizations are objective entities, made up of tangible and relatively stable structures that exist independently of the individuals who work in them (this is called a realist ontology). The characteristics of organizations influencing HCI may therefore be measured from unambiguously observable parameters such as the numbers of levels in the organizational hierarchy or the type of production technology. The "interpretive" (or hermeneutic) position, on the other hand, assumes that organizations consist of the interaction of the beliefs of those who work in and with them and that "reality" is simply a set of labels we associate with these socially–constructed beliefs (this is called a nominalist ontology). Thus the characteristics of organizations that influence HCI would be seen as being based on the "subjective" interpretations of organizational participants, such as their view of the attitude towards computer use in the organization or of the status conferred by computer use.

Depending on which ontological position is chosen, very different conclusions will be reached about the types of knowledge we can have about the way that humans interact with computers. Thus the "positivist" viewpoint would see the relationship between the parameters of organization and human interaction with computers as explainable in terms of law–like generalizations. From the "interpretivist" position, however, there is no objective, reliable "truth" to be found, only different interpretations of a situation.

These conclusions finally lead to quite different views on how we can obtain this knowledge. Researchers adopting the "positivist" position are likely to seek methods of establishing "proof" of the generalizations, based on the tradition of the natural sciences. Surveys, experimental tests and other standardized research instruments are therefore typically the favoured techniques. The concern of researchers adopting the second position, in contrast, will be with identifying and describing individuals' interpretations. Techniques such as semi– or unstructured interviews and observation are therefore likely to be favoured.

The two positions are not compatible and both would claim to be able to explain the other. Thus, a "positivist" would argue, for example, that interpretations will be observable through consistent patterns of behaviour, while an "interpetivist" would argue that the influence of parameters, such as levels of organizational hierarchy, ultimately operate through the interpretations of particular individuals. Any individual piece of HCI research will therefore involve a choice about which of these perspectives to adopt, even if this is not always recognized.

Another important dimension of variation between the different disciplines that Burrell and Morgan (1979) identify, concerns their views on the nature of society (and hence of the organizations which exist within it). Once again we may distinguish two positions, one of which emphasises social order and the other which emphasises social conflict. The first position views society as relatively stable, well–integrated and consensual, while the second sees it as characterized by radical change, endemic conflict and the domination of certain interest groups by others.

In terms of these dimensions we may identify traditional HCI research as generally "positivist" in its approach, adopting a "scientific" methodology in pursuit of enduring "truths" about the way that humans interact with computers. It also tends to view organizations (where it considers them at all) as relatively ordered, consensual systems with functional aims and objectives, such as efficiency or productivity. A similar perspective is also widely adopted in Organization Studies. For example, it may be seen to underpin Scientific Management, and, perhaps more relevant to HCI, it is the dominant perspective in research on IS (Orlikowski and Baroudi, 1992). A number of the approaches we have identified as contributing to Organizational Analysis, however, have important "interpretivist" elements, and some forms of Organization Studies view society as inherently conflictual. Research in these traditions is therefore based on a rather different set of assumptions from mainstream HCI.

11.4 Application to HCI

Despite its relative lack of recognition in the HCI field, the history of organizationally–oriented HCI research is a surprisingly long one. In the UK, for example, social psychological research on HCI has been conducted by the HUSAT group at Loughborough University since the early 1970s (see for example Eason, 1974, 1988). Similar research has been conducted in the US by groups at Carnegie Mellon University (Sproull and Kiesler, 1991) and Bell Labs (Kraut and Streeter, 1990). Most of this research is broadly "positivist", typically employing quasi–experimental studies and surveys to obtain "objective" measurements of organizations.

More "interpretive" approaches to organizationally–oriented research, based on social anthropology, have been developed at Xerox PARC, following the pioneering study of Suchman (1987). This is discussed in more detail in Chapter 8. This type of research has become increasingly influential in the field, particularly with the growth of interest in Computer Supported Cooperative Work.

Another strand of "interpretive" research which has contributed to organizationally–oriented HCI has come from theoretically–based analyses of the nature of the design process. For example Winograd and Flores (1986) describe the creation of computer tools as the designing of new organizational conversations. This concept was extended by Ehn (1988) who considered design as a "language game" between designer and users. This in turn influenced the development of the "contextual design" approach of Wixon, Holtzblatt and Knox, (1990).

Ehn's work is also part of another influential contribution to organizationally–oriented HCI which has been developed in Scandinavia (see Floyd *et al*, 1989 for a review). This generally adopts a social conflict model of organizations, focusing on participative design and more radical trade–union oriented approaches. Some US researchers such as Grudin (1990b) who have worked in Scandinavia have sought to develop less conflictual versions of these approaches to gain greater international recognition of this work.

While this brief overview of the application of different forms of Organizational Analysis in HCI cannot claim to be comprehensive, it does illustrate its theoretical diversity. Rather than attempt to describe each of the types of Organizational Analysis, however, we will concentrate on one particular form, "Cognitive Mapping" as developed by Eden (1989). This is an interpretive approach, which seeks to develop a representation of users' situated understanding of their particular context. It also recognises the existence of conflicting interest groups in organizations and seeks to facilitate negotiations between them. It may therefore be seen as illustrating a number of features of Organizational Analysis in general.

11.5 Cognitive Mapping

The technique of Cognitive Mapping, originally developed by Eden (1989) as a technique for use in strategic decision making, is based on the "Personal Construct Theory" of Kelly (1955). This has three key assertions: that people make sense of their world through contrast and similarity; that people seek to explain their world (why is it so? what made it so?); and that people seek to understand the significance of their world by organizing concepts hierarchically. In the traditional application of Personal Construct Theory, individuals are asked to express their view of the world in terms of constructs, each having a positive and negative pole (expressing the concept and its perceived opposite). The relationship between the constructs is then evaluated through an exhaustive paired or three–way comparison to develop what are known as Repertory Grids.

Eden (1989) adopts Kelly's concept of constructs, but uses them in a much less rigid way. Constructs are identified from the statements individuals use in describing a situation during an interview and are represented as brief phrases in natural language. Each construct has a positive and negative "pole" which are shown separated by three full stops (see Figure 11.2). Where the latter is not evident from the interviewee's comments, it is taken to be implicit (for example construct 41 in Figure 11.2).

Rather than carry out the Repertory Grid comparison, the links between constructs are identified from the chain of argument employed in describing the situation. The relationship between constructs is assumed to take the form of explanations and consequences as shown in Figure 11.1. The relationship may be positive (i.e. construct A reinforces construct B), negative (construct A operates in the opposite direction to construct B – reinforcing the negative pole), or connotative (implying a relationship between the constructs, but of unknown or neutral effect) e.g. between constructs 41 and 43 in Figure 11.2.

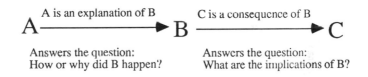

Figure 11.1 Examples of relationships between constructs from a cognitive map.

The product of a Cognitive Mapping exercise is therefore a map (in the style of a directed network) made up of nodes (consisting of phrases used by the individual to describe the situation) and arcs (links identified from the individual's description of the situation). The structure and content of the map is validated by discussing it with the interviewee.

The mapping is initially carried out with pencil and paper during a semi–structured interview which usually lasts about an hour. The large number of constructs generated in such an interview (typically about 100) often results in a very "messy" picture/map being generated. This then needs to be "tidied–up" both for analysis and feedback to the interviewee. As part of this tidying process the map can be transferred to a specific computer package (GraphicsCOPE), which has been developed to operationalise Cognitive Mapping. It enables much easier handling of large numbers of constructs and introduces a much higher degree of flexibility in manipulation of the maps. As each construct is typed into GraphicsCOPE it is assigned a number for ease of identification (as shown in Figure 11.2).

Following the tidying of the map (using GraphicsCOPE), the information is then presented back to the interviewee, either as hardcopy or on the computer screen, for amendment and/or confirmation that it is an appropriate representation of their viewpoint. Rather than working with the whole map, particular chains of argument that are much easier to comprehend can be separated out. The feedback session is also an opportunity for reflection and negotiation over the content and structure of the map.

In practical terms maps of more than about 30 concepts are too difficult to deal with as a whole and GraphicsCOPE includes analytical routines which can aid the identification of: clustering of concepts; the beginnings and ends of chains of arguments (described as "assertions" and "goals"); constructs which have many others associated with them (described as "issues"); and constructs which are branching points in a chain of argument ("option points"). This analysis can help to guide the validation and interpretation of the map.

In its application to strategic decision making, Cognitive Mapping is used as part of a more general method known as Strategic Options Development and Analysis (SODA). In this approach different stakeholders whose views have been individually mapped are brought together in a meeting (a SODA workshop). The individual maps are compared and a collective map is negotiated which seeks to merge those of the individuals. Where there is uncertainty or different views about the meaning of constructs these can be examined in the individual maps and debated among the meeting participants. By retaining elements of the original (individual) maps in the collective map, the individual participants' sense of ownership of the group viewpoint is encouraged. By providing a rich representation of individual viewpoints the similarities and differences between different stakeholders can be studied and debated. Apart from the process and affective benefits of such negotiation, the collective map can serve as an agenda for strategic action by identifying shared goals, problems and options.

11.5.1 Example problem[1]

The wiring systems for modern aircraft involve thousands of different lengths of wire of hundreds of different types. These must be cut to the right lengths from reels and "stuffed" into the appropriate plugs. A number of different machines are used to handle different types of wire. All the plugs and wires needed to make up the "kit" used in a particular electrical sub–assembly are bagged together for delivery to the assembly shop. About twenty per cent of the kits are particularly complex and are made to order, while the remainder are made in batches to optimize the assembly task. Other kits also need to be made up for spares, to incorporate last–minute design changes and to allow for items failing quality inspections.

In the ABC aircraft company the task of scheduling the wire cutting and stuffing was done using cards produced by the Planning Department. These were placed in a box in the kitting area, from which they were taken by the machine operators. No due date was given on the cards so staff would either take the next one in the box, or start a particular kit as directed by the shop supervisor. With the increasing competition in the international aircraft market, the ABC management were concerned to increase the efficiency of their manufacturing process and each department was under pressure to reduce costs. In the electrical Kitting Shop two major areas of potential cost savings were identified: excessive inventory levels and low utilization of staff and machinery resources. The Manufacturing Systems division were asked to advise on how to improve the kitting process and recommended the introduction of a computer–based scheduling system in the Planning Department. This would take data from the production schedule for each aircraft and calculate the precise order in which each kit should be made up. A specialist software company was employed to produce the system. They had an established scheduling product, but this needed to be customized to meet the specific needs of the ABC Kitting Shop. One aspect of this customization was the design of the interface.

Initially attention was focused on what information needed to be presented to the Factory Planners, in what form, to facilitate the scheduling task. As investigations continued, however, it became clear that a whole range of further issues were involved. For example, the shop supervisor was extremely reluctant to participate in the project and was highly critical of the proposed system. It was also

---

[1] The details of this problem and the description of the use of Cognitive Mapping are fictitious although it is based on a number of actual cases, in the aircraft industry and in IS design, in which the author has been involved.

found that the estimated times for the completion of particular tasks were extremely unreliable. Frequent breakdowns of one old machine meant that some tasks took considerably longer than expected, while skilled operators could sometimes rearrange jobs in ways that were not recognized in the official schedule so as to cut down set–up times and speed throughput. Individual operators would also arrange their own work to suit their own preferred work pattern by, for example, leaving early or having longer rest breaks.

It was soon recognized that however good the interface design, the scheduling system was likely to be unsuccessful if it did not address these issues and that a broader analysis was therefore necessary. The first stage in this analysis was to identify the "stakeholders" in the situation (those groups or individuals who could influence the outcome of the project). An initial list of these was identified as: the ABC management (who had control of the budget), the Manufacturing Systems division (who had commissioned the project), the Planning Department, the Kitting Shop supervisor (who would be expected to take responsibility for running the new system), and the machine operators (whose work would be organized by it).

Interviews were held with the relevant individuals or representatives from each of the stakeholder groups to produce cognitive maps of their thinking about the new scheduling system (an extract from one of these is shown in Figure 11.2). With the agreement of the interviewees the interviews were also recorded on audio tape. The manager of the Electrical Division was chosen as the representative of the company management (although not directly involved in senior company management, he was considered sufficiently aware of their views to be able to explain them and also sufficiently interested in the project that he would be willing to give time to be interviewed). He saw the project as part of the company's cost reduction initiative. Targets had been set for all Divisions and he was determined to meet his. Anything that could help with this would be valuable, although he was somewhat sceptical of the cost–saving effect of computer–based systems, having seen too many of them run over budget and time and not produce the results. He had agreed to the development of the scheduling system, however, because he believed that the kitting shop was inefficient and out–of–date and the scheduling system would "shake them up".

The project manager in the Manufacturing Systems Division saw the introduction of the scheduling system as part of a much larger programme of computerization of the whole manufacturing process. She argued that the real problem was not making the kitting operation twenty per cent more efficient, but making the organization more receptive to change. ABC had drifted on for too long with the same old ways of doing things and now needed a complete change of culture, getting everybody in the company ready and willing to think for themselves. Computer–based systems like the one being developed for scheduling could help the process. They should not fossilize existing ways of doing things, but offer exciting new opportunities, she argued.

The Factory Planner for the Electrical Division knew relatively little about the Kitting Shop as he had only recently joined the Department as a graduate trainee. The current scheduling system was recognized to have one or two problems, although he felt these were relatively minor in terms of the production system as a whole which was his main concern. He understood that the schedules were based on time and motion studies done several years previously that probably needed updating, and thought that the planning cards were badly designed. He was pleased to be involved in the development of the computer–based system as it would look good on his CV. It also showed user participation, which was very important. The new system would help the planners because it would give them better control over production and provide them with more accurate information. It would also help the kitting staff by giving them more guidance on how to organise their work.

The Kitting Shop supervisor described his job as getting the work done. All he needed to know was what kits were wanted and he would make sure that they were ready in time. He knew his staff well and could rely on them to help out when necessary. He was particularly proud of his ability to get out the extra quality and design rework kits at short notice. He was very suspicious of the new computer system, which he saw as taking his job away from him. The system wouldn't work in any case, he argued, because the data it used was "rubbish".

The kitting staff, their representative stated, were also concerned about the new system, which they saw as interfering in the way they liked to work. Everyone was a hard worker, but different family arrangements and personal preferences meant that people had different priorities. When the pressure was on, however, everyone pulled together. Although individuals were supposed to specialise on a particular machine, people liked to change around to get some variety in what was otherwise a fairly dull job. This also meant that if someone was ill or needed to take time off then they could cover for each other.

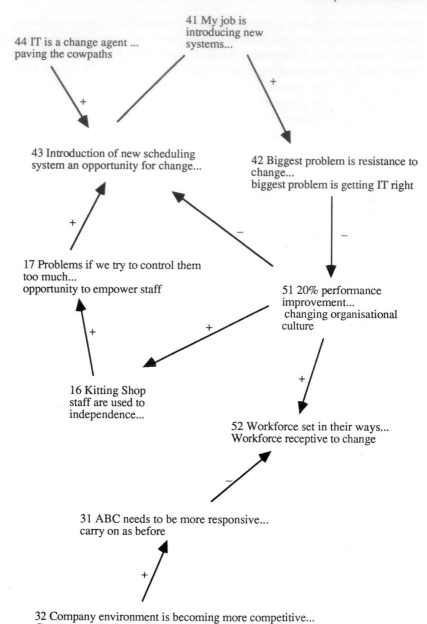

Figure 11.2 Part of cognitive map of the Manufacturing Systems project manager.

They knew the work could be done faster, but they weren't going to tell anyone the tricks of the trade, and in any case a lot of the holdups were because of the unreliable old machinery. If the new scheduling system meant that they would be forced to "follow orders" much more, she argued, then some of the best staff would leave, while others would "follow the orders to the letter" and this would lead to total chaos.

Having prepared "tidy" maps of the different viewpoints these were fed back to the individual interviewees for clarification and agreement. Most agreed with the broad structure of the maps and felt that they gave a fair picture of their views in a way that they had not thought about before. One or two of the interviewees, however, identified aspects of their maps that they considered were inaccurate. In a few cases this was due to errors on the part of the mapper, for example misunderstanding a statement or making unwarranted assumptions. In most cases, however, the problem was due to statements which needed further elaboration to avoid a misleading impression. For example, the supervisor's comment about the data being "rubbish" was expanded to indicate that this was true only for some particular cases. Other data were considered to be reasonably accurate, although the values used for task durations did not always take account of the variations in set–up times that were possible with some particular machine and job combinations.

A meeting was then arranged at which the stakeholders were presented with each other's maps (some of the sensitive comments, for example about the reputation of the Kitting Shop and the tricks of the trade, were edited out with the agreement of the interviewees). At this meeting it was evident that each group had a substantially different picture of the process and of what the scheduling system could and should do. Discussion therefore focused on whether these viewpoints were compatible and whether a system could therefore be designed that would meet everybody's needs.

Comparison of individual goals showed that the views fell broadly in two camps sharing a number of similar constructs: a management side and a worker's side. The priority of the former was changing the production process to improve efficiency, while for the latter it was to maintain some control over their work. It was recognized that if greater productivity could be achieved whilst leaving the workers with detailed control over schedules then these priorities need not be incompatible. Indeed the flexibility of the production staff could support the Manufacturing Systems manager's goal of getting people to think for themselves. Although the Factory Planner's goal of controlling production would not be met by this, not wishing to oppose the Division Manager he chose to adopt the management view.

The design task was then agreed to be to produce a scheduling system with two separate components: a rough–cut scheduler for the Factory Planner that would enable him to estimate whether the Kitting Shop should be able to produce the required kits, and a more detailed scheduler to be used by the Shop supervisor with whatever inside information he had available to decide on the actual sequence of the jobs. The system would then feed back information on the actual performance of the Shop to the Factory Planner. In this way he would be able to develop an indirect understanding of the capability of the Shop and adjust the loading accordingly, while the Kitting Shop staff, retaining control of their work, would be motivated to try to meet higher productivity targets. With better information on due dates and allocation of materials to specific jobs, greater control could also be exercized over inventory levels. Another of the Manufacturing Systems Division projects on the computerization of the Electrical Stores was also expected to contribute to this.

Having agreed the broad structure of the system, the specific design of the interfaces for the two components could then be started. Information contained in the cognitive maps was used to assist this process, by providing the designers with a representation of how the users saw the scheduling activity. For example "issues" identified in the maps generally indicated major concerns, such as performance of the Kitting Shop against targets or allocation of materials to jobs, which needed to be represented in the interface, and addressed in the design process. The maps also allowed designers to see how these issues related to broader concerns of the type identified by the Project Manager in Figure 11.2 such as the change in ABC's market position. In some cases it was necessary to take the maps back to individual stakeholders for further discussion and elaboration of these issues.

Maps could also be used as a form of team memory in the design process (Walz, Elam and Curtis, 1993). For example, by mapping interviews with users a much richer representation of their views was developed than would typically be provided by normal note–taking. In addition, once transferred to GraphicsCOPE the analysis routines could be used to explore the user's views in more depth and a readily–accessible record of the interview produced for later reference. If necessary these maps were used to support negotiation between different users about specific design questions. Finally, another use of mapping was within the design team itself to record decisions and the discussions leading to them.

11.5.2 Main features of the approach as illustrated by the example

Although Cognitive Mapping originated in social psychology, it was developed within the management science/operational research branch of Organization Studies. It is an explicitly interpretive approach. Eden (1989) quotes Thomas and Thomas (1928), "if men define situations as real, then they are real in their consequences" as summarising the perspective it adopts. Its main concern is with representing the thinking of individuals about a problem situation and then using these representations to enable reflection on this thinking, either individually or in a group.

The representations are very informal, being constructed from the natural language descriptions of the problem situation given by the individuals in semi– or un–structured interviews (as shown in Figure 11.2). Rather than being seen as a definitive characterization of their thinking, maps are seen as "negotiative devices" that can contribute to the individuals' ongoing process of understanding of the situation and it is expected that this understanding will develop and change as a result. For example the Supervisor's blanket criticism of the data was revized to identify a more subtle categorization. Cognitive mapping therefore recognises and seeks to make use of the way that representations of the world contribute to the construction of our social "reality".

Consequently, the approach is openly interventionist. Thus the analyst is not seen as a detached, objective observer and recorder of the situation, but as an active participant in its development. This does not mean, however, that analysts deliberately try to manipulate the situation to suit their own objectives, rather they acknowledge their influence and seek to use it to support the users' thinking and reflection. This places considerable demands on the mapper in facilitating the interviewees' understanding while avoiding, as far as possible, imposing their own interpretations. The feedback process is used to check how successful this has been.

Cognitive mapping is an essentially practical technique that has been developed for use in real organizational settings, not just in laboratories or with fellow researchers. The real problems of working in such environments, such as availability influencing the choice of interviewees or the mixed personal and professional motivations of individuals, have therefore to be acknowledged and accommodated. Rather than pursuing a complete and enduring understanding of the situation, which in any case it is argued is unattainable, a pragmatic approach is adopted which seeks a workable consensus on which individuals are prepared to act.

Achieving such a consensus will usually require individual maps to be compared and combined. As we saw, in this, Cognitive Mapping treats organizations as essentially orderly systems in which consensus is possible, although this is usually recognized to be contingent on the particular conditions and membership of the group. The retention of individual ownership of elements of a "merged" map (by including constructs from different individuals' maps) however, is recognized as important in keeping discussion rooted in individuals' interpretations. Otherwise negotiations can come to be focused on the content of the collective map itself rather than the substantive issues which it is seeking to address.

As its origins in strategic decision–making suggest, though, this does not mean that Cognitive Mapping ignores the political nature of consensus formation (shown, for example, in the ABC Planner's decision to back the management position). Rather, higher priority is given to facilitating the development of a mutually acceptable solution, than to resolving structural inequalities which transcend the particular situation. The informal character of maps may help with this by making them easier for users to see as a partial and situated representation of their individual views, rather than a definitive statement of their official position.

Finally, the approach is systemic, seeing the organizational context as a complex inter–relationship of factors that cannot be considered in isolation. The "interpretivist" character of Organizational Analysis also means that the boundaries of this system and the factors to be included cannot be defined objectively *a priori*, but depend on the viewpoint of the individuals involved. In practice this means that anything that is mentioned by stakeholders in their discussion of the context, such as the organizational change issues mentioned by the ABC Project Manager, needs to considered as potentially relevant and suitable for inclusion in the analysis.

11.6 Comparison with some other approaches

Before comparing Cognitive Mapping with some of the other approaches described in this book, it should be reiterated that this is only one of the possible forms of Organizational Analysis. Others may be quite different in their assumptions and methods. For example, Ethnography could also have been used to obtain data about the organizational processes in ABC (and, as Jeanette Blomberg's discussion of the attorneys' view of document production in Chapter 8 illustrates, may have revealed similar simplistic views on the part of those distant from actual work process). The discussion below should therefore be taken to refer to the particular features of Cognitive Mapping, rather than Organizational Analysis as a whole, unless indicated otherwise.

Similarly, the discussion of other approaches should be taken to refer to their application in HCI as described in the other chapters of this book rather than to the theoretical perspectives from which these are derived. Given their very different aims, assumptions and concerns, this inevitably has something of the character of a comparison of apples and oranges (if not chalk and cheese), but may be helpful in appreciating the particular stance adopted in Organizational Analysis. As a final caveat, it should also be evident from the description of the approach that the use of the term cognitive in this context is very different from that of Andrew Howes in Chapter 5. Rather than the detail of the cognitive processes underlying particular generic behavioural properties, the focus is on the broad structure of individuals' understandings of the organizational context in which they work.

11.6.1 Organizational Analysis and other approaches

In all forms of Organizational Analysis the interaction at the interface is seen as one small part of the much larger process of interaction involved in the use of a computer–based IS in organizations. Compared with traditional HCI, therefore, it considers a much broader range of issues. For example, much of the description of the problem situation given above would probably be considered to be, at best, marginally useful background for many forms of HCI analysis. Indeed Tetzlaff and Mack (1991) describe the level of detail considered in contextual analyses of this sort as "distressing". From the point of view of Organizational Analysis, however, such a "rich description" of actual work practices in real organizational settings over a period of time is essential to an understanding of how individuals interact with computers.

Only Ethnography and Activity Theory of the other approaches described in this book adopt such a wide and sustained view of the system which they are seeking to address. Indeed, some ethnographers might argue that, even allowing for the editing needed to make the description suitable for inclusion in this chapter, it is still rather "thin" in its presentation of potentially significant features of the situation. Of the remainder of the approaches, Conversation Analysis of the sort described in Chapter 9 shares the concern of Organizational Analysis with the complex "ecology" of interaction in real work settings, but is generally too fine–grained to be practical in focusing on more than the detail of particular episodes. Cognitive Science approaches, in contrast, have traditionally been laboratory–based, while Formal Methods are derived from abstract mathematical principles. Although some forms of Task Analysis may be conducted in work settings, the boundary of the relevant context is generally very tightly drawn.

Organizational Analysis also takes a very broad view of the design task. In many forms of HCI, design is taken to consist of the systematic analysis of a specific, pre–defined activity which will involve a computer–based IS intended to support a particular organizational operation. The aim of this analysis is seen as the identification of principles which should guide the development of an effective interface to this IS. From this perspective, therefore, Organizational Analysis might be seen as a way of helping to define this activity; a prelude to the real interface design task. From an Organizational Analysis perspective, however, this viewpoint is unsatisfactory. While not denying the need for a detailed interface design activity, many decisions about how to support the organizational operation, will have to be taken before this stage is reached. It may also be argued (Henderson, 1991) that the design process extends beyond implementation to include the way in which users incorporate a new system into their work. A broader view of design is necessary, therefore, if important factors influencing the interface are not to be excluded from consideration.

The breadth of view adopted in Organizational Analysis may be traced to its systemic perspective, which is shared with other contextual approaches such as Ethnography, Conversation Analysis and Activity Theory. This may be contrasted with the reductionist perspective of approaches such as Task Analysis and Cognitive Science which seek to understand interaction behaviour in terms of separate components. Many of these latter approaches also adopt a natural science model of knowledge acquisition based on the testing of falsifiable claims. From a contextual perspective, however, such knowledge is unattainable, not just in practice (as it is impossible to replicate or experimentally control for a particular organizational context), but also theoretically (as all that can be achieved is a working understanding of the particular system at hand).

Ethnography and Conversation Analysis (but not Activity Theory which has an essentially realist, materialist ontology) are also similar to Organizational Analysis, at least as exemplified by Cognitive Mapping, in adopting an "interpretivist" perspective. This is criticized by Carroll (1989b) as making the design process "essentially mystical", since it offers "no systematic methodology, no conceptual framework and no explicit way to abstract from particular experiences". As Wixon, Holtzblatt and Knox, (1990) argue, however, while "mystical" transcendence of the everyday condition may be a feature of the design process (which is often reported to rely on inexpressible gut feelings), this would seem unlikely to be effective as the sole basis for a practical design method. The social process of building understanding is therefore also an important part of the interpretive approach. Unlike Ethnography and Conversation Analysis, however, Cognitive Mapping is concerned with action and intervention in the problem situation rather than simply its description.

Another difference between Organizational Analysis and Ethnography and Conversational Analysis is in its conception of power and the attention it gives to organizational power relationships. This may be seen to derive from the influence of Organization Studies. Thus the different resources and interests of the various actors in the organizational context are seen as a potentially important factor in HCI and interface design is itself viewed as a political process. The influence of culture and language are also considered, but these are seen as additional aspects of the problem situation that are sustained and changed by social actors over time, rather than the primary focus, as in Ethnography or Conversation Analysis. The political character of Organizational Analysis is in even greater contrast with traditional "scientific" HCI methods, such as Cognitive Science or Formal Methods, in which power relationships are generally ignored, or even denied.

Cognitive Mapping is also very different from these methods in the informal nature of the representation it uses. Compared with approaches such as Formal Methods or Task Analysis, which strive for a complete, rigorous and unambiguous description of interaction, Cognitive Mapping promotes negotiation to achieve a description that is good enough for whatever purpose it is needed, arguing that it will always be contingent on the particular circumstances and open to multiple interpretations. Cognitive maps are also less formalistic than the representations provided by Activity Theory. Compared with the straight (or annotated) text descriptions of ethnography, however, they may be seen as imposing a greater degree of external structure in terms of the mapping conventions.

11.7 Recent developments and directions for the future

The use of Cognitive Mapping in HCI need not be restricted to helping to decide on the appropriate interface, but may also contribute to the design process by supporting communication between members of the design team. For example, maps may be used to record design discussions, or more actively to support design decision–making. Research on the use of Cognitive Mapping for requirements analysis (Jones and Brooks, 1994) suggests that there are several roles in which mapping may be applied, depending on the relationship between the design team members and the users, and the type of support required.

As we have argued, Organizational Analysis is a fairly recent development in HCI and applications have been relatively few and far between. The future prospects for the approach are therefore mainly related to its greater uptake in the field. Some authors, such as Grudin (1990a), have predicted that this will be the major focus of HCI in the 1990s. Evidence from the use of Cognitive Mapping, however, suggests that this is likely to be a slow process, particularly in view of the significant theoretical differences between such approaches and traditional HCI. Despite the considerable interest, particularly in the CSCW field, in Social Anthropology approaches such as Ethnography which also adopt an interpretive perspective, it remains to be seen how far they are actually incorporated into HCI design in practice. Social Psychological approaches to Organizational Analysis which have a theoretical perspective rather closer to traditional HCI may therefore continue to be favoured.

There would seem to be a danger in this, however, of HCI becoming identified with a narrow technological perspective, as Bannon (1992) argues, and thereby being superseded by CSCW as the main focus of attention (and funding) for research and practice. Such an outcome would seem undesirable not just in terms of the future of HCI as a field, but also in terms of the failure to develop an appropriate understanding of a fundamental aspect of the use of computer–based IS in organizations. The development of practical bridges between technology– and organizationally–oriented approaches in HCI would therefore seem to be a priority.

11.8 Further reading

Eden, C. (1989). Using cognitive mapping for strategic options development and analysis (SODA). In J. Rosenhead (ed.), *Rational Analysis for a Problematic World: Problem Structuring Methods for Complexity, Uncertainty and Conflict*, pp. 21–42. Chichester: John Wiley.

A couple of chapters in this collection on problem structuring methods provide a useful introduction to the theory and practice of Cognitive Mapping.

Vaske, J. J. and Grantham, C. E. (1990). *Socializing the Human–Computer Environment*. Norwood, NJ: Ablex.

One of the few HCI books which specifically addresses organizational issues. It covers most of the main approaches mentioned in this chapter, but is strongest on social psychology (the specialism of its authors).

Whiteside, J. and Wixon, D. (1987). Discussion: improving Human Computer Interaction – a quest for cognitive science. In J. Carroll (ed.),*Interfacing Thought: Cognitive Aspects of Human Computer Interaction.*, pp. 337–352. Cambridge, MA: Bradford/MIT Press.

An interesting chapter in a collection of papers, mostly from a cognitive science perspective, which raises many of the HCI issues which Organizational Analysis seeks to address.

References

Abowd, G. D. (1990). Agents: communicating interactive processes. In G. Cockton and B. Shakel (eds), *Human–Computer Interaction – INTERACT'90*, pp. 143–148. Amsterdam: Elsevier .

Abowd, G. D. (1991). *Formal Aspects of Human–Computer Interaction*. Technical Monograph PRG–97, Oxford University, Programming Research Group, D.Phil. thesis.

Abowd, G. D. and Dix, A. J. (1992). Giving undo attention. *Interacting with Computers*, 4(3), 317–342.

Agar, M. (1980). *The professional stranger*. New York: Academic Press.

Agar, M (1986). Speaking of ethnography. *Qualitative Research Methods*, 2, 11–78.

Alexander, H. (1987). *Formally–based Tools and Techniques for Human–Computer Dialogues*. London: Ellis Horwood.

Anderson, J. R. (1993). *The Architecture of Cognition*. Cambridge, Mass.: Harvard University Press.

Anderson, J.R. (1987). Causal analysis and inductive learning. In *Proceedings of the Fourth International Workshop on Machine Learning*, P. Langley (ed), pp. 288–299. San Mateo, CA: Morgan Kaufmann.

Anderson, J.R. (1993). *Rules of the Mind*. Hillsdale, NJ: Erlbaum.

Anderson, P. (1991). A semiotic approach to the construction and assessment of computer systems. In H. Nissen, H. Klein and R. Hirschheim, (1991). *Information Systems Research: Contemporary Approaches and Emergent Traditions*. Amsterdam: Elsevier.

Anderson, R. J. (1994). Representations and requirements: The value of ethnography in system design. In *Human Computer Interaction*, 9(2), 151–182. Hillsdale, NJ: Lawrence Erlbaum Associates.

Anderson, R. J., Hughes, J. A. and Sharrock, W. W. (1989). *Working for profit: The social organization of calculations in an entrepreneurial firm*, Aldershot, UK: Avebury.

Anderson, W. and Crocca, W. (1992). Experiences in reflective engineering practice: Co–development of product prototypes. In *Proceedings of the Participatory Design Conference*, M. Muller and S. Kuhn (eds), pp. 13–22. Boston, MA: CPSR.

Annett, J. and Duncan, K. D. (1967). Task analysis and training design. *Occupational Psychology*, 41, 211–221.

Annett, J., Duncan, K. D., Stammers, R. B., and Gray, M. J. (1971). *Task Analysis*. London: HMSO.

Archer, Jr., J., Conway, R. and Schneider, F. B. (1984). User recovery and reversal in interactive systems. *ACM Transactions on Programming Languages*, 6(1), 1–19.

Argyris, C. (1980). *The inner contradictions of rigorous research*, New York: Academic Press.

Arnkil, E. (1988). Learning activity and the zone of proximal development in social work. In M. Hildebrand–Nilshon and G. Ruckriem (eds), *Proceedings of the 1st International Congress on Activity Theory*, vol. 3. Berlin: System Druck.

Atkinson, J. M. and Heritage, J. (eds) (1984). *Structures of Social Action: Studies in Conversation Analysis*, Cambridge: Cambridge University Press.

Bannon, L. J. (1991). From human factors to human actors: The role of psychology and human computer interaction studies in system design. In J. Greenbaum and M. King (eds) *Cooperative Design of Computer Systems*. Hillsdale NJ: Lawrence Erlbaum.

Bannon, L. J. (1992). Perspectives on CSCW: From HCI and CMC to CSCW. In: *Proceedings of the International Workshop on Human Computer Interaction*, St Petersburg, Russia.

Barnard, P. J. (1987). Cognitive resources and the learning of human–computer dialogues. In *Interfacing Thought: Cognitive Aspects of Human–Computer Interaction*, J.M. Carroll (ed). Cambridge, MA: MIT Press.

Barnard, P. J. (1990). Bridging between basic theories and the artefacts of human–computer interaction. In J. M. Carroll (ed) *Designing Interaction – Psychology at the Human–Computer Interface*, Cambridge: Cambridge University Press.

Barnard, P. J., Hammond, N. V., Morton. J., Long, J. and Clark, I. A. (1981). Consistency and compatibility in human–computer dialogue. *International Journal of Man–Machine Studies*, 15, 87–134.

Bartlett, F. C. (1932). *Remembering: A Study in Experimental and Social Psychology*. Cambridge: Cambridge University Press.

Basalla, G. (1988). *The evolution of technology*. New York: Cambridge University Press.

Bass, L and Coutaz, J. (1991). *Developing Software for the User Interface*, The SEI Series in Software Engineering, Reading MA: Addison–Wesley.

Bateson, G. (1972). *Steps to an Ecology of Mind*. New York: Ballantine.

Bellotti, V. M. E. (1990). A framework for assessing applicability of HCI techniques. In D. Diaper, D. Gilmore, G. Cockton and B. Shackel (eds), *Human–Computer Interaction – INTERACT'90*, pp. 881–885, Amsterdam: Elsevier.

Bentley, R., Hughes, J. A., Randall, D., Rodden, T., Sawyer, P., Shapiro, D., Sommerville, I. (1992). Ethnographically–informed system design for air traffic control. In J. Turner, and R. Kraut, (eds), *Proceedings of CSCW'92*. pp. 123–129. New York: Association for Computer Machinery.

Berlekamp, E. R., Conway, J. H., and Guy, R. K. (1982). *Winning Ways for your mathematical plays*, *Vol. 1*. New York: Academic Press.

Berry, D. C., and Broadbent, D. E. (1990). The role of instruction and verbalisation in improving performance on complex search tasks. *Behaviour and Information Technology*, 9, 175–190.

Bibby, P. A. and Payne, S. J. (1993). Internalization and the use specificity of device knowledge. *Human–Computer Interaction*, 8, 25–56.

Bjerknes, G., Bratteteig, T., and Espeseth, T. (1991). Evolution of finished computer systems: The dilemma of enhancement. *Scandinavian Journal of Information Systems*, 3, 25–45.

Bjerknes, G., Ehn, P., and Kyng, M. (1987) *Computers and Democracy: A Scandinavian Challenge*, Aldershot: Avebury.

Bloch, M. (1977). The past and the present in the present. *Man*, 12, 278–292.

Blomberg, J. (1987). Social interaction and office communication: Effects on user evaluation of new technologies. In R. Kraut, (ed),*Technology and the transformation of white–collar work*, pp. 195–210. Hillsdale, NJ: Lawrence Earlbaum Associates.

Blomberg, J. (1988a). The variable impact of computer technologies on the organization of work activities. In I. Greif, (ed), *Computer–supported cooperative work: A Book of readings*, pp. 771–781. San Mateo, CA: Morgan Kaufmann.

Blomberg, J. (1988b). Social aspects of operability: Ethnography of photocopiers. Paper Presented at the American Association for the Advancement of Science Annual Meeting. Boston.

Blomberg, J. (1994). Broadening participation in technology design: The politics and problematics of technology and organizational transformation. Presented at American Anthropological Association Meeting, Atlanta, Georgia.

Blomberg, J., Giacomi, J., Mosher, A. and Swenton–Wall, P. (1993). Ethnographic field methods and their relation to design. In D. Schuler and A. Namioka, (eds), *Participatory design: Principles and practices*, pp. 123–155. Hillsdale, NJ: Lawrence Erlbaum Associates.

Blomberg, J., Suchman, L. and Trigg, R. (1994). Reflections of on work–oriented design. In *Proceedings of PDC'94*, Chapel Hill, NC: CPSR.

Blum, M., and Naylor, J. (1968). *Industrial Psychology – Theoretical and Social Foundations*, New York: Harper and Row.

Boden, D. and Zimmerman, D. H. (1991). *Talk and Social Structure: Studies in Ethnomethodology and Conversation Analysis*, Cambridge: Polity Press.

Bodker, S. (1989). A human activity approach to user interfaces. *Human–Computer Interaction*. 4, 171–195.

Bodker, S. (1991).*Through the Interface: a Human Activity Approach to User Interface Design*, Hillsdale, NJ: Lawrence Erlbaum.

Bodker, S., Christiansen, E., Ehn, P., Markussen, R., Morgensen, P. and Trigg, R. (1993). The AT–Project: practical research in cooperative design. Computer Science Department, Aarhus University. Daimi PB 454.

Boehm, B. (1988). A spiral model of software development enhancement. *IEEE Computer*, 21, 61–72.

Boland, R. (1985). Phenomenology: a preferred approach to research on information systems. In E. Mumford, R. Hirschheim, G. Fitzgerald and A. Wood–Harper (eds), *Research Methods in Information Systems*. Amsterdam: Elsevier.

Bourdieu, P. (1977). *Outline of a Theory of Practice*. Cambridge: Cambridge University Press.

Bowers, J. and Benford, S. D. (eds) (1991). *Studies in computer supported cooperative work: Theory, practice and design*, Amsterdam: North–Holland.

Broadbent, D. E. (1971). *Decision and Stress*. London: Academic Press.

Broadbent, D. E. (1980). The minimisation of models. In A. J. Chapman and D. M. Jones, (eds) *Models of Man*, pp. 113–128. Leicester: British Psychological Society

Brooks., F. P. (1975). *The mythical man–month.*, Reading, MA: Addison–Wesley.

Brown, J., Collins, A. and Duguid, P. (1989) Situated cognition and the culture of learning. *Educational Researcher*. January–February, 32–42.

Brown, J.S., Burton, R.R., and deKleer, J. (1982). Pedagogical, natural language and knowledge engineering techniques in SOPHIE I, II, and III. In D. Sleeman and J.B. Brown (eds), *Intelligent tutoring systems*. pp. 227–282, New York: Academic Press.

Brun–Cottan, F., Forbes, K., Goodwin, C., Goodwin, M., Jordan, B., Suchman, L. and Trigg, R. (1991). The Workplace Project: Designing for diversity and change (Videotape). Xerox Palo Alto Research Center, Palo Alto, CA.

Buchanan, D. and Boddy, D. (1983). *Organisations in the Computer Age.*, Aldershot: Gower.

Burrell, G. and Morgan, G. (1979). *Sociological Paradigms and Organisational Analysis*, Portsmouth, NH: Heinemann Educational.

Button, G. (1990). Going up a Blind Alley: conflating Conversation Analysis and Computational Modelling. In P. Luff, G. N. Gilbert and D. M. Frohlich, (eds), *Computers and Conversation*, pp. 67–90. London and New York: Academic Press.

Button, G. and Lee, J. R. E. (eds) (1986). *Talk and Social Organisation*. Avon: Multilingual Matters.

Button, G. and Sharrock, W. (forthcoming). On Simulacrums of Conversation: Towards a Clarification of the Conversation Analysis for Human Computer Interaction. In P. Thomas (ed), *Social Aspects of HCI Design*, Cambridge: Cambridge University Press.

Byrne, M.D., Wood, S.D., Sukaviriya, P., Foley, J.D., and Kieras, D.E. (1994) Automatic interface evaluation. In B.Adelson, S.Dumais, J.Olson (eds) *Proceedings of Human Factors and Computing Systems: CHI'94*. pp. 232–237, New York: Association for Computer Machinery.

Callon, M., Law, J., and Rip, A. (eds) *Mapping the Dynamics of Science and Technology: Sociology of Science in the Real World*. London: MacMillan.

Card, S. K., Moran, T. P., and Newell, A. (1983). *The Psychology of Human Computer Interaction*. Hillsdale, New Jersey: Lawrence Erlbaum Associates.

Card, S. K., Mackinlay, J. D. and Robertson, G. G. (1990) The design space of input devices. In J. C. Chew and J. Whiteside (eds) *CHI'90 Conference Proceedings: Human Factors in Computing Systems*, pp. 117–124, New York: Association for Computer Machinery.

Carroll, J.M. (1982) Learning using and designing command paradigms. *Human Learning: Journal of Practical Research and Applications*, 1, 31–63.

Carroll, J.M. (1989) Feeding the interface eaters. In Sutcliffe, A. and Macauley, L. (eds), *People and Computers V*, pp. 35–48. Cambridge: Cambridge University Press.

Carroll, J.M. (1989). Evaluation, description and invention: Paradigms for human–computer interaction. In M.C. Yovits (ed), *Advances in Computers*, 29, Orlando, FL: Academic Press, pp. 47–77.

Carroll, J.M. (1990). *The Nurnberg Funnel: Designing minimalist instruction for practical computer skill*. Cambridge, MA: MIT Press.

Carroll, J.M. (1994a). Designing scenarios for human action. *Performance Improvement Quarterly*, 7(3), 64–75.

Carroll, J. M. (1994b). Making *use* a design representation. *Communications of the Association for Computer Machinery*, 37, 29–35.

Carroll, J. M. and Carrithers, C. (1984). Training wheels in a user interface. *Communications of the Association for Computing Machinery*, 27, 800–806.

Carroll, J.M. and Campbell, R. L. (1986). Softening up hard science: Reply to Newell and Card. *Human–Computer Interaction*, 2, 227–249.

Carroll, J.M. and Campbell, R. L. (1989). Artifacts as psychological theories: The case of human–computer interaction. *Behaviour and Information Technology*, 8, 247–256.

Carroll, J.M. and Kellogg, W.A. (1989). Artifact as theory–nexus: Hermeneutics meets theory–based design. In K. Brice and C.H. Lewis (eds) *Proceedings of CHI'89: Conference on Human Factors in Computing Systems*. pp. 7–14. New York: Association for Computer Machinery.

Carroll, J.M., Kellogg, W.A., and Rosson, M.B. (1991). The task–artifact cycle. In J.M. Carroll (ed), *Designing Interaction: Psychology at the human–computer interface*. pp. 74–102. New York: Cambridge University Press.

Carroll, J.M. and Rosson, M.B. (1985). Usability specification as a tool in iterative development. In H. Hartson (ed) *Advances in human–computer interaction* 1, Norwood, NJ: Ablex, pp. 1–28.

Carroll, J.M. and Rosson, M.B. (1987). Paradox of the Active User. In J.M. Carroll (ed) *Interfacing Thought*. Cambridge, MA: MIT Press.

Carroll, J.M. and Rosson, M.B. (1990). Human computer interaction scenarios as a design representation. *Proceedings of HICSS–23: Hawaii International Conference on System Sciences.*, pp. 555–561, Los Alamitos, CA: IEEE Computer Society Press.

Carroll, J.M. and Rosson, M.B. (1991). Deliberated evolution: Stalking the View Matcher in design space. *Human–Computer Interaction*, 6, 281–318.

Carroll, J.M. and Rosson, M.B. (1992). Getting around the task–artifact cycle: How to make claims and design by scenario. *ACM Transactions on Information Systems*, 10, 181–212.

Carroll, J.M., Singley, M.K. and Rosson, M.B. (1992). Integrating theory development with design evaluation. *Behaviour and Information Technology*, 11, 247–255.

Carroll, J.M., Thomas, J.C., and Malhotra, A. (1979). A clinical–experimental analysis of design problem solving. *Design Studies*, 1, 84–92.

Castells, M. (1989) *The Informational City: Information, Technology, Economic Restructuring and the Urban–Regional Process*. Oxford: Basil Blackwell.

Cawsey, A. (1990). A Computational Model of Explanatory Discourse: local interactions in a plan–based explanation. In Luff, P., Gilbert, G. N. and Frohlich, D. M. (eds), *Computers and Conversation*, pp. 223–236. London and New York: Academic Press.

Chaiklin, S. and Lave, J. (eds) (1993) *Understanding Practice: Perspectives on Activity and Context*. Cambridge: Cambridge University Press.

Chalfonte, B. L., Fish, R. E., Kraut, R. (1991). Expressive richness: a comparison of speech and text as media for revision. In S.P. Robertson, G.M. Olson and J.S. Olson(eds) *Reaching Through Technology – CHI'91 Conference Proceedings:Human Factors in Computing Systems, New Orleans, Louisiana*. pp. 21-26, Reading MA: Addison–Wesley.

Chapanis, A. (1986). Interactive human communication. In *Computer Supported Cooperative Work: A Book of Readings*, Greif, I. (ed), pp. 127–140. California: Morgan Kaufman.

Ciborra, C. (1987) Research agenda for a transaction cost approach to information systems. In R. Boland and R. Hirschheim, (eds) *Critical Issues in Information Systems Research*. Chichester: John Wiley.

Clark, H.H. and Schaefer, E.F. (1989). Contributing to discourse. *Cognitive Science*, 13, 259–294.

Clegg, C. (1991).*Psychology and Information Technology*. Memo no 1254. Sheffield: MRC/ESRC Social and Applied Psychology Unit.

Clifford, J. (1988). *The predicament of culture: Twentieth–century ethnography, literature, and art*. Cambridge: Harvard University Press.

Clifford, J. and Marcus, G. (eds) (1986). *Writing culture: The poetics and politics of ethnography*. Berkeley, CA: University of California Press.

Cole, M., John–Steiner, V., Scribner, S. and Souberman, E. (eds). (1978) *Mind in Society: The Development of Higher Psychological Processes*. by L. Vygotsky. Cambridge Mass: Harvard University Press.

Conein, B., de Fornel, M. and Quere, L.(eds) (1989). *Analyse de L'Action et Analyse de la Conversation. Volume 1 and II*. Paris: Reseaux CNET.

Coulter, J. (1979). *The Social Construction of Mind: Studies in Ethnomethodology and Linguistic Philosophy*. London: Macmillan.

Coulter, J. (1989). *Mind In Action*. Cambridge: Polity Press.

Coulter, J. (1990). (eds) *Ethnomethodological Sociology. Bibliography compiled by B. J. Fehr and J. Stetson with the assistance of Y. Mizukawa*, Aldershot: Edward Elgar Publishing.

Coutaz, J. (1987). PAC, an Object Oriented Model for Dialog Design. In Bullinger, H. –J. and Shackel, B. (eds), *Human–Computer Interaction – INTERACT '87*, pp. 431–436. Amsterdam: North–Holland.

Crossman, E. R. F. W. (1956). Perceptual activities in manual work. *Research*, 9, 42–49.

Crossman, E. R. F. W. (1960). *Automation and Skill*. London, H.M.S.O.

Currie, R. M. (1977). *Work Study*. London: Pitman.
Daft, R. and Weick, K. (1984) Towards a model of organisations as interpretation systems. *Academy of Management Review*, 9, 284–295.
Dejong G. and Mooney, R. (1986). Explanation–based learning: An alternative view. In R.S.Michalski, J.G.Carbonell, and T.M. Mitchell, *Machine Learning: An Artificial Intelligence Approach*. Los Altos, CA: Morgan Kaufmann: 145–176.
Diaper, D (1989). Task Analysis for Knowledge Descriptions (TAKD); the method and an example. In: D. Diaper (ed) *Task Analysis for Human–Computer Interaction*, pp. 108–159. Chichester : Ellis Horwood.
Digitalk (1989). *Smalltalk/V PM Tutorial and Programming Handbook*. Los Angeles, CA: Digitalk.
Dix, A. J. (1991). *Formal methods for interactive systems*. London: Academic Press.
Dix, A. J. (1992). Beyond the interface. In Larson, J. and Unger, C. (eds),*Engineering for Human–Computer Interaction*, pp. 171–190. Amsterdam: North–Holland.
Dix, A. J. (1994). LADA a logic for the analysis of distributed action. In *Proceeding of the Eurographics Workshop on the Specification and Design of Interactive Systems*, Carrara, Italy.
Dix, A. J., Finlay, J. E., Abowd, G. D., and Beale, R (1993). *Human–Computer Interaction*. London: Prentice Hall.
Dix, A. J. and Runciman, C. (1985). Abstract models of interactive systems. In *HCI'85: People and Computers I: Designing the Interface*, Johnson, P. and Cook, S. (eds), pp. 13–22. Cambridge: Cambridge University Press.
Draper, S.W. (1986). Display managers as the basis for user machine communication. In D.A. Norman and S.W. Draper (eds), *User Centred System Design*. Hillsdale, NJ: Erlbaum.
Drew, P. and Heritage, J. (eds) (1992). *Talk at Work: Interaction in Institutional Settings*. Cambridge: Cambridge University Press.
Dreyfus, H. (1979). *What computers can't do: The limits of artificial intelligence.*. New York: Harper and Row.
Dreyfus, H. L. (1992). *What Computers Still Can't Do: A Critique of Artificial Reason*. Cambridge, MA: MIT Press.
Drury, C., Paramore, B., Cott, H. V., Grey, S., and Corlett, E. (1987). Chapter 3.4 – Task Analysis. In G. Salvendy (eds), *Handbook of Human Factors*, pp. 370–401. New York: John Wiley and Sons.
Duff, S.C. (1989). Reduction of action uncertainty in process control systems: The role of device knowledge. In Megaw, E. (ed) *Contemporary Ergonomics*. pp. 213–219, London: Taylor and Frances.
Duncan, K. D. (1972). Strategies for the Analysis of the Task. In J. Hartley (eds), *Programmed Instruction: An Education Technology*, London: Butterworth.
Duncan, K. D. (1974). Analytical Techniques in Training Design. In E. Edwards and F. P. Leeds (eds), *The Human Operator and Process Control*. London: Taylor and Francis.
Eason, K. D. (1974). The manager as a computer user. *Applied Ergonomics*, 5(1), 9–14.
Eason, K.D. (1988). *Information Technology and Organisational Change*, London: Taylor and Francis.
Eden, C. (1989). Using cognitive mapping for strategic options development and analysis (SODA). In Rosenhead, J. (ed), *Rational Analysis for a Problematic World: Problem Structuring Methods for Complexity, Uncertainty and Conflict*, pp. 21–42. Chichester: John Wiley.
Edmonds E. (ed) (1992). *The Separable User Interface*. London: Academic Press.
Ehn, P. (1988). *Work–oriented design of computer artifacts*. Hillsdale, NJ: Lawrence Erlbaum Associates.

Ehn, P. and Kyng, M. (1991). Cardboard computers: Mocking it up and hands on the future. In *Design at work: Cooperative design of computer systems.*, Greenbaum, J. and Kyng, M. (eds), pp. 169–195. Hillsdale, NJ: Lawrence Erlbaum Associates.

Ehn, P., Molleryd, B. and Sjogren, D. (1990). Playing in Reality: A paradigm case. *Scandinavian Journal of Information Systems*, 2, 101–120.

Englebeck, G.E. (1986). *Exceptions to generalisations: Implications for formal models of human–computer interaction.* Unpublished master's thesis, University of Colorado, Department of Psychology, Boulder.

Engestrom, R. (1987). *Learning by Expanding: an Activity Theoretical Approach to Developmental Research.* Helsinki: Orienta–Konsultit.

Engestrom, R. (1990). *Learning, Working and Imagining: Twelve Studies in Activity Theory.* Helsinki: Orienta Consultit.

Engestrom, Y. (1991). Developmental work research: reconstructing expertise through expansive learning. In M. Nurminen and G. Weir (eds) *Human Jobs and Computer Interfaces.* Amsterdam: Elsevier.

Engestrom, Y. (1993). Developmental studies of work as a testbench of activity theory: the case of primary care medical practice. In S. Chaiklin and J. Lave (eds) *Understanding Practice: Perspectives on Activity and Context.* Cambridge: Cambridge University Press.

Engestrom, Y. and Engestrom, R. (1986). Developmental work research: the approach and an application in cleaning work, *Norsk Pedagogik*, 1, 2–15.

Engestrom, Y., Engestrom, R. and Saarelma, O. (1988), Computerised medical records, production pressure and compartmentalisation in the work activity of health centre physicians. *Proceedings of the 2nd Conference on Computer– Supported Cooperative Work.* New York: Association for Computer Machinery. Reprinted in Engestrom, R. (1990) *Learning, Working and Imagining: Twelve Studies in Activity Theory.* Helsinki: Orienta Consultit.

Festinger, L. (1957). *A theory of cognitive dissonance.* New York: Harper and Row.

Filippi, G. and Theureau, J. (1993). Analyzing cooperative work in an urban traffic control room for the design of a coordination support system. In Michelis, G., Simone, C. and Schmidt, K. (eds), *Proceedings of the Third European Conference on Computer–Supported Cooperative Work*, pp. 171–186. Dordrecht: Kluwer.

Fischer, G., Lemke, A.C., Mastaglio, T. and Morch, A.I. (1990). Using critics to empower users. In J.C. Chew and J. Whiteside (eds), *Proceedings of CHI'90: Conference on Human Factors in Computing Systems*, pp. 337–347, New York: Association for Computer Machinery.

Fischer, G., Lemke, A.C., McCall, R., and Morch, A.I. (1991). Making argumentation serve design. *Human–Computer Interaction*, 6, 393–419.

Flanagan, J. C. (1954). The critical incident technique. *Psychological Bulletin*, 51, 327–358.

Floyd, C., Mehl, W–M., Reisin, F–M., Schmidt, G. and Wolf, G. (1989). Out of Scandinavia: Alternative approaches to software design and system development. *Human–Computer Interaction*, 4(4), 253–349.

Floyd, C., Zullighoven, H., Budde, R., and Keil–Slawik, R. (eds) (1992). *Software development and reality construction.* New York: Springer–Verlag.

Foley, J. D., Van Dam, A., Feiner, S. K., J. F. Hughes and R. L. Phillips (1994). *Introduction to Computer Graphics.* Addison–Wesley.

Forsythe, D. (1992). Using Ethnography to build a working system: Rethinking basic design assumptions. In *Proceedings of the 16th Symposium on Computer Applications in Medical Care (SCAMC 92)*, pp. 505–509. New York: McGraw–Hill.

Forsythe, D. and Buchanan, B. G. (1991). Broadening our approach to evaluating medical information systems. In *Proceedings 15th SCAMC*, Clayton, P. (ed), pp. 8–12. New York: McGraw–Hill.

Foushee, H. C. and Helmreich, R. L. (1989). Group interaction and flight crew performance. In Wiener, E. L. and Nagel, D. C. (eds), *Human Factors in Aviation*, pp.189–227. San Diego: Academic Press.

Foushee, H. C., Lauber, J. K., Baetge, M. M., and Acomb, D. B. (1986). *Crew performance as a function of exposure to high–density short–haul duty cycles*. NASA Technical Memo 88322. Moffett Field, CA: NASA Ames Research Center.

Freeman, P. (1987). *Software perspectives: The system is the message*. Reading, MA: Addison Wesley.

Friedman, A. (1989). *Computer Systems Development: History, Organisation and Implementation*. Chichester: John Wiley.

Frohlich, D. M. and Luff, P. (1990). Applying the Technology of Conversation to the Technology for Conversation. In *Computers and Conversation*, Luff, P., Gilbert, G. N. and Frohlich, D. M. (eds), pp. 189–222. London and New York: Academic Press.

Frohlich, Monk and Drew (forthcoming). Repair and the management of Human–Computer Interaction. *Human–Computer Interaction*.

Gagne, R.M., and Briggs, L.J. (1979). *Principles of instructional design*. New York: Holt, Rinehart and Winston.

Gagne, R., Briggs, L., and Wager, W. (1988). *Principles of Instructional Design* (Third ed.). New York: Holt, Rinehart and Winston.

Gale, S. (1990). Human aspects of interactive multimedia communication. *Interacting with Computers*, 2, 175–189.

Galegher, J., Kraut, R. and Edigo, C. (1990). *Intellectual Teamwork*. Hillsdale, NJ: Erlbaum.

Gantt, M and Nardi, B. (1992). Gardeners and gurus: Patterns of cooperation among CAD users. In Bauersfeld, P., Bennett, J. and Lynch, G. (eds), *Proceedings CHI '92*. pp. 107–117. New York: Association for Computer Machinery.

Garfinkel, H. (1967). *Studies in Ethnomethodology*. Englewood Cliffs, NJ: Prentice–Hall.

Gaver, W. W., Moran, T., Maclean, A., Lovstrand, L., Dourish, P., Carter, K. A. and Buxton, W. (1992). Realizing a video environment: EuroPARC's RAVE system. In P. Bauersfeld, J. Bennet, G. Lynch (eds) *Proceedings of Human Factors in Computing Systems, CHI'92*, pp. 27–35, Reading MA: Addison Wesley.

Gaver, W. W., Sellen, A., Heath, C. C. and Luff, P. (1993). One is not enough: Multiple Views in a Media Space. In Ashlund, S., Mullet, K., Henderson, A., Hollnagel, E. & White, T. *InterCHI'93 Conference proceedings*, pp. 335–341, New York: Association for Computer Machinery.

Geertz, C. (1973). *The interpretation of cultures*. New York: Basic Books.

Geertz, C. (1983). *Local knowledge: Further essays in interpretive anthropology*. New York: Basic Books.

Gergen, K. (1985). Social pragmatics and the origin of psychological discourse. In K. Gergen and K. Davis, (eds) *The Social Construction of the Person*. New York: Springer–Verlag.

Gibbs S. and Verrijn–Stuart, A. (1991). *Multi–user Interfaces and Applications*. Amsterdam: North Holland.

Giddens, A. (1993). *Sociology*. Cambridge: Polity Press.

Gilb, T. (1988). *Principles of software engineering management*. Reading, MA: Addison Wesley.

Gilbert, G. N., Wooffitt, R. and Fraser, N. (1990). Organising Computer Talk. In *Computers and Conversation*, Luff, P., Gilbert, G. N. and Frohlich, D. M. (eds), pp. 237–260. London and New York: Academic Press.

Goffman, E. (1974). *Frame Analysis. An Essay on the Organisation of Experience*. London: Harper and Row.

Goodwin, C. (1979). The interactional organisation of a turn at talk. In Psathas, G. (ed), *Everyday Language: Studies in Ethnomethodology*, New York: Irvington.

Goodwin, C. (1981). *Conversational Organization: Interaction between Speakers and Hearers*. New York: Academic Press.

Goodwin, C. and Goodwin, M. H. (1992). Professional Vision. In *Proceedings of International Conference on Discourse and the Professions*, 25th September.

Goodwin, C. and Goodwin, M. (in press). Formulating planes: Seeing as a situated activity. In *Communication and Cognition at Work*, Engestrom, Y. and Middleton, D. (eds). New York: Cambridge University Press.

Gould, S.J. (1990). *Wonderful life: The Burgess shale and the nature of history*. New York: Norton.

Gray, P. and Took, R. K. (eds) (1992). *Building Interactive Systems: Architectures and Tools*. Workshops in Computing Series, Berlin: Springer–Verlag.

Gray, W.D, John, B.E. and Atwood, M.E. (1992). The precis of Project–Ernestine or an overview of a validation of GOMS. In P.Bauersfeld, J.Bennet, and G.Lynch (eds) *Proceedings of CHI92 Conference on Human Factors in Computing Systems*. Reading, MA: Addison Wesley.

Greatbatch, D., Luff, P., Heath, C. C. and Campion, P. (1993). Interpersonal Communication and Human–Computer Interaction: an examination of the use of computers in medical consultations. *Interacting With Computers*. 5, 193–216.

Green, M. (1986). A Survey of Three Dialogue Models. *ACM Trans. on Graphics*, 5(3), 244–275.

Green, T.R.G. (1990). Limited theories as a framework for human–computer interaction. In D. Ackermann and M.J. Tauber (eds) *Mental Models and Human–Computer Interaction 1*. Amsterdam: Elsevier Science Publishers, North Holland.

Green, T.R.G., Bellamy, R.K.E. and Parker, J.M. (1987). Parsing and gnisrap: a model of device use. In G.M. Olson, S. Sheppard, and E. Soloway (eds), *Empirical Studies of Programmers: Second Workshop*. Norwood: Ablex.

Green, T.R.G., Payne, S.J., Gilmore, D. and Mepham, M., (1985). Predicting expert slips. In B.Shackel (ed) *Proceedings of Human–Computer Interaction, INTERACT'84*. pp. 519–525, Amsterdam: North Holland.

Greenbaum J. and Kyng, M. (1991). *Design at Work. Cooperative Design of Computer Systems*. Hillsdale NJ: Erlbaum.

Greif, I. (1988). *Computer–supported cooperative work: A book of readings*. San Mateo, CA: Morgan Kaufmann.

Grudin, J. (1990a). The computer reaches out: the historical continuity of interface design. In Chew, J.C. and Whiteside, J. (eds), *Empowering People: Proceedings of CHI '90*, pp. 261–268. New York: Association for Computing Machinery.

Grudin, J. (1990b). Obstacles to user involvement in interface design in large product development organisations. In Diaper, D.; Gilmore, D.; Cockton, G. and Shackel, B. (eds), *Human–Computer Interaction: Interact '90*, pp. 219–224. Amsterdam: North Holland.

Grudin, J. (1990c). Groupware and cooperative work: Problems and prospects. In Laurel, B. (ed), *The art of human–computer interface design*, pp. 171–185. Reading, MA: Addison–Wesley.

Grudin, J. and Bernard, P. (1984). The cognitive demands of learning and representing names for text editing. *Human Factors*, 26, 407–422.

Gugerty, L. (1993). The use of analytic models in human–computer–interface design. *International Journal of Man–Machine Studies*, 38, 625–660.

Haraway, D. (1988). Situated knowledges: The science question in feminism and the privileges of partial perspective. *Feminist Studies*, 14, 575–599.

Harper, R., Hughes, J. and Shapiro, D., (1991). Harmonious Working and CSCW: An Examination of computer technology and air traffic control, In Bowers, J. M. and Benford, S. D. (eds), *Studies in computer supported cooperative work: Theory, practice and design*, pp. 225–234. Amsterdam: North–Holland.

Harrison, M.D. and Thimbleby, H.W., (eds) (1990). *Formal Methods in Human Computer Interaction*. Cambridge: Cambridge University Press.

Hayes, P. and Reddy, D. (1983). Steps Towards Graceful Interaction in Spoken and Written Man–machine Communication. *International Journal of Man–Machine Studies*. 19, 231–284.

Heath, C. (1982). Preserving the consultation: medical record cards and professional conduct. *Sociology of Health and Illness*. 4, 56–74.

Heath, C. (1986). *Body Movement and Speech in Medical Interaction*. Cambridge: Cambridge University Press.

Heath, C., Jirotka, M., Luff, P. and Hindmarsh, J. (1993). Unpacking collaboration: The interactional organization of trading in a city dealing room. In *Proceedings of the Third European Conference on Computer–Supported Cooperative Work*, Michelis, G., Simone, C. and Schmidt, K. (eds), pp. 155–170. Dordrecht: Kluwer Academic Publishers.

Heath, C. and Luff, P. (1991). Collaborative activity and technological design: Task coordination in London underground control rooms. In Bannon, L., Schmidt, K. and Robinson, M. (eds), *Proceedings of the Second European Conference on Computer–Supported Cooperative Work*, pp. 65–80. Dordrecht: Kluwer Academic Publishers.

Heath, C. C. and Luff, P. (1992a). Collaboration and control: Crisis Management and Multimedia Technology in London Underground Line Control Rooms. *CSCW Journal*. 1, 69–94.

Heath, C. C. and Luff, P. (1992b). Media Space and Communicative Asymmetries: Preliminary Observations of Video Mediated Interaction. *Human–Computer Interaction*, 7, 315–346.

Heath, C. and Luff, P. (1993). Disembodied conduct: Interactional asymmetries in video–mediated communication. In Button, G. (ed), *Technology in working order*, pp. 35–54. London: Routledge.

Heath, C. C. and Luff, P. (forthcoming). Converging Activities: Line Control and Passenger Information on London Underground. In Engestrom, Y. and Middleton, D. (eds), *Distributed Cognition*, Cambridge: Cambridge University Press.

Heath, C. C., Luff, P. and Sellen, A. (1994). Reconfiguring Media Space. In *Proceedings of POTS to PANS Symposium*, March 28 – 30.

Heidegger, M. (1962). *Being and time*. (trans. by J. Macquarrie and E. Robinson). New York: Harper and Row.

Henderson, A. (1991). A development perspective on interface, design and theory. In *Designing Interaction: Psychology at the Human–Computer Interface*. Carroll, J.M. (ed), pp. 254–268. Cambridge: Cambridge University Press.

Heritage, J. C. (1984). *Garfinkel and Ethnomethodology*. Cambridge: Polity Press.

Hirschheim, R. and Klein, H. (1989). Four paradigms of informations systems development. *Communications of the Association for Computer Machinery*. 32, 1199–1216.

Hirshhorn, L. and Gilmore, T. (1992) The new boundaries of the 'boundaryless' company,*Harvard Business Review*, May–June, 105–115.

Hollingshead, A. B., McGrath, J. E., and O'Connor, K. (1993). Group task performance and communication technology: a longitudinal study of computer–mediated versus face–to–face work groups. *Small Group Research* 24, 307–333.

Hopgood, F. R. A. and Duce, D. A. (1980). A Production System Approach to Interactive Graphic Program Design. In *Methodology of Interaction*, Geudj, R. A., ten Hagen, P. J. W., Hopgood, F. R. A., Tucker, H. A. and Duce, D. A. (eds), pp. 247–263. Amsterdam: North–Holland.

Hopper, R. (1991). (ed). *Conversation Analysis and Ethnography*. Special Issue of *Research on Language and Social Interaction*.

Howes, A. (1993) Recognition–based problem solving. *Proceedings of the Fifteenth Annual Meeting of the Cognitive Science Society*, pp. 551–556, New Jersey: Lawrence Erlbaum Associates.

Howes, A. (1994) A Model of the acquisition of menu knowledge through exploration. In B.Adelson, S.Dumais, J.Olson (eds) *Human Factors in Computing Systems CHI94.*, pp. 445–451, New York:Association for Computer Machinery.

Howes, A. and Payne, S.J. (1990a) Display–based competence: Towards user models for menu–driven interfaces. *International Journal of Man–Machine Studies*, 33 (6), 637–655.

Howes, A. and Payne, S.J. (1990b) Semantic analysis during exploratory learning. In J.C. Chew and J. Whiteside (eds) *CHI'90 Conference Proceedings: Human Factors in Computing Systems (Special Issue of the SIGCHI bulletin)*. pp. 399–406. New York: Association for Computer Machinery.

Howes, A. and Payne, S.J. (1990c) Supporting exploratory learning. In D. Diaper, D. Gilmore, G. Cockton and B. Shackel (eds), *Human–Computer Interaction – INTERACT'90*, pp. 881–885, Amsterdam: Elsevier Science Publishers, B.V

Howes, A. and Young, R.M. (1991) Predicting the learnability of task–action mappings. In S.P. Robertson, G.M. Olson and J.S. Olson(eds) *Reaching Through Technology – CHI'91 Conference Proceedings:Human Factors in Computing Systems, New Orleans, Louisiana*. pp. 113–118, Reading MA: Addison–Wesley.

Hughes, J. A., King, V., Rodden, T. and Andersen, H. (1994). Moving out of the control room: ethnography in system design. In *Proceedings of CSCW '94*.

Hughes, J. A., Randall, D. W. and Shapiro, D. Z. (1992). Faltering from ethnography to design, *Proceedings of CSCW'92*, Turner, J. and Kraut, R. (eds), pp. 115–122. New York: Association for Computer Machinery.

Hughes, J. A., Randall, D. W. and Shapiro, D. Z. (1993). From Ethnographic Record to System Design, *Computer Supported Cooperative Work*, 1(3), 123–141.

Hughes, J.A., Somerville, I., Bentley, R. and Randall, D. (1993). Designing with ethnography: making work visible. *Interacting with Computers*, 5, 239–253.

Hutchins, E. L. (1990). The Technology of Team Navigation. In *Intellectual Teamwork: The Social and Technological Foundations of Cooperative Work*, Kraut, R. E., Galegher, J. and Egido, C. (eds), pp. 191–221. Hillsdale, New Jersey: Lawrence Erlbaum Associates.

Jewkes, J., Sawers, D., and Stillerman, R. (1958/1969). *The sources of invention*. New York: Macmillan.

Jick, H., Jick, S. S., and Derby, L., E. (1991). Validation of information recorded on general practitioner based computerised data resource in the United Kingdom. *British Medical Journal*, 766–768.

Johannson, G. and Aronsson, G. (1980). *Stress reactions in computerised administrative work*. Reports of the Department of Psychology, University of Stockholm, No. 50.

John, B.E. (1989). Cumulating the science of HCI: From S–R compatibility to transcription typing. *Proceedings of CHI'89 Human Factors in Computing Systems*. New York: Association for Computer Machinery.

Johnson, C. W. (1992). *A Principled Approach to the Integration of Human Factors and Systems Engineering for Interactive Control System Design*. YCST 92/05, University of York, Department of Computer Science, D.Phil. thesis.

Johnson, P. (1992) *Human–Computer Interaction: Psychology, Task Analysis and Software Engineering*. London: McGraw–Hill.

Johnson–Laird, P.N. (1983) *Mental Models*. Cambridge: Cambridge University Press.

Jones, C. B. (1980). *Software Development: A Rigorous Approach*. Prentice Hall.

Jones, M.R. and Brooks, L. (1994). *Addressing Organisational Context in Requirements Analysis Using Cognitive Mapping*. Research Paper in Management Studies 93/94 No 17. Cambridge: University of Cambridge

Jordan, B. (in press). Ethnographic workplace studies and computer supported cooperative work. In Shapiro, D., Tauber, M. and Traunmueller, R. (eds). *The Design of computer–supported cooperative work and groupware systems*, Amsterdam: Elsevier Science.

Jordan, B. and Henderson, A. (in press). Interaction analysis: Foundations and practice. *Journal for the Learning Sciences*.

Joseph, I. (forthcoming). Les Liens Faibles. *Sociologie du Travail*.

Jungk, R. and Mullert, N. (1987). *Future workshops: How to create desirable futures*. London: Institute for Social Inventions.

Kabbash, P., MacKenzie, I. S. and Buxton, W. (1993). Human performance using computer input devices in the preferred and non–preferred hands. In Ashlund, S., Mullet, K., Henderson, A., Hollnagel, E. & White, T. *InterCHI'93 Conference proceedings*, pp. 474–481, New York: Association for Computer Machinery.

Kanter, R. (1989).*When Giants Learn to Dance*. London: Simon and Schuster.

Kelly, G.A. (1955).*The Psychology of Personal Constructs: a Theory of Personality*. New York: Norton.

Kendon, A. (1979). Some methodological and theoretical aspects of the use of film in the study of social interaction. In *Emerging Strategies in Social Psychological Research*, Ginsburg, G. P. (eds) New York: Wiley.

Kendon, A. (1982). The organization of behavior in face–to–face interaction: Observations on the development of a methodology. In *Handbook of Methods in Nonverbal Behavior Research*, Scherer, K. and Ekman, P. (eds). Cambridge: Cambridge University Press.

Kendon, A. (1990). *Conducting interaction: Studies in the Behaviour of Social Interaction*. Cambridge: Cambridge University Press.

Kerlinger, F. N. (1973). *Foundations of Behavioural Research*. New York: Holt, Rinehart, and Winston.

Kieras, D.E. and Polson, P.G. (1985). An approach to the formal analysis of user complexity. *International Journal of Man–Machine Studies*, 22, 365–394.

Kintsch, W. (1988). The role of knowledge in discourse comprehension: A construction–integration model. *Psychological Review*, 95, 163–182.

Kirwan, B. and. Ainsworth, L. K. (1992). *The Task Analysis Guide*. London: Taylor and Francis.

Kitajima, M. and Polson, P.G. (1992). A computational model of skilled use of a graphical user interface. In Bauersfeld, P., Bennett, J. & Lynch, G. (eds)*Proceedings of CHI92 Conference on Human Factors in Computing Systems.*, pp. 241–249, New York: Association for Computer Machinery.

Kling, R. (1991). Cooperation and control in computer supported work. *Communications of the Association for Computer Machinery*. 34(12), 83-88.

Knorr–Cetina, K. (1981). Introduction: the micro–sociological challenge of macro–sociology: towards a reconstruction of social theory and methodology In K. Knorr–Cetina and A. Cicourel (eds), *Advances in Social Theory and Methodology. Towards an Integration of Micro– and Macro–Sociologies*. London: Routledge and Kegan Paul.

Kondo, D. (1986). Dissolution and reconstitution of self: Implications for anthropological epistemology. *Cultural Anthropology*, 1, 74–96.

Kozulin, A. (1990). *Vygotsky's Psychology: a Biography of Ideas*. New York: Harvester Wheatsheaf.

Kraemer, K. L. and Pinsonneault, A. (1990). Technology and groups: assessment of the empirical research. In Galegher, J., Kraut, R. E., and Egido, C. (eds), *Intellectual Teamwork: Social Foundations of Cooperative Work*, pp. 373–404. Hillsdale, N.J.: Lawrence Erlbaum.

Kragt, H., and Landeweerd, J. (1974). Mental Skills in Process Control. In E. Edwards and F. Lees (eds), *The Human Operator in Process Control*, pp. 135 - 145. London: Taylor and Francis.

Krasner, G. E. and Pope, S. T. (August 1988). A Cookbook for Using the Model–View Controller User Interface Paradigm in Smalltalk–80. *Journal of Object–Oriented Programming* , 1(3).

Kraut, R., Galegher, J. and Egido, C. (1988). Relationships and tasks in scientific research collaboration. *Human Computer Interaction*, 3, 31–58.

Kraut, R.E. and Streeter, L.A. (1990). Satisfying the need to know: interpersonal information access. In Diaper, D., Gilmore, D., Cockton, G. and Shackel, B. (eds) *Human–Computer Interaction: Interact '90*, pp. 909–915. Amsterdam: North Holland.

Kuhn, T.S. (1962a). *The structure of Scientific revolutions*. Chicago: University of Chicago Press.

Kuhn, T.S. (1962b). Comment. In *The rate and direction of inventive activity: Economic and social factors*. Universities–National Bureau Conference Series, No. 13. Princeton: Princeton University Press, pp. 450–457.

Kurtenbach, G. and Buxton, W. (1993). The limits of expert performance using hierarchic marking menus. In *CHI'93 Conference Proceedings*. New York: Association for Computer Machinery Press.

Kuutti, K. (1991). Activity theroy and its application in information systems research and design. In H. E. Nissen, H. Klein and R. Hirscheim (eds) *Information Systems Research Arena of the 90s*. Amsterdam: Elsevier.

Kuutti, K. (forthcoming). Activity theory, tranformation of work and information systems design. In Engestrom, Y. and Punamaki, R–L. (eds) *Perspectives on Activity Theory: Papers Presented at the 2nd International Congress on Acvity Theory*. Cambridge: Cambridge University Press.

Kuutti, K. and Arvonen, T. (1992). Identifying CSCW applications by means of activity theory concepts: a case example. In *Sharing Perspectives –Proceedings of the CSCW '92 Conference*. New York: Association for Computer Machinery Press.

Kvale, S. (1992). Postmodern psychology: a contradiction in terms?. In S. Kvale, (ed) *Psychology and Postmodernism*. London: Sage.

Kyng, M. (1991). Designing for cooperation: Cooperating in design. *Communications of the Association for Computer Machinery*, 34(12), 64–73.

Kyng, M. (1994). Making Representations Work. In Suchman, L. (ed), *Representations of Work, HICSS Monograph, Hawaii International Conference on System Sciences*, pp. 19–35. New York: Association for Computer Machinery.

Lammers, S. (1986). *Programmers at work*. Microsoft Press, Redmond, WA.

Landauer, T. K. (1987). Relations between cognitive psychology and computer system design. In *Interfacing Thought: Cognitive Aspects of Human Computer Interaction*, Carroll J. M. (ed), pp. 1–25. Cambridge Mass: Bradford Books (MIT Press).

Landauer, T.K. (1991). Let's get real: a position paper on the role of cognitive psychology in the design of human useful and usable systems. In J.M. Carroll (ed), *Designing Interaction: Psychology at the human–computer interface*. New York: Cambridge University Press.

Landauer, T. K. and Nachbar, D. W. (1985). Selection from alphabetic and numeric menu trees using a touch screen: Breadth, depth, and width. In *CHI'85 Conference Proceedings*. New York: Association for Computer Machinery Press.

Lansdale, M.W. (1991). Remembering about documents: memory for appearance, format, and location. *Ergonomics, 34* (8), 1161–1178.

Larkin, J.H. (1989). Display–based problem solving. In D. Klahr, and K. Kotovsky (eds), *Complex Information Processing; The Impact of Herbert A. Simon.*, pp. 319–342, Hillsdale, NJ: Erlbaum.

Larson, J. A. (1992). *Interactive Software: Tools for Building Interactive User Interfaces.* Yourdon Press, Englweood Cliffs, New Jersey.

Lash, S. and Urry, J. (1987). *The End of Organised Capitalism.* Oxford: Polity Press.

Lashley, K.S. (1951). The problem of serial order in behaviour. In L.A. Jeffress (ed), *Cerebral mechanisms in behaviour.* pp. 112–136. New York: Wiley.

Latour, B. (1987) *Science in Action.* Milton Keynes: Open University Press.

Lave, J. (1988). *Cognition in Practice.* Cambridge: Cambridge University Press.

Law, J. (1992). Notes on the theory of actor–network: ordering, strategy and heterogeneity, *Systems Practice, 9,* 378–393.

Lave, J, and Wenger, E. (1991). *Situated Learning: Legitimate Peripheral Participation.* Cambridge: Cambridge University Press.

Leach, J. (1991). *Running Applied Psychology Experiments.* Milton Keynes: Open University Press.

Lee, W.O. (1993). Adapting to interface resources and circumventing interface problems: knowledge development in a menu search task. In J.L. Alty, D.Diaper and S.Guest (eds) *People and Computers VIII Proceedings of the HCI'93 Conference*, pp. 61–77, Cambridge: Cambridge: Cambridge University Press.

Lee, W.O. and Barnard, P.J. (1993) Precipitating change in system usage by function revelation and problem reformulation. In J.L. Alty, D.Diaper and S.Guest (eds), *People and Computers VIII (Proceedings of the HCI'93 Conference)*, pp. 35–47, Cambridge: Cambridge University Press.

Lektorsky, V. (ed) (1990) *Activity: Theories, Methodology and Problems.* Orlando: Deutsch Press.

Leont'ev, A. (1978). *Activity, Consciousness, and Personality.* Englewood Cliffs: Prentice Hall.

Lewis, C.H. (1986). A model of mental model construction. *Proceedings of Human Factors in Computing Systems, CHI'86*, New York: Association for Computer Machinery Press.

Lewis, C.H. (1988). Why and how to learn why: Analysis–based generalisation of procedures. *Cognitive Science, 12,* 211–256.

Lewis, C.H. and Rieman, J. (1993). *Task–Centered User Interface Design.* Shareware book available via anonymous ftp from ftp.cs.colorado.edu.

Lieberman, H. (1986). Using Prototypical Objects to Implement Shared Behaviour in Object Oriented Systems. In *Proc OOPSLA '86, SIGPLAN Notices,* 21(11), 214–223.

Long, J. (1989). Cognitive ergonomics and human–computer interaction. In J.Long and A.Whitefield (eds) *Cognitive Ergonomics and Human–Computer Interaction*. Cambridge: Cambridge University Press.

Luff, P. and Heath, C. (1993). System use and social organization: Observations on human–computer interaction in an architectural practice. In Button, G. (ed), *Technology in working order*, pp. 184–210. London: Routledge.

Luff, P., Heath, C. C. and Greatbatch, D. (1994). Work, Interaction an Technology: the naturalistic analysis of human conduct and requirements capture. In Jirotka, M. and Goguen, J. (eds), *Requirements Engineering: Social and Technical Issues*, pp. 255–284. London: Academic Press.

Mack, R.L. and Nielsen, J. (April, 1987). *Software integration in the professional work environment: Observations on requirements, usage, and interface issues*. (IBM Research Report, RC 12677). Yorktown Heights, New York: IBM T.J.Watson Research Center.

Mackay, W. (1990). Users and customizable software: A co–adaptive phenomenon. Unpublished PhD dissertation. Sloan School of Management, MIT, Boston.

Malone, T. and Rochart, J. (1991). Computers, networks and the corporation *Scientific American*, September, 265, 92–99.

May, J., Barnard, P.J. and Blandford, A. (1993). Using structural descriptions of interfaces to automate the modelling of user cognition. *User Modelling and User Adapted Interaction*, 3, 27–64.

Mayes, J.T., Draper, S.W., McGregor, M.A. and Oatley, K. (1988). Information flow in a user interface: The effect of experience and context on the recall of MacWrite screens. In D.M. Jones and R. Winder (eds) *People and Computers IV*. pp. 275-289, Cambridge: Cambridge University Press.

McCarthy, J. (1994). The state–of–the–art CSCW: CSCW systems, cooperative work, and organisation. *Journal of Information Technology*, 9, 73-83.

McCarthy, J. C., Miles V. C., and Monk, A. F. (1991). An experimental study of common ground in text–based communication. In S.P. Robertson, G.M. Olson and J.S. Olson(eds) *Reaching Through Technology – CHI'91 Conference Proceedings:Human Factors in Computing Systems, New Orleans, Louisiana*. pp. 209–215, Reading MA: Addison–Wesley.

McCarthy J. C., and Monk, A. F. (1994). Measuring the quality of computer mediated communication. *Behaviour and Information Technology*, 13, 311-319.

McClumpha, A. (1992). Human factors and flight deck automation. In *People and Computers VII: Proceedings of HCI'92*, Monk, A. F., Diaper, D. and Harrison, M. D. (eds), pp. 489–491. Cambridge: Cambridge University Press.

McKendree, J. and Anderson, J. R. (1987). Effect of practice on knowledge and use of Basic Lisp. In Carroll, J. M. (ed), *Interfacing Thought: Cognitive Aspects of Human Computer Interaction*, pp. 1–25. Cambridge Mass: Bradford Books (MIT Press).

Menzies I. (1960). A case–study in the functioning of social systems as a defense against anxiety, *Human Relations*, 13, 95–121.

Miller, G.A., Galanter, E. and Pribram, K. (1960) *Plans and the Structure of Behaviour*. New York: Holt, Rinehart and Wilson.

Miller, R. B., (1962). Task description and analysis. In R. M. Gagne (ed), *Psychological principle in systems development*, New York: Wiley.

Miller, R. B., (1966). Task taxonomy: science or technology. In W. T. Singleton, R. S. Easterby and D. C. Whitfield (eds), *The human operator in complex systems*, London, Taylor and Francis.

Miller, R. B., (1974). *A method for describing task strategies* (No. AFHRL–TR–74–26), Alexandria, VA, American Institute for Research.

Mitchell, T.M. (1986). Explanation–based generalisation: A unifying view. In R.S.Michalski, J.G.Carbonell, and T.M. Mitchell (eds), *Machine Learning: An Artificial Intelligence Approach*, pp. 47–80, Los Altos, CA: Morgan Kaufmann.

Mogensen, P. (1992). Towards a prototyping approach in systems development. *Scandinavian Journal of Information Systems*, 4, 31–53.

Mogensen, P. (1994). Challenging Practice: An approach to cooperative analysis. Ph.D. dissertation, Computer Science Department, Aarhus University. DAIMI PB – 465.

Mogensen, P and Trigg, R. (1992). Artifacts as triggers for participatory analysis. In Muller, M. J., Kuhn, S. and Meskill, J. A. (eds), *Proceedings of PDC'92*. pp. 55–62. Cambridge: CPSR.

Monk, A.F. and Dix, A. (1987). Refining early design decisions with a black–box model. In Diaper D. and Winder R. (eds) *People and Computers 3*, pp. 147-158, Cambridge: Cambridge University Press.

Morgan, C. (1987). Specification Statements and Refinement. *IBM Jnl. Res. Dev.*, 31(5).

Muller, M. and Kuhn, S. (eds) (1993). Special Issue on Participatory Design. *Communications of the Association for Computer Machinery*, 36(4).

Multhauf, R.P. (1959). The scientist and the improver of technology. *Technology and Culture*, 38–47.

Mumford, E. (1983).*Designing Human Systems for New Technology: The ETHICS Method*. Manchester: Manchester Business School.

Myers, B. A. (1987). Creating Interaction Techniques by Demonstration. *IEEE Computer Graphics and Applications*, 51–60.

Nardi, B. (1993). *A small matter of programming: Perspectives on end user computing*. Cambridge, MA: MIT Press.

Nardi, B. and Miller, J. (1990). An ethnographic study of distributed problem solving in spreadsheet development. In *Proceedings of CSCW'90*, pp. 197–208, New York: Association for Computer Machinery Press.

Nardi, B. and Miller, J. (1991). Twinkling lights and nested loops: Distributed problem solving and spreadsheet development. *International Journal of Man–Machine Studies*, 34, 161–184.

Nardi, B. and Zarner (1991). Beyond models and metaphors: Visual formalisms in user interface design. In *Proceedings of the 24th Hawaii International Conference on System Sciences* 2, 478–491. Koloa, Hawaii.

Nazareth, I., King, M., Haines, A., Rangel, L. and Myers, S. (1993). Accuracy of Diagnosis of Psychosis on General Practice Computer System. *British Medical Journal*, 307, 32-34.

Nelson, R. (1962). The link between science and invention: The case of the transistor. In *The rate and direction of inventive activity: Economic and social factors*. Universities–National Bureau Conference Series, No. 13. Princeton: Princeton University Press.

Newell, A. (1980). The problem space as a fundamental category. In R. Nickerson (ed), *Attention and performance V111*. Hillsdale, N.J:Erlbaum.

Newell, A. (1990). *Unified Theories of Cognition*. Cambridge, MA: Harvard University Press.

Newell, A. and Card, S.K. (1985). The prospects of psychological science in human–computer interaction. *Human–Computer Interaction, 1*(3), 209–242.

Newman, W.M. (1988). The representation of user interface style. In D.M.Jones and R.Winder (eds), *People and computers IV* Cambridge, U.K.: Cambridge University Press, pp. 123–143.

Norman, D. A. (1988). *The Psychology of Everyday Things*. New York: Basic Books.

Norman, D.A. (1981). Categorization of action slips. *Psychological Review*, 88, 1–15.

Norman, D.A. (1986). Cognitive engineering. In D.A.Norman and S.W. Draper (eds), *User centered system design*, pp. 31–62, Hillsdale, NJ: Lawrence Earlbaum.

Norman, M. and Thomas, P. (1990). The Very Idea: informing HCI design from Conversation Analysis. In Luff, P., Gilbert, G. N. and Frohlich, D. M. (eds), *Computers and Conversation*, pp. 51–66. London and New York: Academic Press.

Nygren, E., Lind, M., Johnson, M., and Sandblad, B. (1992). The art of the obvious. In P. Bauersfeld, J. Bennet, G. Lynch (eds) *Proceedings of Human Factors in Computing Systems, CHI'92*. pp. 235–239, Reading MA: Addison Wesley.

Olsen Jr., D. R. (1984). Pushdown automata for user interface management. *ACM Trans. Graphics*, 3(3), 177–203.

Olsen Jr., D. R. (1986). MIKE: The Menu Interaction Kontrol Environment. *ACM Trans. Graphics*, 5(4), 318–344.

Olsen Jr., D. R. (1989). A Programming Language Basis for User Interface Management. In *Proc CHI `89: Human Factors in Computing Systems*, Brice, K. and Lewis, C. H. (eds), pp. 171–176, New York: Association for Computer Machinery.

Olsen Jr, D. R. (1990). Propositional Production Systems for Dialog Description. In *Proc CHI '90*, Addison Wesley, pp. 57–63.

Olsen Jr., D. R. (1992). *User Interface Management Systems: Models and Algorithms*. San Mateo: Morgan Kaufmann.

Orlikowski, W. J. and Baroudi, J. J. (1991). Studying Information Technology in organisations: research approaches and assumptions. *Information Systems Research*, 2(1), 1–28.

Orr, J. (1990). Talking about machines: An ethnography of a modern job. Ph.D. Thesis Cornell University, PARC Technical Report SSL–91–07 [P91–00132], Xerox PARC, Palo Alto, CA.

Orr, J. and Crowfoot, N. (1992). Design by Anecdote: The use of ethnography to guide the application of technology practice. In Muller, M. J., Kuhn, S. and Meskill, J. A. (eds), *Proceedings of PDC'92*. pp. 31–37. Cambridge, MA: CPSR.

Ortner, S. (1984). Theory in Anthropology since the Sixties, *Comparative Studies in Society and History*, 26, 126–166.

Parnas, D. L. (1969). On the Use of Transition Diagrams in the Design of a User Interface for an Interactive Computer System. In *Proc 24th National Association for Computer Machinery Conference*, pp. 379–385. New York: Association for Computing Machinery.

Parsons, T. (1951). *The Social System*. Glencoe, Illinois: The Free Press.

Patrick, J. (1992). *Training – Research and Practice*. London: Academic Press.

Payne, S.J. (1987). Complex problem spaces: modelling the knowledge needed to use interactive devices. In H. Bollinger and B. Shackel (eds) *Proceedings of Human–Computer Interaction, INTERACT'87*, pp. 203–208, Amsterdam: North–Holland.

Payne, S.J. (1990) Looking HCI in the I: A simple notation for describing interactions at the user interface. In D. Diaper, D. Gilmore, G. Cockton and B. Shackel (eds), *Human–Computer Interaction – INTERACT'90*, pp. 881–885, Amsterdam: Elsevier Science Publishers.

Payne, S.J. (1991). Display–based action at the user interface. *International Journal of Man–Machine Studies*, 35, 275–289.

Payne, S.J. and Green, T.R.G. (1986). Task–action grammars: A model of the mental representation of task languages. *Human–Computer Interaction*, 2, 93–133.

Payne, S.J. and Green, T.R.G. (1989). The structure of command languages: an experiment on task–action grammar. *International Journal of Man–Machine Studies*, 30, 213–234.

Payne, S.J., Squibb, H., Howes, A. (1990). The nature of device models: The yoked state space hypothesis and some experiments with text editors. *Human–Computer Interaction*, 5, 415–444.

Pelto, P. (1970). *Anthropological Research*. New York: Harper and Row.

Piore, M. and Sable, C. (1984) *The Second Industrial Divide*. New York: Basic Books.

Polson, P. G. and Kieras, D. E. (1985). A quantitative model of the learning and performance of text editing knowledge. In *CHI'85 Conference Proceedings*. New York: Association for Computer Machinery Press.

Polson, P.G. and Lewis, C.H. (1990). Theory–based design for easily learned interfaces. *Human–Computer Interaction*, 5, 191–220.

Polson, P.G., Lewis, C., Rieman, J. and Wharton, C. (1992) Cognitive walkthroughs: a method for theory–based evaluation of user interfaces. *International Journal of Man–Machine Studies*, 36, 741–773.

Pope, S.T., Goldberg, A., and Deutsch, L.P. (1987). Object–oriented approaches to the software lifecycle using the Smalltalk–80 system as a CASE toolkit. In *Proceedings of the Fall Joint Computer Conference — Exploring Technology: Today and Tomorrow*. (October, 25–29, Dallas, Texas), pp. 13–20, IEEE Press.

Pugh, D.S. and Hickson, D. J. (1989).*Writers on Organisations*. London: Penguin.

Pylyshyn, Z.W. (1984) *Computation and Cognition: Toward a Foundation for Cognitive Science*. Cambridge, MA: MIT Press.

Raeithal, A. (1992). Activity theory as a foundation for design. In Floyd, C., Zullighoven, H., Budde, R. and Keil–Slawik, R. (1992) *Software Development and Reality Construction*. Berlin: Springer–Verlag.

Rao R., Card, S. K., Johnson, W., Klotz, L., and Trigg, R. (1994). Protofoil: Storing and finding the information worker's paper documents in an electronic file cabinet. In Adelson, B., Dumais, S. and Olson, J. (eds), *Proceedings of CHI'94*, pp. 180–185. New York: Association for Computer Machinery.

Raskin, J. (1994). Holes in history: A personal perspective on how and why the early history of today's major interface paradigm has been so often misreported, *Interactions*, 1 (3), 11–16.

Raudaskoski, P. (1990). Repair Work in Human–Computer Interaction: a conversation analytic perspective. In *Computers and Conversation*, Luff, P., Gilbert, G. N. and Frohlich, D. M. (eds), pp. 153–174. London and New York: Academic Press.

Reason, J. (1979) Actions not as planned: The price of automatization. In G. Underwood and R. Stevens (eds), *Aspects of Consciousness*. Vol. 1. London: Academic Press.

Reason, J. (1990). *Human Error*. Cambridge: Cambridge University Press.

Reich, R. (1991) *The Work of Nations: Preparing Ourselves for 21st–Century Capitalism.*, London: Simon and Schuster.

Reisner, P. (1981). Formal Grammar and Human Factors Design of an Interactive Graphics System. *IEEE Trans. Software Engineering*, SE–7(2), 229–240.

Rieman, J., Lewis, C., Young, R.M. and Polson, P. (1994). Why is a raven like a writing desk? lessons in interface consistency and analogical reasoning from two cognitive architectures. In *Proceedings of Human Factors in Computing Systems CHI'94*. pp. 438–444, New York: Association for Computer Machinery Press.

Roberts, T.L. and Moran, T.P. (1983). The evaluation of text editors: Methodology and empirical results. *Communications of the Association for Computer Machinery*, 26, 265–283.

Rosaldo, R. (1989). *Culture and truth: The remaking of social analysis*. Boston: Beacon Press.

Rosch, E., Mervis, C.B., Gray, W., Johnson, D., and Boyes–Braem, P. (1976). Basic objects in natural categories. *Cognitive Psychology*, 7, 573–605.

Rosson, M.B. and Alpert, S.R. (1990). The cognitive consequences of object–oriented design. *Human–Computer Interaction*, 5, 345–379.

Rosson, M.B. and Carroll, J.M. (1993). Extending the task–artifact framework. In H.R. Hartson and D. Hix (eds), *Advances in Human–Computer Interaction*, 4, pp. 31–57, Norwood, NJ: Ablex.

Rosson, M.B. and Carroll, J.M. (1994). Narrowing the specification–implementation gap in scenario–based design. In J.M. Carroll (ed), *Scenario–based design: Envisioning work and technology in system development*. New York: John Wiley and Sons.

Rosson, M.B., Carroll, J.M. and Bellamy, R.K.E. (1990). Smalltalk scaffolding: A case study in minimalist instruction. In J.C. Chew and J. Whiteside (eds) *Proceedings of CHI'90: Conference on Human Factors in Computing Systems*, pp. 423–429, New York: Association for Computer Machinery.

Rosson, M.B., Maass, S., and Kellogg, W.A. (1988). The designer as user: Building requirements for design tools from design practice. *Communications of the Association for Computer Machinery*, 31, 1288–1298.

Rouncefield, M., Hughes, J., Rodden, T., Viller, S., (1994). Working with 'constant interruption': CSCW and the small office. In Proceedings of CHI'94. New York: Association for Computer Machinery.

Rumelhart, D.E. and Norman, D. (1982). Simulating a skilled typist: A study of skilled motor performance. *Cognitive Science*, 6, 1–36.

Sacks, H. (1964). Sociological Description. *Berkeley Journal of Sociology*, 8, 1–16.

Sacks, H., Schegloff, E. A. and Jefferson, G. (1974), A simplest systematics for the organization of turn-taking in conversation. *Language*, 50, 696-735.

Sanderson, P. M., Haskell, I., Flach, J. M. (1992). The complex role of perceptual organization in visual display design theory. *Ergonomics*, 35, 1199–1219.

Schank, R. and Abelson, R. (1977) *Scripts, Plans, Goals and Understanding*. Hillsdale: Lawrence Erlbaum.

Schegloff, E. A. (1988). Between macro and micro: contexts and other connections. In Griesen, B., Alexander, J., Munch, R. and Smelser, N. (eds), *The Macro–micro Link*, pp. 207–236. Berkeley and Los Angeles: University of California Press.

Schegloff, E. A. (1991). Reflections on Talk and Social Structure, in Boden, D. and Zimmerman, D. (eds), *Talk And Social Structure: Studies in Ethnomethodology and Conversation Analysis*, Cambridge: Polity Press.

Schegloff, E.A. and Sacks, H. (1974). Opening up Closings. In Ethnomethodlogy: Selected Readings, Turner, R (ed). Penguin: Hardmondsworth.

Schiele, F and Green, T.R.G. (1990). HCI formalisms and cognitive psychology: The case of task–action grammar. In Harrison and Thimbleby (eds), *Formal methods in HCI*. pp. 9–62. Cambridge: Cambridge University Press.

Schon, D.A. (1983). *The reflective practitioner: How professionals think in action*. New York: Basic Books.

Schuler, D. (ed) (1994). Special issue on Social Computing, *Communications of the Association for Computer Machinery*, 37 (1), 52–63.

Schuler, D. and Namioka, A. (eds) (1993). *Participatory design: Principles and practices.* Hillsdale, NJ: Lawrence Erlbaum Associates.

Scribner, S. (1986). Thinking in action: some characteristics of practical thought. In R. Sternberg and R. Wagner, (eds) *Practical Intelligence: Nature and Origins of Competence in the Everyday World*. Cambridge: Cambridge University Press.

Sellen, A. J. (1992). Speech patterns in video–mediated conversations. In P. Bauersfeld, J. Bennet, G. Lynch (eds) *Proceedings of Human Factors in Computing Systems, CHI'92.*, pp. 49–59, Reading MA: Addison Wesley.

Seymour, W. D. (1966). *Industrial Training for Manual Operation*. London: Pitman.

Shapiro, D. (1994). The limits of ethnography: Combining social sciences for CSCW. In *Proceedings of CSCW'94*. New York: Association for Computer Machinery.

Shepherd, A. (1985). Hierarchical task analysis and training decisions. *Programmed Learning and Educational Technology*, 22, 162–176.

Shepherd, A. (1986). Issues in the training of process operators. *International Journal of Industrial Ergonomics*, 1, 49–64.

Shepherd, A. (1989). Analysis and training in information technology tasks. In D. Diaper (eds), *Task Analysis for Human–Computer Interaction*, pp. 15 – 55, Chichester: Ellis Horwood.

Shepherd, A. (1993). An approach to information requirements specification for process control tasks. *Ergonomics*, 36 (11), 805–817.

Shepherd, A., and Duncan, K. D. (1980). Analysing a complex planning task. In K. D. Duncan, M. M. Gruneberg, and D. Wallis (eds), *Changes in Working Life* Chichester: Wiley.

Shneiderman, B. (1982). The Future of Interactive Systems and the Emergence of Direct Manipulation. *Behaviour and Information Technology*, 1(3), 237–256.

Simonsen, J. and Kensing, F. (1994). Take users seriously, but take a deeper look: Organizational and technical effects from designing with an intervention and ethnographically inspired approach. In *Proceedings of PDC'94*. Chapel Hill, NC: CPSR.

Singley, M.K. and Carroll, J.M. (1995). Synthesis by analysis: Five modes of reasoning that guide design. In Moran, T.P. and Carroll, J.M., (eds) *Design rationale: Concepts, techniques, and use*. Erlbaum, Hillsdale, N.J.

Singley, M.K., Carroll, J.M., and Alpert, S.R. (1991). Psychological design rationale for an intelligent tutoring system for Smalltalk. In Koenemann–Belliveau, J., Moher, T., and Robertson, S.P. (eds), *Empirical Studies of Programmers, Fourth Workshop*, pp. 196–209, Norwood, N.J.: Ablex.

Spivy, J. M. (1989/1992). *The Z Notation – A Reference Manual*. Engelwood Cliffs, NJ: Prentice Hall.

Sproull, L. and Kiesler, S. (1991). *Connections: New Ways of Working in the Networked Organisation*. Cambridge, MA: MIT Press.

Starr, S. (1992). The Trojan door: organisations, work and the 'open black box'. *Systems Practice*, 5, 395–410.

Stefik, M., Bobrow, D. G. and Kahn, K. M. (January 1986). Integrating Access–Oriented Programming into a Multi–Paradigm Environment. *IEEE Software* 3(1), 10–18.

Stein, L. A. (1987). Delegation is Inheritance. In *Proc OOPSLA '87*, pp. 138–146. Association for Computer Machinery.

Still, A. and Costall, A. (1991). (eds) *Against Cognitivism: Alternative Foundations for Cognitive Psychology*. London: Harvester Wheatsheaf.

Strauss, A. (1978). A social world perspective. *Studies in Symbolic Interaction*, 1, 119–128.

Suchman, L. (1983a). Office procedures as practical action: Models of work and system design. *ACM Transactions on Office Information Systems*, 1(4), 320–328.

Suchman, L. (1983b). The role of common sense in interface design. In Marshall, D. and Gregory, J. (eds), *Office automation: Jekyll or Hyde? Highlights of the International Conference on Office Work and New Technology*, pp. 96–101. Cleveland, Ohio: Working Women Education Fund.

Suchman, L. (1987). *Plans and Situated Actions: the Problem of Human Machine Communication.* Cambridge: Cambridge University Press.

Suchman, L. (1993). Centers of coordination: A case and some themes. Presented at the NATO Advance Research Workshop on Discourse, Tools and Reasoning, Lucca, Italy, Nov 2–7.

Suchman, L. (1994a). Representations of work: A preface. In *Representations of Work, HICSS Monograph*, Hawaii International Conference on System Sciences. Suchman, L. (ed), pp. 1–2.

Suchman, L. (1994b). Working relations of technology production and use. In *Computer Supported Cooperative Work*, 2(1–2), 21–39.

Suchman, L. (forthcoming). Constituting Shared Workspaces. In *Cognition and Communication at Work*, Engestrom, Y. and Middleton, D. (eds), London: Sage.

Suchman, L. and Trigg, R. (1991). Understanding practice: Using video as a medium for reflection and design. In *Design at work: Cooperative design of computer systems.*, Greenbaum, J. and Kyng, M. (eds), pp. 65–89. Hillsdale, NJ: Lawrence Erlbaum Associates.

Sufrin, B. (1982). Formal specification of a display editor. *Science of Computer Programming*, 1, 157–202.

Sukaviriya, P. 'Noi', Foley, J. D. and Griffith, T. (1993). A Second Generation User Interface Design Environment: The Model and the Runtime Architecture. In Ashlund, S., Mullet, K., Henderson, A., Hollnagel, E. & White, T. *InterCHI'93 Conference proceedings*, pp. 375–382, New York: Association for Computer Machinery.

Swenton–Wall, P. and Mosher, A. (1994). Representations of work: Bringing designers and users together. In *Proceedings of PDC'94*. Chapel Hill, NC: CPSR.

Szekely, P. (April 1987). Separating the User Interface from the Functionality of Application Programs. In Carroll J M and Tanner, P P (eds), *Proc CHI + GI 1987*, *ACM SIGCHI Bulletin*, 18(2), 45–46.

Szekely, P. (April 1993). Beyond Interface Builders: Model–Based Interface Tools. In Ashlund, S., Mullet, K., Henderson, A., Hollnagel, E. & White, T. *InterCHI'93 Conference proceedings*, pp. 383–390, New York: Association for Computer Machinery.

Teitelbaum, R.C. and Granda, R.E. (1983) The effects of positional constancy on searching menus for information. *In Proceedings of Human Factors in Computing Systems CHI'83* (Boston), pp. 150–153, New York: Association for Computer Machinery.

Tetzlaff, L. and Mack, R.L. (1991). Discussion: perspectives on methodology in HCI research and practice. In Carroll, J.M. (ed), *Designing Interaction: Psychology at the Human–Computer Interface*, pp. 286–314. Cambridge: Cambridge University Press.

Thimbleby, H. W. (1990). *User Interface Design.* New York: Association for Computer Machinery Press, Addison–Wesley.

Thimbleby, H. W. (1993). Combining systems and manuals. In J. L. Alty, D. Diaper and S. Guest (eds), *HCI '93: People and Computers VIII*, pp. 479–488. Cambridge: Cambridge University Press.

Thomas, P. J. (1990). *Conversation Analysis in Interactive Computer System Design.* Ph.D. Thesis. University of Hull.

Thomas, W.I. and Thomas, D.S. (1928).*The Child in America: Behaviour Problems and Progress.* New York: Knopf.

Toikka K., Hyotylaines, R. and Norros, L. (1986). Development of work in flexible manufacturing. *Norsk Pedagogik*, 1, 16–25.

Tolman, C. and Maiers, W. (eds) (1991). *Critical Psychology: Contributions to an Historical Science of the Subject*. Cambridge: Cambridge University Press.

Took, R. K. (1990). Surface Interaction: A Paradigm and Model for Separating Application and Interface. In J.C. Chew and J.Whiteside (eds) *Empowering People – CHI'90 Conference Proceedings: Human Factors in Computing Systems (Special Issue of the SIGCHI Bulletin)*. pp. 35–42, New York: ACM.

Took, R. K. (1992). The Active Medium: A Conceptual and Practical Architecture for Direct Manipulation. In *Building Interactive Systems: Architectures and Tools*, Gray P. and Took, R. K. (eds), pp. 7–22. Workshops in Computing Series, Berlin: Springer–Verlag.

Torbert, W. (1976). *Creating a community of inquiry*. New York: John Wiley and Sons.

Trigg, R., Bodker, S. and Gronbaek, K. (1991). Open–ended interaction in cooperative protytyping: A video–based analysis. *Scandinavian Journal of Information Science*, 3, 63–86.

Trist, E. and Bamforth, K. (1951). Some social and psychological consequences of the longwall method of coal getting. *Human Relations*, 4, 3–38.

Tullis, T.S. (1986). A system for evaluating screen formats. *Proceedings of the Human–Factors Soceity 30th Annual Meeting*, pp. 1216–1220, Santa Monica, CA: Human Factors Society.

Van Maanen, J. (1988). *Tales of the Field*. Chicago: University of Chicago Press.

Vaske, J.J. and Grantham, C.E. (1988). *Socialising the Human–Computer Environment*. Norwood, NJ: Ablex

Vitter, J. S. (1984). USandR: A new framework for redoing. *IEEE Software*, 1(4), 39–52.

Walz, D.B., Elam, J., and Curtis, B. (1993). Inside a software design team: knowledge acquisition, sharing and integration. *Communications of the Association for Computer Machinery*, 36(10), 63–76.

Wasserman, A. I. (1985). Extending state transition diagrams for the specification of human–computer interaction. *IEEE Transactions on Software Engineering*, SE–11(8), 699–713.

Weick, K. (1985) Cosmos versus chaos: sense and nonsense in electronic contexts. *Organisational Dynamics*. Autumn, 50–64.

Weiser, M. (1993). Some computer science issues in ubiquitous computing. In *Communications of the Association for Computer Machinery*, 36(7), 75–84.

Wertsch, J. (1979). *The Concept of Activity in Soviet Psychology*. Armonk, N.Y.: M.E. Sharpe.

Wertsch, J. (1985). *Vygotsky and the Social Formation of Mind*. Cambridge, MA: Harvard University Press.

Wexelblat, A. (1987). Report on scenario technology. *MCC Technical Report STP–139–87*. Austin, TX: MCC.

Whalen, J. (1992). Technology and the Coordination of Human Activity: Computer–Aided Dispatch in Public Safety Communications. In *Proceedings of Discourse and the Professions*, March.

Whalen, J. (1993). Accounting for 'standard' task performance in the execution of 9–1–1 operations. Paper presented at the annual meetings of the American Sociological Association, Miami, August 1993.

Whalen, J. (in press). Expert systems versus systems for experts: Computer–aided dispatch as a support system in real world environments. In Thomas, P. J. (ed), *Social and interactional dimensions of human–computer interfaces*, Cambridge: Cambridge University Press.

Whiteside, J. and Wixon, D. (1987). Discussion: improving Human Computer Interaction – a quest for cognitive science. In Carroll, J. (ed), *Interfacing Thought:*

Cognitive Aspects of Human Computer Interaction, pp. 337–352. Cambridge, MA: Bradford/MIT Press.

Wickens, C. D. (1992). *Engineering Psychology and Human Performance*. New York: Harper Collins.

Wiecha, C., Bennett, W., Boies, S., Gould, J. and Greene, S. (1990). ITS: A Tool for Rapidly Developing Interactive Applications. *ACM Trans. on Information Systems*, 8(3), 204–236.

Williams, E. (1977). Experimental comparisons of face–to–face and mediated communication: a review. *Psychological Bulletin*, 84(5), 963–975.

Williams, J. C. (1992). A method for quantifying ultrasonic inspection effectiveness. In Kirwan, B. and. Ainsworth, L. K. (eds). *The Task Analysis Guide*, London: Taylor and Francis.

Wilson, P (1991). Computer supported cooperative work (CSCW): origins, concepts and research initiatives. *Computer Networks and ISDN Systems*, 23, 91–95.

Wilson, S., Johnson, P., Kelly, P., Cunnigham, C. and Markopoulos, P. (1993). Beyond Hacking: A Model Based Approach to User Interface Design. In Alty, J., Diaper, D. and Guest, S. (eds), *People and Computers VIII, Proc HCI '93*, pp. 217–231, Cambridge: Cambridge University Press.

Winograd, T. and Flores, F. (1986). *Understanding Computers and Cognition: A New Foundation for Design*. Norwood, NJ: Ablex.

Wirfs–Brock, R., Wilkerson, B. and Wiener, L. (1990). *Designing object–oriented software*. Englewood–Cliffs, New Jersey, Prentice Hall.

Wixon, D.; Holtzblatt, K. and Knox, S. (1990) Contextual design: an emergent view of systems design. In Chew, J.C. and Whiteside, J. (eds), *Empowering People: Proceedings of CHI '90*, pp. 329 336. New York: Association for Computing Machinery.

Wolf, M. (1992). *A thrice–told tale: Feminism, postmodernism, and ethnographic responsibility*. Sandford, CA: Stanford University Press.

Woodcock, J and Loomes, M. (1989). *Software Engineering Mathematics*. London: Pitman.

Yang, Y. (1988). Undo support models. *International Journal of Man–Machine Studies*, 28(5), 457–481.

Young, R.M. (1981). The machine inside the machine: Users' models of pocket calculators. *International Journal of Man–Machine Studies*, 15, 51–85.

Young, R.M., Barnard, P., Simon, T. and Whittington, J. (1989) How would your favourite user model cope with these scenarios? *SIGCHI Bulletin*, 20 (4), 51–55.

Young, R.M., Green, T.R.G. and Simon, T. (1989). Programmable user models for predictive evaluation of interface designs. In K.Brice and C.Lewis (eds) *Proceedings of CHI'89 Human Factors in Computing Systems*, pp. 15–19, New York: Association for Computer Machinery.

Young, R.M., Howes, A. and Whittington, J. (1990). A knowledge analysis of interactivity. In D. Diaper, D. Gilmore, G. Cockton and B. Shackel (eds), *Human–Computer Interaction – INTERACT'90*. pp. 881–885, Amsterdam: Elsevier Science Publishers.

Young, R.M. and Simon, T. (1987). Planning in the Context of Human–Computer Interaction. In D.Diaper and R.Winder (eds) *People and Computers III*. pp. 362–370, Cambridge: Cambridge University Press.

Young, R.M. and Whittington (1990). Using a knowledge analysis to predict conceptual errors in text–editor usage. In J.C. Chew and J.Whiteside (eds) *Empowering People – CHI'90 Conference Proceedings: Human Factors in Computing Systems (Special Issue of the SIGCHI Bulletin)*. pp. 91-97, New York: Association for Computing Machinery.

Zimmerman, D. H. (1992). The interactional organization of calls for emergency assistance. In Drew, P. and Heritage, J. (eds), *Talk at Work: Interaction in institutional settings*, pp. 418–469. Cambridge: Cambridge University Press.
Zuboff, Z. (1988). *In the Age of the Smart Machine: the Future of Work and Power*. New York: Basic Books.

Index